D1234192

From Little Houses to Little Women

From

LITTLE HOUSES

to

LITTLE WOMEN

REVISITING A
LITERARY CHILDHOOD

Nancy McCabe

UNIVERSITY OF MISSOURI PRESS
London

University of Missouri Press, Columbia, Missouri 65201
Printed and bound in the United States of America
5 4 3 2 1   18 17 16 15 14

Cataloging-in-Publication data available from the Library of Congress
ISBN 978-0-8262-2044-8

∞ This paper meets the requirements of the
American National Standard for Permanence of Paper
for Printed Library Materials, Z39.48, 1984.

Jacket design: Jennifer Cropp
Interior design and composition: Richard Farkas
Typefaces: Centaur MT

For Sara King

and Sophie McCabe

and in memory of Lucille McCabe, Shirley Carlson,
and Gena Shipley

all champion readers

Contents

Acknowledgments

Thanks to the many people who assisted with this project, which would not have happened at all without my friend Sara King, with whom I have been discussing books for almost thirty years. Carol Newman, Dani Weber, Liza Greville, Tracee Howell, Livingston Alexander, Anna Smith, Marietta Frank, Donna Dombek, and Lisa Fiorentino read chapters and gave me valuable feedback during the writing process, and Abigail Arnold helped with the initial stages of documenting sources. Mahita Gajanan and Micquel Little were great company on the trip to Prince Edward Island. Thanks to those who hosted us on our other trips, including Lee and Deb Martin, Karen Hindhede and Jim Kaisen, and Anna Smith. Conversations with Lee Tobin McClain as well as Sena Jeter Naslund, Dania Rajendra, Katy Yocom, and others at Spalding University's low residency MFA in Writing Program helped me maintain enthusiasm and pushed me in new directions. I am grateful to the other administrators of the wonderful Spalding program, Kathleen Driskell and Karen Mann, for creating an atmosphere where great discussions take place. Thanks also to Jeff Guterman and the Division of Communication and the Arts and Steve Hardin and the Office of Academic Affairs at the University of Pittsburgh at Bradford as well as the UPB Faculty Development Committee and the Pennsylvania Council for the Arts; several generous grants enabled me to purchase out-of-print books and make the three trips described in these chapters. I'd also like to thank the University of Missouri Press, especially Clair Willcox, Mary Conley, Sara Davis, and Alayna Cohen for their work on this book.

Most of all, I am indebted to my aunts, Gena Shipley and Shirley Carlson, my cousin, Jody Shipley, and my mom, Lucille McCabe, for introducing me to many of these books. And I'd especially like to thank my patient daughter, Sophie, who accompanied me on all of these journeys.

From Little Houses to Little Women

Prologue

WHEN MY DAUGHTER WAS STILL A TODDLER and I was overwhelmed by the chores and errands and tasks of a single parent with a full-time job, I found myself reminiscing fondly about the books I'd read when I was young. Having a child made me miss my own childhood—not the miseries of forgotten homework or lost retainers or shifting friendships, but the joys of the uninterrupted hours that I spent reading.

Back then I'd floated across seamless surfaces of prose, absorbed in books without an eye on the clock or an ever-present guilt about neglected duties. Now, my job required heavy reading, but that was work, more like swimming: I had to be aware of each stroke, of the tricky rhythms of breath. I was tired of being tightly scheduled and hyper-organized. I was tired of being too busy to while away at least an occasional afternoon with a book. I just wanted to plop down and read for hours and hours. But there was so little time. So, I checked out a book from the library called *How to Be Less Busy*. It made brief sense to me that maybe I'd find ways to carve out more time for reading by reading a book about it.

Ultimately, though, I was just too busy to read it, although I did skim a chapter or two. Its premise was that being busy makes us feel important; therefore, we have trouble letting go of it. Since I couldn't blow off grading papers, attending meetings, paying bills, calling the plumber, or taking my daughter for her allergy shot, though, I thought, I should at least get to feel self-important about it.

My friend Sara, also a single mom, got nostalgic, too, and we enthusiastically exchanged e-mails containing lists, memories, and adult impressions of books we'd read and plans for rereading piles of old favorites. "Remember Mrs. Piggle-Wiggle's upside-down house with a chandelier in the middle of the floor that all the kids pretended was a campfire?" I wrote to Sara, who was rereading *Little Women*. "I found myself getting emotional about the last chapter," she replied. "I identified with that feeling that work can be put on hold but life can't. It's funny that at the same time I'm rereading and reflecting on Louisa May Alcott, Isaac is enjoying an earlier-reader form of smarminess, a Scholastic series called 'The Best Me I Can Be,' which includes titles like 'I Am Responsible!' 'I Can Cooperate!' and 'I Am Generous!'"[1]

Sara and I had been discussing books since we met as new graduate teaching assistants in the English department at the University of Arkansas in the fall of 1985. It felt magical to be around so many people who loved books and writing, but I felt boring by comparison: I had a degree from a state university no one had heard of and I'd been in an unhappy marriage for two years. I felt washed up at age twenty-two, if grateful to have escaped nine miserable months as a housewife in Pratt, Kansas, where I'd plowed through *Portrait of a Lady* after hearing that it was a prerequisite for anyone going to graduate school. During a brief stint as a receptionist, I'd also secretly read the entire Danielle Steele oeuvre on my lunch breaks, which somehow made me feel as if I'd given up on life.

From the beginning, Sara and I talked about books with a mutual feverish passion, and so our friendship eventually outlasted my disastrous marriage and the crazy boyfriend she acquired during that first year. I remember hanging out by the pool at my Hill Street apartment complex, talking about writing and books and discovering that we'd read many of the same ones as children. We bought bags of hefty trashy novels at the Dickson Street Bookshop and passed them back and forth. We propped copies of *Ulysses* in front of us by a lake on a cold day, and then, instead of reading, we talked about all of the books we'd rather be reading. We continued that conversation throughout the next two decades, most recently as exhausted mothers of babies and then toddlers. Like most of my best friendships, this one was built on books, inspired and cemented by a mutual love of reading.

My own mother and aunts—my first models for adult female friendships—had also shared a bond over books. Gathered around the kitchen table, they used to talk rapidly, intensely, urgently, sometimes all at the same time. Sometimes, forgetting that anyone else was watching, they fell back into old roles: my mom the responsible, stern older sister; Aunt Gena the alternately playful and resentful middle sibling whose allegiances kept shifting; Aunt Shirley the sickly youngest child who wheedled and whined and demanded attention. Even when they were apart, my mother carried on long conversations with her sisters, standing at the kitchen phone mounted on the wall, spinning the spiraling cord round and round her finger while they exchanged information and opinions and stories about their kids and books and sewing and, later, their teaching jobs. My mom and aunts, I realize, looking back, were the reason I loved so many books, especially *Little Women* and Laura Ingalls Wilder's *Little House* series.

Aunt Shirley, who taught fifth grade, made a special point to read those books nominated for the William Allen White award, given annually based on a vote by Kansas schoolchildren. I read many of the same books she did and listened with awe to the strength of her opinions. Aunt Shirley impressed on me that I had a civic duty to vote, and so I did, every year. As an adult, as I began to reread books from my childhood, revisiting books she had loved felt like a way of bringing back to life the aunt who had died when I was seventeen.

I imagined that I would pass on books to my own daughter someday, but in the meantime, rereading old favorites, I would recover a joy and pleasure in reading it had sometimes seemed I'd lost, even if I could never get back the leisure of childhood. And that's what I wanted—the leisure without the loneliness and boredom that led me, when I was young, to pile up books and page through them. My despair used to gradually vanish, as did the hours and daylight when I finally surfaced from stories, full of the deep sense of well-being they left behind.

My entire adult life, I had hauled many childhood books from state to state, house to house, but never rereading them, as their mere presence was gratifying. Each packed shelf was like a neighborhood full of houses in which I'd once lived. Now, searching for a place to start rereading, I pulled down a couple of books, volumes that exuded an enigmatic aura of vaguely recalled mystery and excitement. Those happened to be 1960s British novels by Ruth Arthur.

The jacket blurb of *Requiem for a Princess* said the book was about a girl named Willow who dreams the whole life of a seventeenth-century occupant of the estate Penliss. It had all of my favorite childhood ingredients: heroines who want to be pianists or dancers or painters, gothic mansions by the sea, the turmoil wrought by an uncovered secret, the healing powers of nature. Eagerly I set forth, gradually deflating. The only thing I was discovering about my past self was that I'd had really, really bad taste. I found myself skimming, faster and faster, hoping for one sentence that would hoist me out of the quicksand of disappointment rapidly sucking me under. Things had to get better, I assured myself.

But the story was flat and rushed and summarized. Where were the crusty bread and goat cheese, the rice pudding and sweet milk, the snowdrops and crocuses and jonquils, the fresh air and sunshine, all of the lush detail of children's books in the nature-heals-all tradition? Where were the ingredients of books like *Heidi* and *The Secret Garden* and *Understood Betsy*, populated by pale weak children transformed to strapping, healthy ones, described in a complimentary, joyful way as fat, with brown skin and red cheeks? And what's the point of setting a book by the sea without crashing waves, misty spray, and sand that pulls each step down so deep that you have to yank your feet free?

Maybe I simply could no longer experience these books in the same way. Maybe it hadn't been my younger self who'd had bad taste. Maybe instead I'd become too much of a perfectionist, too nitpicky. But still, I wondered what I'd been thinking, straining my back and then paying movers to haul these books around for so many years.

Setting out to recapture a former mindset, I just found myself appalled by that earlier self, who seemed like a distant, somewhat embarrassing relative with whom I hesitated to be associated.

I became even more doubtful that I wanted to hang out with my former self when, rereading *Mrs. Dalloway* for my book club, I realized how regularly I'd missed the point. I mean, I was only eleven when I read Ruth Arthur. But at seventeen, when I first encountered Virginia Woolf, I wrote a paper describing Clarissa Dalloway as "superficial," "shallow," and "snobbish." "She spends her day in a useless way, as she has spent her whole life, preparing for a party," I wrote. I condemned her as a "fake" person, lacking humanity and shying away "from any emotional or intellectual contact with others." Somehow I viewed Peter Walsh, Clarissa's rejected former suitor, as an unimpeachable center of authority, responding to her with what I now see as a highly suspect mixture of yearning, admiration, venom, and self-justifying disdain.

Rereading *Mrs. Dalloway* in my forties, I connected far more to the compromises and satisfactions of age than to the idealism of youth. Now, through the lens of middle age and the declining health and deaths of my parents, I was taken with the novel's revelations about the loss of privacy and autonomy inherent in growing old and frail, its underlying persistent awareness of mortality, Clarissa Dalloway's free-floating anxiety and dread and her equally meaningful moments of deep contentment. I found myself underlining words: "No pleasure could equal . . . straightening the chairs, pushing in one book on the shelf, this having done with the triumphs of youth, lost herself in the process of living, to find it, with a shock of delight, as the sun rose, as the day sank."[2]

I wondered: what had happened between the ages of eleven and seventeen? Why, at eleven, was I so willing to identify wholeheartedly with even a poorly drawn heroine, whereas by the age of seventeen, I was eager to take sides against a female protagonist, giving far more credit to the perspective of a more minor male character? Maybe that eleven-year-old could remind me of important things that I'd forgotten.

So I tackled Ruth Arthur's *A Candle in Her Room*, which had to be a reasonably decent book, right? After all, a used copy went for a minimum of $98.00 on Amazon. According to the cover, the story featured an evil doll who casts a spell over three generations of girls at Pembrokeshire. I remember once, against my better judgment, reading *A Candle in Her Room* late at night. After that, I couldn't sleep. All the glittering little eyes of the collectible dolls given to me by my Aunt Shirley stared down, their plastic smiles suddenly full of malice.

Now, as an adult, I started rereading, chuckling in a detached, highly intellectual and professorial way at allusions to the *Aeneid*, especially when Dido the doll is finally ruined in a fire, much the way Virgil's Dido immolates herself on a funeral pyre. I read on with half a brain, the other half pondering what I should fix for dinner. And then suddenly, whoosh! A detail jolted my memory. It unfurled like a tightly wound ribbon suddenly released.

A little girl orphaned in World War II keeps imagining herself in the house where her mother grew up. An old woman who lives in the house repeatedly envisions a little girl standing in the room with her. Eventually the old woman embarks on a journey, determined to find the child from her vision. The little girl, it turns out, is the old woman's great-niece, and when the two are finally united, they recognize each other from their mutual visions even though they've never met in the flesh. Those mutual visions had retained a powerful hold on me my whole life.

In my early twenties, when my then-husband was hired as a photographer at a small-town newspaper, I left an apartment I loved on Kellogg Street in Wichita to move with him to a crumbling duplex in Pratt, Kansas. But every night, I dreamed that I was in the Kellogg Street apartment again, wandering through the back hall that connected the kitchen to the bedroom and bathroom. I never figured out why I saw myself there as opposed to a more emotionally loaded location—the bedroom or living room or kitchen, perhaps—but the dream persisted.

A college friend had taken over my lease, and when I was visiting Wichita, he invited me over. At my request, he gave me a tour. "We have a friend who says he's psychic," he said as we passed through the back hall I'd dreamed about. "He says there's a ghost in this hall."

Cold pine needles brushed against my spine. *That's me,* I thought. *I'm that ghost.* With that thought, my unhappiness started to clarify itself, my recognition that the marriage I'd left this hall to save might not be worth saving.

Many years later, I dreamed about a baby. I went searching for her, eventually adopting my daughter. If I'd never read *A Candle in Her Room,* I'd probably still believe that love and longing could hold mysterious power. But would I have half-believed that it was possible, through dreams energized by the intensity of these emotions, to project a self somewhere else? How much did a novel I read as a child plant the seeds for the unfolding of these profound events—leaving my marriage, becoming a parent?

I felt as if I had spent some time with my silly younger self and discovered that she wasn't so silly after all. That she had the capacity to look at the world from a distinctly female point of view, that she hadn't learned yet to diminish or down-play that vision. That that willingness to bury herself in characters had shaped her imagination in influential ways.

I was hooked. I wanted to know more about this, more about how my val-ues, particularly my belief in creativity and imagination, had come from the books I read.

I read and read: the first chapter book I remembered checking out of the Wich-ita Public Library, the first chapter book I had checked out of the Seltzer School library, the classics I'd regularly received in the mail from the Children's Book of the Month Club, books about big noisy families and stories about the perform-ing arts and series books, those glorious series that let me live with favorite charac-ters through installment after installment: Nancy Bruce, Jennifer Hill, Betsy Ray, Randy Melendy, Beany Malone, Donna Parker, Nancy Drew, Jo March, Anne Shirley. And Laura Ingalls! Laura Ingalls was more than a character to me; I'd re-read the *Little House* books every year, until they were a part of me on a cellular level, focused on the same Great Plains that were the landscape of my own childhood and intimately interwoven with my own family heritage.

As I read, I existed in a relentless state of déjà vu, as if every word had been stored in my memory, etched forever in some place I could no longer readily access, long-forgotten details appearing like retrieved memories. Used copies of books ar-rived in padded envelopes, and as I cracked limp spines, pages sizzled with familiar-ity, my synapses firing off like crazy firecrackers of memory exploding. With each book, I took up the threads of a lost world. I discovered how these books imparted the values of previous generations and had made me a somewhat peculiar child out of step with my times, how they had offered me models for living that remain with me today, how I'd both internalized and resisted messages about family bonds, fe-male sacrifice and other gender expectations, piousness, conformity, originality, and independence. How this tied in with lives centered on art and imagination, themes that I had seemed to seek out regularly. Or maybe I hadn't sought them out. Maybe every children's book in existence was actually some version of a *Kunstlerroman*, I wrote to Sara, a novel documenting the coming of age of the artist, a template for how to move forward into a creative life.

As I came of age, the specter of death had been ever-present. My Aunt Shirley had lupus, a disease that we knew would kill her. Lupus, I learned, meant "wolf." In books like the *Little House* series, wolves were dangerous predators. Their howls had chilled the blood of pioneers, who, I'd learn later, had driven them from the prairies, almost driven them to extinction. I thought of wolves as deceptive and menacing creatures from fables and fairy tales, animals that appeared in sheep's clothing and grandmothers' bonnets, stealing the innocence of little girls.

My aunt was the first person I ever knew who wore her unfulfilled dreams right out where everyone could see them. She'd always wanted a daughter, but she couldn't have children. So she married a widower with two pre-teen daughters and later adopted a son, and she loved those children ferociously, but she never lost her desire for that baby girl she would never have. Her nieces also stepped in as substitute daughters, two cousins and me. And our role in her life obligated us to love the same books she did.

And I tried, but sometimes I mixed up the wolf who was stalking my aunt with my aunt herself. I didn't want to be afraid of her, but often, I was, mixing up being afraid of her with being afraid of the death she represented.

The summer I was thirteen, Aunt Shirley invited my cousin Jody and me along on a trip to visit the places that Laura Ingalls Wilder had lived and written about in Minnesota and South Dakota. This journey, both exciting and disappointing for reasons I couldn't quite remember years later, was one of many that instilled in me a fascination with tourist spots related to books and writers. Every year as I was growing up, my family took a two-week vacation, each trip carefully planned to include at least one amusement park, museum, zoo, and presidential or author home. These ranged from Andrew Jackson's Hermitage near Nashville to Mark Twain sites in Missouri, Herbert Hoover's birthplace in Iowa, the Eisenhower museum complex in Kansas, and Laura Ingalls Wilder's farmhouse in Missouri. In 1977, my parents decided to take an eight-hour detour on the way to Disney World so that we could drive through Plains, Georgia, home of newly elected president Jimmy Carter. We had also, a few years before, stood in line for five hours to file past Harry S. Truman's casket in Independence, Missouri. Much to my disappointment, the casket was closed, and I missed out on viewing a presidential corpse.

We took a train all the way to California to go to Disneyland—and to spend a day visiting the ruins of Jack London's Wolf House in Sonoma County. Once or twice when I was in my twenties, my mother and I stopped at the birthplace of Harold Bell Wright, author of a book that had influenced her childhood, *The Shepherd of the Hills*, near Branson, Missouri. My mother winced as I hooted at the placards on the furniture, like the one that said something like, "This desk is where Wright's wife kept track of all the little details dear to a housewife's heart."

The upshot of all of my parents' matter-of-fact literary tourism was that I learned to view writers as people who were as important as presidents. As an adult

I lost interest in amusement parks and zoos but love to look at places through the vision of those who have visited or lived there. I explored Barcelona by lying on the couch in my Barcelona apartment, reading Carlos Ruiz Zafón novels. Every now and then, I looked up and smiled, pretending to be a typical Spanish citizen for the benefit of the tour bus that routinely stopped outside my window, which was on the level with the upper deck. Then I walked around the city, seeing its twisting alley-sized back streets and gorgeous, garish architecture through Zafón's gothic vision. One of my favorite memories of traveling in China was taking a sleeper train through the countryside, reading Polly Evans's account of taking a sleeper train through the Chinese countryside.

I'm drawn to places, as well, that represent artistic inspiration and achievement. I get excited knowing I'm standing on Coronado Island near San Diego, where Frank Baum did some of his writing right there at the Hotel de Coronado. Or that he was born in Chittenango, New York, according to Mapquest only four hours and one minute from my house, a town with yellow brick sidewalks. When I lived in Lincoln, Nebraska, how could I resist driving a mere three hours to Red Cloud to visit Willa Cather's stomping grounds? Or, while visiting a friend in Illinois, spending a morning at the Carl Sandburg house in Galesburg, a town that was also a favorite setting for science fiction writer Jack Finney? Once years ago, Sara and I biked around the Hemingway house in Key West, trying to spot the famous six-toed cats, though we didn't pay to enter the gates to see the urinal Hemingway had turned into a water fountain or the boxing ring he'd set up in his front yard. More recently, I arranged a lunch stop in Putnam, Connecticut, just so I could see the tiny museum dedicated to Gertrude Chandler Warner of *Boxcar Children* fame housed in—what else?—a boxcar. If I'm driving from Pennsylvania to Kansas, I've been known to route myself through Hannibal, Missouri, to visit Mark Twain sites, including a white picket fence that visitors can sign after making a donation.

I loved some of these writers and books. I merely liked some of them. There are a few that I actively hated. But there's something that gets my brain revved and pulse pounding and blood pumping when I view even the most pathetic, most ridiculous museum full of dioramas and paintings and film clips and clothing related to the life and work of writers, hearing stories about their childhoods and philosophies and work habits, discovering the events and places that shaped them.

So when I started rereading children's books, when I re-entered the lives in particular of favorite heroines, I found myself yearning to travel to the settings of those books. It was as if the tourist sites that had sprung up might be living manifestations of stories that I once loved, of stories that had once themselves seemed like physical locations, places to which I could escape. They were, for me, as real as real life. As with my original impulse to reread books, maybe my initial motivation for embarking on these travels had something to do with nostalgia. Maybe I was seeking to make literal the metaphorical experience of being lost in stories, of meeting again characters who had seemed three-dimensional, flesh and blood, like old, good friends, like a part of me.

Sometimes I found myself troubled at the ways that author-related tourist attractions promoted interpretations antithetical to my own. Still, these visits became another way to rediscover the self I was when I first read the books and to understand and interrogate their messages more deeply. So I took an Anne-tastic tour of Prince Edward Island, home of *Anne of Green Gables* author Lucy Maud Montgomery. I spent a morning in Mankato, Minnesota, on which Betsy-Tacy series author Maud Hart Lovelace based her fictional town of Deep Valley. I drove to Louisa May Alcott's childhood home in Concord, Massachusetts. And, most significantly, I undertook a long pilgrimage through the Midwest, retracing my disillusioning journey when I was thirteen, to Laura Ingalls Wilder homes and museums that carve a path from Wisconsin to Kansas to Minnesota to South Dakota to Missouri.

What started out as a dialogue with a friend turned into multiple journeys, and this book is the story of those: my returns to hundreds of books I once loved, my trip to Laura Ingalls Wilder sites in search of a younger self, my travels to other writers' home and museums. All of these journeys intersected, became inextricably intertwined. Initially motivated by a desire to return to a pre-ironic state, an unconfined part of childhood, where the whole world felt spread out before me and I had all the time I could ever want, I discovered far more. These books and characters had shaped me in a thousand surprising small ways but in larger ones, too: in them, I'd figured out who I wanted to be, found sources of creativity, templates for transcending limitations, and models for leading a creative life, one in which small pleasures and profound insights could go hand in hand. I related even more to the passage I'd underlined from *Mrs. Dalloway* as these books reminded me how to be, at least in my mind, less busy, to lose myself in the process of living, and then, to find it: "with a shock of delight, as the sun rose, as the day sank."[3]

CHAPTER ONE

Beginning the Journey

WHEN I WAS THREE, I sat on our long gold couch while my mother read to me from first editions of *Little House in the Big Woods* and *Little House on the Prairie* with Helen Sewell illustrations. Though I too had blond hair, I seethed with indignation over Mary's smug assurance that her golden hair was prettier than Laura's brown. When Laura lashed out at her sister and was the one punished, the injustice stung me. A gift of peppermint candy became exciting, though such a present would have seemed like a paltry Christmas gift in my own time. I was horrified by the stories Ma told about the pressures on girls of her generation to be little ladies. I was riveted when obnoxious attention-seeking cousin Charley was attacked by yellow jackets. That episode later became inseparable from the Garth Williams illustration of Charley lying on the bed, mummified by bandages.

My friends and cousins and I frequently re-enacted scenes from what we called the "Laura and Mary" books, pretending my bed was a covered wagon. I usually played Laura, identifying with her struggles to be good, but sometimes I preferred the release of being Nellie Oleson, Laura's double who unleashes her delicious mean-girl impulses. I happily anticipated the debut of the TV series *Little House on the Prairie*, which to my great chagrin got so many things wrong—especially, I thought, its portrayal of the Olesons. In the show, the mother is an exaggerated shrewish stereotype, the father a caricature of an ineffectual, hen-pecked husband. And Nellie becomes a smug, flat character with her unnatural if period-appropriate ringlets like stacks of gold coins.[1]

Not only did I know the books inside and out, I felt I had an additional special claim on them: my mother and aunts had grown up thirty miles down the road from Rocky Ridge Farm while Wilder was writing her stories. Though my mother's family drove by the farm sometimes, they didn't discover the books until the 1950s. After that, though, as young adults, they read them again and again, integrating the stories into their histories and mine.

My mother and her sisters felt a strong kinship to Wilder, sharing with her a rural and impoverished upbringing, their early childhood spent outside Raymond-ville, Missouri, in a ramshackle wood frame house insulated by old newspapers. Their father, who'd been partially blinded when sand blew into his eye during his five months in the army, was like Pa: a strong, capable giant of a man, even if he sometimes raged at their mother, even if he might appear to outsiders something of a drifter, a poor provider, a "robust man careless in his dress," according to one medical examination. As in Wilder's early books, there were three daughters, al-though also two sons.

My mother signed her first teaching contract at the age of nineteen, though this was old when stacked against Laura's fifteen. My mother always told me that she'd insisted on omitting the word "obey" from her wedding ceremony, and I copied her and made the same request for the vows of my own short-lived marriage. My mother also liked to quote the lines:

Backward, turn backward
Oh Time in thy flight
Make me a child again
Just for tonight.[2]

I don't remember when I realized that the poem my mom liked to quote came straight from a song performed at a community gathering in *Little Town on the Prairie*. I don't remember when I realized that my mother's story of her wedding had been directly influenced by *These Happy Golden Years*, when Laura insists on the omission of the word "obey" from her wedding vows, telling Almanzo that she could never obey anyone.[3]

No wonder Wilder always felt like a sort of spiritual grandmother to me, since her lore had been passed down through my family as our own. No wonder I felt such ownership of these books. I felt outraged and robbed when I encountered oth-ers who held the belief that the series belonged to them. What a shock it is to me, even in adulthood, to find that every book of criticism, every essay related to Wild-er, opens with a story of a similar intense feeling of connection. Even my former student Dania writes about knowing, as a child, that if Laura had been born in the seventies, she'd have been "a half-Indian, half-Jewish little lefty kid from the sub-urbs of New York City just like me!"

Eventually I would discover another connection to Wilder: my childhood home was built in 1965 on land that had once belonged to the Osage Indians, in a dif-ferent part of Kansas from the Osage Diminished Reserve where the Ingallses had squatted and then left in 1870. The Indians sold the land that became my childhood neighborhood, 160 acres, for $200 in 1872, when the Osage were forced to relocate to a reservation in Oklahoma. So the medium-sized house on the prairie in which I'd read voraciously as a child was, unbeknownst to me, part of the ancestral home of the Indians about whom I was reading.

My sense of possession first kicked in full force when, as a young teenager, I incited my cousin to collaborate on a protest letter to Michael Landon. We misspelled his name "Micheal" before we launched our litany of crimes against accuracy committed by the TV show *Little House on the Prairie*. We informed him that the name "Caroline" was not pronounced the same as "Carolyn"; that Jack was a bulldog, not a fuzzy little terrier; and that Pa was supposed to have a beard and not be so young and cute (no offense, Mr. Landon). We were disgusted by Mary's Hollywood-style breakdown over her loss of sight. In actuality, we contended, she had docilely accepted her fate. "She was never married and certainly never pregnant," we concluded, annoyed about the show's super-sweet happily-ever-after that put less emphasis on Mary's hard-won education than her factually nonexistent romantic life.

"Michael" Landon never responded. In a printed interview months later, he made a snide comment about the many fans who scolded him for not sticking more closely to the books. He dismissed those books and their fans with a disdainful comment about Wilder's boring plotlines, saying something along the lines of "Sometimes all that happens in a chapter is that a character goes to the creek." So maybe it was true that more drama was required to sustain a TV show, and possibly Mary's rage and frustration at her loss of sight were greatly underplayed in the books, which only report the event in retrospect, but I still felt personally affronted by Landon's comments.

So what happened? One moment I was the world's self-appointed foremost thirteen-year-old Laura Ingalls Wilder authority who took seriously my responsibility to defend her work. One moment I was brimming with excitement because my aunt had decided to take my cousin and me to the places that Wilder had lived. But then, sometime during that journey with my aunt three years before she died, my enchantment with the series came to an abrupt halt. After the trip, I never read the books again.

That summer years ago, my aunt and uncle and their son Erik and my other cousin Jody and I drove up from Kansas through Nebraska and Iowa into Minnesota. My aunt wore wide-brimmed hats to protect her from the sun and sagged against my uncle while resting on benches. I was acutely aware that she was ill, that she was dying, but pretended not to notice the dark truth looming over us all, impossible to put into words.

As a young teenager during that drive, I was no doubt crossing a threshold beyond which children's books could no longer fully satisfy my raging hormones. I remember our trip as a series of cafés and motels: grilled cheese sandwiches at diners with fly-specked windows and fans circulating hot air, nights in crowded air-conditioned motel rooms, my horrifyingly shirtless uncle snoring nearby. And over it all, a profound pall of ordinariness: my aunt was dying, passing her last years in such mundane activities as driving around in the heat to tourist attractions on a brown, weedy, relentlessly flat prairie to learn about mundane people. As I stood before museum exhibits, most of the Ingallses struck me as shockingly boring, grim, thick waisted, fussy, even bigoted. This was what life came down to, something so opposite the slim, spirited Laura's youthful dreams.

In the wake of these impressions, which felt like a betrayal of my dying aunt, my relationship with her couldn't help but shift. I was growing up, moving on, viewing the world in increasingly complex ways, rejecting the nostalgia with which she regarded the books. Naturally, the series had ceased to speak to me in quite the same way, although the suddenness with which I severed myself from them still feels underscored with an exaggerated sense of disillusionment.

Even in adulthood, my attempts to read the *Little House* series to my daughter repeatedly stalled. I couldn't seem to achieve what I'd been able to with childhood books that meant less to me: I couldn't re-create that unalloyed pleasure and fierce possessiveness that marked my early relationship with Wilder's work. My feelings about those novels were too bound up in my memory of that trip, my sense of being deeply, strangely, let down.

In my early twenties, encountering Michael Dorris's essay on the series's portrayal of American Indians, I related to his sense of betrayal. My own similar feelings as a white teenager remained more nebulous to me than his understandable adult discomfort with the embedded politics that erased the humanity of the Osage Indians and reinforced an attitude of white entitlement. A few years later, in his biography of Wilder's daughter Rose Wilder Lane, William Holtz also shook up many assumptions on which my childhood was built when he asserted that Lane had ghostwritten the novels. My relationship with the books became even more complicated as I reconsidered my ingrained belief that they were simply apolitical accounts of Wilder's life that had been written by a relatively inexperienced author with amazing stores of raw talent. I also had to rethink the assumption that single authorship automatically accorded books more authority and artistic value than collaboration.

In my forties, as I began to reread childhood favorites, I steered clear of the *Lit-*

tle House series after many failed attempts to share them with my daughter. It had started when she was five, and I read aloud *Little House in the Big Woods.* She was less than enthralled. I pushed on to *Little House on the Prairie* while she was in the bathtub. Some books had so captivated her—*The Ersatz Elevator, Because of Winn Dixie, In the Year of the Boar and Jackie Robinson*—that she demanded that I keep reading while the water turned chilly. "Go on," she said, and ran more hot water. At the ends of the books she emerged looking aged, fingers and toes shriveled, skin white and as soft as Kleenex.

But with *Little House on the Prairie*, the bathwater didn't even have the chance to turn tepid. After one chapter each night, she was out of there, dripping impatiently on the rug as she called for her towel. In today's sophisticated, high-concept page-turning children's book market, I thought, from her perspective as a child of China and the eastern US, episodic stories about the grind of pioneer life and its corresponding comforts must seem dull.

We did watch a new TV movie of *Little House on the Prairie*, and I even made it through a few episodes of the saccharine series on DVD before I turned her loose to stomach them on her own. We began *On the Banks of Plum Creek*, but it didn't take.

I had by then been rereading childhood books for several years, and I had a sense of reluctant inevitability that I was going to have to return to this series. After all, though my worldview had been shaped by many, many books, none had influenced me quite as profoundly as these, the ones that figured in my earliest memories. Eventually it became clear to me that I didn't just want to reread these formative books; it seemed somehow important to return to the places that had inspired them. About that time, I received a state arts grant and the time seemed right—would I ever again have the money to do a trip like this? We made another stab at *Plum Creek* and got to the end three months later, two weeks before we were scheduled to leave. Reading aloud, I was finding the books so familiar that they felt redundant, like a part of my past that I just needed to let go of. I regretted planning the trip.

Finally, a week and a half before our departure date, I buckled down. Once I started, I flew through the series, senses heightened, memories sparking; my love for the books was mysteriously restored as I experienced a new pull toward the theme of undergoing, again and again, the process of making a home. Every few years, in a new state, I've planted my china-shepherdess equivalent on my own mantel-equivalent, created a new network of friends and a new home on a reverse trek from that of my ancestors, relocating from Kansas to Arkansas to Missouri to Nebraska, briefly detouring to the southeast, ending up in the northeast. My relationship to the books reconfigured itself in light of my adult experience.

I also recognized details from the books in unexpected ways. There are a few mentions of Ma's Delaine dress, a holdover from her fashionable, independent life before marriage. I didn't remember the dress, but now I knew where my cousin Jody got one of her childhood favorite girl names, Delaine. I remembered wishing I could, like Mary, believe in the superiority of my blond hair, never described by anybody as "golden." I recalled finding wooden beads in the dirt at a camp I attended when I was nine, sure they were Indian beads just like the ones Laura and Mary find.

The mood of the books began to infect me, a gratitude for small pleasures. I began to think in Wilder's language; everything was "happy," "cozy," "pretty," "snug," and "sweet." I had such a feeling of plenty when I carried groceries—"*provisions*," I thought—down to my basement freezer. I felt new appreciation for the patterns of sunlight swimming on the walls of my living room, for the red geraniums in a pot on my porch, for quiet hours of reading and evening walks.

When I was halfway through the series, I was seized by an impulse to explore the woods above our house. We'd lived there six years, so it seemed high time to find out what was nearby. Pa and Laura's shared wanderlust, their yearning toward adventure, had sizzled from the pages into my fingertips, entering my bloodstream as surely as if Wilder had passed her DNA on to me.

I was much more excited about the woods than Sophie. It was 90 degrees, and she immediately started complaining that she was hot and tired. The path climbed steeply uphill, scored with deep muddy ruts from four-wheelers. Every few feet, tucked back into trees, overgrown with weeds, old oil derricks stood like miniature windmills robbed of their blades.

We followed a set of cables stretching way up the mountain, ending at a small engine house, the whole contraption rusted over. Northwestern Pennsylvania was the US's chief oil producer from the mid-1800s until early in the twentieth century, when much of the country's oil industry shifted to Texas. In the 1870s, there were 4,000 oil wells in Bradford, nearly half the number of the town's human population today.

The path plunged steeply downhill, blackberry thickets tangling along the edges where the trail flattened out. I wondered if we should turn back before we got lost, but we pressed on and suddenly found ourselves at a clearing where the whole town spread beneath our feet. Black rooftops with their brick chimneys, white pipes, and pine needle puddles descended the hill like stair steps. In the valley below, downtown rose up, a few six- and eight-story buildings against the backdrop of the opposite hills.

Then the end of the trail spilled us out onto a street. Nearby, an eerie clanking repeated and repeated—an empty swing in a breeze? A child's loose bicycle wheel?

The noise was too rhythmic to be either. We crept toward the sound, ears perked for children's voices among the steady clank, clank, clank. Sophie glanced at me, wide eyed. We squinted through the trees, expecting ghosts. Instead we came upon a little oil rig, cables alternating as they creaked up and down.

Turning the corner, we found ourselves looking down on the roof of Sophie's school. "We could walk to school this way," I said. I pictured her tramping through the woods like a storybook pioneer girl. Rather than wait for the bus, it's usually easier for us to take the sidewalks a few blocks along the busy streets below. But this way, we could stroll through the stillness, watching the leaves change in the fall, feeling, under our feet, the earth turn hard and frozen, our footsteps marking white stretches of snow. The *Little House* series had infected me, reminding me what it was like to feel like a character in a book, heightening my alertness to history and nature, my appreciation of details, of beauty.

"Mmm," was all Sophie said in reply to my half-cocked notion about walking this way every day.

We leave for our trip on an overcast day in July 2007. We live on the Pennsylvania/New York border, just a few miles south of Cuba, New York. That's the area that, 150 years ago, the family of a young teenager named Charles Ingalls also left to head west. I picture them setting out on a summer day from the pine-forested hills of Allegheny County, canvas stretched over the top of the wagon, a baby on the box behind the seat, children crouching in the swaying bed. The wagon probably held a couple of trunks of family possessions and supplies: porcelain bowl and pitcher, treasured family photos, a musket and fiddle, coffee beans and corn meal and molasses, salt pork and dried fruits.

Here's what I imagine: the wagon hot and stuffy, even with the sides rolled up to let in a breeze, the children watching the two lines stretching endlessly behind them where the wagon wheels have flattened the grass. Wheels creak and hooves clip clop through the vast silence of the roadless prairie, moving about two miles an hour, covering maybe fifteen miles in a day. Birds rise into the overturned blue bowl of sky like pepper emptied suddenly from a shaker. Clouds scud above and quick rabbits rustle through grass, and sometimes near creeks the children spot muskrat houses or beaver dams. And from the height of bird flight, the speed of clouds, the number of rabbits, the thickness of mud walls, Charles Ingalls learns to gather information about the length and harshness of the season ahead. This is one of the skills he will pass on to his daughter, Laura Ingalls Wilder, whose stories will teach generations about westward migration and white settlement of the American frontier.

I think about this as I load up our Rent-a-Wreck, a Ford Taurus with 132,000 miles and an alarming tendency to rattle and groan during left turns. I've packed more stuff than any wagon could hold, though only a fraction of the contents of my house. I tuck the cooler on the front seat floor. It contains two days' worth of lunches: cheese and turkey, mini-bagels, apples and grapes. Finally my nine-year-old daughter and I set out toward Erie, straddling the Pennsylvania/New York border through the Alleghenies. Forested hills, like nubby green wool, meet a gray sky that gradually clears, woolly hills poking up against cottony clouds.

Following directions printed out from MapQuest, I pause to check an Internet weather report on my cell phone. The temperature is currently in the low 70s. I watch gas prices descend through Ohio, from $2.99 to $2.98 to $2.95 a gallon. We zip past moving vans and RVs—"Sunseeker," these lumbering vehicles are labeled, and "Pioneer Spirit."

In the backseat, Sophie watches her portable DVD player. I shuffle through my shoebox of CDs for the one I always play first on any trip, my Women on the Road compilation. I have chosen mostly songs communicating ambivalent messages I relate to, messages that when juxtaposed become downright schizophrenic, about loss and yearning, freedom and independence, solitude and companionship. The Indigo Girls set out on an adventure, getting out the map and laying their fingers down on random destinations. Dar Williams is traveling again, conflicted about the solo nature of her journey. Patsy Cline is moving along, she's got to be free. The road is Bonnie Raitt's middle name. Kirsti MacColl has been driving all day but is getting no further away. Kristin Hall is following her compass in the dark.[4] And so on. I am a woman traveling alone with a child, and the music gives me courage. As we set out to retrace the journey of Laura Ingalls Wilder, I imagine that the endless stretch of Ohio would be intolerable without music.

As we drive across Ohio, I think about how my aunt was forty-two, just a little younger than I am now, when we embarked on our Laura Ingalls Wilder trip. Like her, I am a reader, a teacher, and a mother through adoption. Her son was eight during the trip, close to my daughter's age.

I idly go on calculating parallels, what my friend Dianne calls numeric convergences. Wilder started writing her books when my mother was three, I figure out, and wrapped up the series when Mom was fourteen. Mom started reading the books to me when I was three; I quit reading them altogether right before my fourteenth birthday. Charles Ingalls would have been about fourteen when his family left Cuba, New York, and migrated to Illinois. Some years later, at thirteen, Almanzo Wilder left Malone, New York, about seven hours northeast of Cuba, with his family, and his life would intersect fatefully with Laura's about ten years later.

I know all of this because, in addition to rereading the series, I skimmed several biographies. I'd forgotten how much of real life had been simplified, altered, fictionalized, and dramatized in the process of converting Wilder's experiences into stories, despite her repeated insistence that everything in the books actually happened. Laura Ingalls took a journey somewhat more convoluted than portrayed in the books: after Charles relocated from Illinois to Wisconsin, where he and Caroline married, they took their young children to live in Missouri, then Kansas territory, then back to Wisconsin. Within a few years, they lit out for Minnesota, eventually backtracked for a brief stay in Iowa, returned to Minnesota, and finally settled in South Dakota. Later, Wilder spent a year in Florida, then the remainder and bulk of her life in Missouri. But in the books, Laura and her family move in a clean line west, from Wisconsin to eastern Kansas to Minnesota to South Dakota.

Now, as I drive, I find myself thinking about the ways these books contributed to my identity as a midwesterner. Although I was brought up in Kansas on the romantic myth of western expansion, it's still a surprise to realize just how seriously pioneers like Wilder took that romance—and the corollary idea that to move east was a kind of backsliding. Those who gave up everything to settle west of the Mississippi, especially the white pioneers who pressed into that last frontier of the untamed prairie, were reputed to be courageous, hardworking, and neighborly. For the sake of a dream, they had sacrificed comfort and security.

Many fellow Kansans refer to the East Coast as "back east," a phrase which perplexed me as a child and young adult. It seemed pretentious, a claim of ancestral connection to what we imagined was a more refined civilization. That word choice retained an awareness of geographic roots but also, I thought, a hint of regret for a lost sophistication. I was proud to the point of contrariness of my pioneer roots, of the hardy grandfather who came to Kansas in a covered wagon, of the tenacious stock from which I'd descended. I was vaguely aware that others did not necessarily feel the same way. Every day after school when I was eleven, I watched reruns of *Gilligan's Island*, whose original theme song listed the desert island's seven castaways as "Gilligan, the Skipper too, the millionaire, and his wife, the movie star, and the rest." The omission of the professor and Mary Ann was probably due to the fact that they were considered lesser stars, but at eleven, I assumed that it was because young women from Kansas and professors were just less significant than millionaires and movie stars. At the time I had no plans to become a professor, so I was oblivious to the implication that he wasn't important, but I felt a little defensive about Mary Ann.

When I landed in a graduate program in Arkansas, fellow students from the East Coast bragged about their Ivy League educations, their European travel, their ancestors who came to America on the Mayflower. I didn't get what the big deal was, or why so many of my classmates felt qualified to dismiss the Midwest as the "flyover," what they insisted even in the face of evidence to the contrary was a barren, treeless land. But, I protested, the ancestors of white midwesterners had also largely arrived from European countries; some had also fought in the American Revolution; but rather than settle and build fortunes and create legacies at prestigious universities, many of them had instead pressed onward, creating a society where class was at least temporarily meaningless. What difference did a family's social position make when survival depended on their ability to overcome hardship and cooperate with each other? I identified when, years later, rereading the books of another favorite childhood author, Maud Hart Lovelace, I came across this passage in *Carney's House Party*:

> No one at Vassar [knew] much even about Minnesota. Some girls thought there were Indians running wild in the streets out there. Moreover, they thought that all culture and refinement ended at the Hudson. . . . They were astonished at how well she played the piano. They were amazed that her clothes were so modish, and it meant nothing to them when Carney explained that she and her mother had bought them in Minneapolis. They confused Minneapolis with Indianapolis and both cities seemed equally remote. "They haven't any *idea* how nice the Middle West is," she thought, with a sudden longing for it. She had returned to Minnesota last summer feeling that nothing she had seen in the East was half so beautiful as that rolling green country, with its generous farms, its groves and fertile pastures, a tree-fringed lake around every turn in the road.[5]

My 1964 *World Book Encyclopedia* says that "Western Frontier Life marks one of the most exciting chapters in American history." It cites the "dreams of gold-hungry prospectors and of homesteaders whose back-breaking labor transformed barren plains into fields of grain" and the "living tradition that symbolizes to men and women everywhere the American achievement of taming a wild and beautiful land." In my early twenties, I didn't know what to make of the dissonance between such glorified language that had shaped my image of my home region and the contrasting views of many who grew up east of the Mississippi. Even my current students who've lived their lives in small Pennsylvania towns have been known to smirk and make fun of me for being from Kansas. These Appalachian students, beleaguered by the stereotypes they face, have embraced some unspoken sense of geographic superiority that deems me, from the Air Capital of the World in the Breadbasket of the Nation, a hick, a bumpkin.

My former classmates and current students did not apparently absorb the wide-ranging legacy of Laura Ingalls Wilder, who ranks even above Frederick Jackson Turner, in the estimation of many, for teaching generations about the American West. Or so Donald Zochert asserts in his biography *Laura*.[6] And while she could not have initially predicted the breadth of her work's influence, Wilder was heavily invested in the romance of westward movement and the shame of retreating east. The trail of the fictionalized Ingalls family seems deliberately constructed to promote that mythology.

My own pride in my heritage has been reshuffled somewhat in the face of East Coast oblivion to the pioneering spirit. A colleague from Pittsburgh once called her native city "The Gateway to the Midwest," a phrase I pounced on, scornful and amused at the implication that a city that seemed to me to be pretty far east was the last vestige of civilization before the vast expanse of nothingness standing between it and the West Coast. It was a shock to confront stereotypes of midwesterners as the insulated ones, the ones beset by appalling ignorance, the ones lacking sophistication and irony. I had no illusions of sophistication but an extremely well-developed sense of irony, and most of these stereotypes were directly opposed to what I'd been brought up to believe about my native landscape and its hardy settlers.

I'd never encountered this attitude of superiority from any of my many childhood pen pals who wrote to me from all over the US. There was, however, the occasional query about the state of cowboy/Indian relations in Kansas. Then there was the whimsical short-term sixth grade correspondent who envisioned Kansas as a beautiful colorful place bisected by roads made of pure gold. I had to gently explain, with all the twelve-year-old tact I could muster, that she was confusing us with Oz, that we were the black and white segments, and no, in actuality Kansas was not a black and white state.

Of course, narratives casting pioneers as larger-than-life enterprising visionaries eventually had to be revealed to be just as precarious as any of our fictions. These myths had to come under fire just as our other myths did, like that Columbus discovered America or that my native Kansas had been on the "right" side of the Civil War. Kansas did, in fact, fight on the Union side, but I knew little about my home state as a site of violent contention between proslavery and antislavery forces; I'd never heard the nickname "Bleeding Kansas."

And my ancestors who'd nobly beat the soil into submission had also, it turned out, participated in the dehumanization and displacement of thousands of Indians. And for what? The last page of David Laskin's *The Children's Blizzard* left my brain reeling. The book, which tells the story of a deadly snowstorm in the upper Midwest in 1888, only seven years after similar blizzards in the same region described in Wilder's *Long Winter*, finally posits that we can now write off white settlement of the plains states as a vast and costly failed experiment. No one ever really tamed the harsh conditions of the prairie, a fact ever more apparent in the last few decades' widespread disappearance of family farms. Perhaps it is time to admit to our mistake, critics contend.[7]

I was startled and uncomfortable with what seemed a wholesale dismissal of my own foundation, though I knew such critiques are underpinned with important questions. I imagined Laura Ingalls Wilder churning the dirt around her grave in Mansfield, Missouri, as she turned over. I didn't mind pricking a few holes in the myths on which my life was built. But was it necessary to deflate them altogether?

Maybe when I was thirteen, it was starting to dawn on me in some nebulous way that yes, it was necessary. Maybe that has something to do with why that long-ago trip felt so anticlimactic.

Now, it takes us seven and a half hours to reach Columbus, where we spend the night at our friends Lee and Deb's. Early Monday we head toward Illinois, pushing the limits of nine-year-old patience, on the road more than seven hours again to visit Karen, Jim, and Abby on the Rock River in Moline, IL. Tuesday, Sophie and I set out through thunderstorms for Wabasha, MN, across the river from Pepin, WI, where *Little House in the Big Woods* takes place. Everything is the deep color of the world after rain—the green, green grass, the velvet blue of the overcast sky, the wet orange cones along the highway, the newly painted yellow lines. At Dubuque, IA, we cross the Mississippi in a blinding rain. It clatters like an old toolbox is being emptied onto the roof.

A sign in Lancaster, WI, says, "Buy a women's bottom and get a women's top free." At La Crosse we pass over the Mississippi yet again, this time into Minnesota, our third casual crossing. In a couple of weeks a bridge will collapse near Minneapolis, killing thirteen people, but for now I'm zipping back and forth across the river, reveling at how easy it is to speed over water the Ingalls family could only cross on ice. Pioneer families left trunks and pianos and rocking chairs strewn along the banks of this river, finding it too great a risk, in the end, to carry such heavy possessions across potentially fragile ice.

In Minnesota, we hug the river all the way up Highway 61. Bluffs swell along one side and railroad tracks follow the river on the other. We head toward the Little House in the Big Woods, my anticipation swelling like the bluffs, because although I'm not sure what I'll find, I'm headed to the place where the books began. And however ambivalent or uncertain I may be today, that is also the place where my love of reading began.

CHAPTER TWO

Rereading Childhood

ONE DAY DURING COLLEGE, I was browsing through a used bookstore when I came across a paperback by Margaret Hodges called *What's for Lunch, Charley?*

A feather brush of memory stirred. Suddenly, I was seven, reaching up to retrieve from a high shelf at the Seltzer School library a book about a boy named Charley. At twenty, I picked up Hodges's book and a small, vulnerable feeling flooded back, accompanied by wild excitement and wonder. I didn't remember anything about the characters or the story. Just that feeling.

I bought the book, intending to reread it, but instead ended up packing it a total of fourteen times in the subsequent eighteen years, unpacking it again in each new home. When I embarked on my project of rereading old favorites, I included *What's for Lunch, Charley?* on my list in addition to the books my mom had read to me when I was a preschooler, like *Little House in the Big Woods, Little House on the Prairie, Summer at Buckhorn,* and *Mrs. Piggle-Wiggle* along with the first chapter book I'd checked out from the Wichita Public Library, Carolyn Haywood's *"B" Is for Betsy.*

Then I settled down to read my copy of *What's for Lunch, Charley?* Its front cover promptly fell off and its middle section hung loose. It took me twenty minutes to review the story of Charley as he comes to realize that Plain Jane Lane, who shares her peanut butter sandwich with him, is more worthy of admiration and attention than Rosabelle, the beautiful quiet new girl with painted fingernails and fancy lunches.

A copy of this book had been disintegrating on my shelves for twenty years, hauled from state to state, house to house, re-alphabetized each time, to come to this? For me to find out that, at seven, I was deeply moved by a tale of two girls vying for a boy's favor? I was mildly horrified.

But an elusive memory kept darting away like a quick slippery fish. I repeatedly had that sensation of a word on the tip of my tongue, a thought sliding to the edge of consciousness but never quite breaking through. It was related to a book I'd glimpsed the week before in a secondhand store in Olean, New York, a children's book by Rebecca Caudill, *Did You Carry the Flag Today, Charley?* It had seemed familiar, but, in a hurry, I'd passed it over. When I went back looking for it, it was gone. Now I ordered a one-cent used copy of it online.

While waiting for that, I turned to *"B" Is for Betsy*, a title that still lit me up with a memory of discovery. Images tumbled forth: Betsy's long braids, her plaid schoolbag. My own red schoolbag, a purchase from Sears right before I started kindergarten. Details permanently embedded in my brain cells had lain dormant for years but now kicked up. Oh, yeah, I thought as I read, how could I have forgotten the bread and jelly sandwiches Betsy packs in her schoolbag pocket every day, or the tea set she wants to buy for her curly-haired friend Ellen?

A battered first edition of *Flag* soon appeared in my mail. Its illustrations were so familiar that the second I opened it, a fierce suppressed excitement overtook me, a dual response: the headiness of adult recognition overlaying a long-buried intense childhood connection. Memories fired along my neurons as I relived the story of a little Appalachian boy named Charley who leaves his remote small home to take a bus to preschool.

Against a backdrop of beautifully described mountains, Charley is a delightfully clever, mischievous, well-meaning kid who can't seem to follow the rules but who loves learning. This evaluation is, of course, the language of my critical, analytical adult self. But, abruptly, that defense peeled away and I was six years old again, standing by the mailbox at the end of my long driveway, waiting for the school bus, bursting with a sense of adventure and independence. I could smell the dirt and the trees. I remembered pretending to be Charley, leaving my own home for a world of learning and books.

There's a wonderful scene where Charley imagines what it would be like to be a rock, another where he paints a picture called "Rainbow in a Puddle at a Filling Station."[1] In the end, nature walks and art and books have opened up possibility and wonder. Learning performs magic, transforming him. I see now how this book transformed me also, tapping into the person I didn't yet know I was, igniting a spark that was already there. Charley and Betsy, both heading off for school, stood on the brink of the same discoveries as I: the joys of reading and learning, the world that books would open up. Now I'd come full circle: listening to stories about Laura read aloud, stumbling upon Betsy and Charley, opened the doors to the reading that would become my greatest and most reliable source of childhood happiness.

At the end of *Did You Carry the Flag Today, Charley?* the title character gets to lead the line to the buses, hoisting the flag. This is a coveted honor awarded to the day's best behaved child, a distinction that hasn't come easily to mischievous Charley. By the time he achieves his goal, he isn't particularly excited, though neither is he blasé. It's just that by then, for him as for my first-grade self and, I imagine, generations of young readers, there were much more meaningful rewards in store.

After I finished that book, my systematic plan fell apart as I returned to the patterns of my childhood, immersing myself in whatever beckoned: Antonia Barber's *The Ghosts*, which I remembered as wonderfully spooky, along with Lois Duncan's *Down a Dark Hall*. Noel Streatfeild's *Dancing Shoes*, which once inspired artistic dreams. Nonfiction books that used to make me wish to belong to a huge, lively family: *Cheaper by the Dozen*, *The Family Nobody Wanted*. Classics like *Heidi*, *Harriet the Spy*, *The Cricket in Times Square*, *Anne of Green Gables*. Series about girls, often out of print. Books that my aunt had given me or that my mother had ordered through the Children's Book of the Month Club or Scholastic Book Services; books I found myself at the library.

I expected to find that books had shaped me philosophically and imaginatively. It was more surprising to note how they'd also affected me on an ordinary material level. For instance, as children, my cousin Jody and I acted out an ongoing saga in which we played sisters who hailed from a nebulous imaginary country, Ockland, whose traditions included a twelfth birthday rite of passage in which girls received a set of "silks." These "silks" were colorful nylon fabric pieces from my mother's scrap box, which was filled to overflowing since my mother sewed every stitch of my clothing until I was twelve—everything but my socks and shoes.

Playing girls from Ockland, we tied our "silks" to skirts fashioned from bed sheets. Suddenly, we were transformed from little girls in plain, functional "sheet skirts" to glamorous ladies in colorful gowns. The silks also gained a rather ominous function when we invented an Ockland coming-of-age ritual: girls used the "silks" to tie together their legs for several hours a day to encourage them to take small, ladylike steps. I won't try to deconstruct all of the implications of the way a coveted decoration turned into a tool of oppression in this game, or what it suggested about the cultural messages we'd received about girls' sexuality. The fun for Jody and me wasn't in creating restrictive customs; it was in then allowing our characters to rebel against them. It took a while to dawn on me that the "silks" were the leftover fabric from my home-sewn panties.

When I started to reread a second grade favorite, Eva Moore's *The Fairy Tale Life of Hans Christian Andersen*, it felt as if a hazy fog hung over me, the outlines of everything vaguely familiar. Then, suddenly, the fog lifted, my vision sharpened, and I recognized the small cozy room where Hans lives with his parents, the illustrations of big-nosed people, the father who makes crooked shoes that fail to secure a dream job as shoemaker to a rich woman, the image of writers as clumsy, hopeless losers whose work can transform them from ugly ducklings into swans.

It was all instantly familiar—but the kicker? To dress Hans up for a special occasion, his mother pins pieces of colorful silk to his white shirt. When I read this, I exploded with laughter. All these years, I'd thought it was a random thing, that idea to make imaginary gowns more fashionable and grown up by tying to them scraps from my panties.

I've always wondered what possessed me, at twelve, to talk my mother into redecorating my room with pink rose-and-trellis wallpaper, an old-fashioned bulbous lamp painted with red roses and turned on with a switch shaped like a gold key, and a dainty new white dresser and desk. Within a couple of years, living in a fussy Victorian room no longer appealed to me, and I was stuck with it. As an adult re-reader, I was able to assign the blame for my mysterious lapse in taste to favorite heroines. Like *The Golden Name Day*'s Nancy Bruce, who chooses wallpaper with yellow roses on it not once, for her room at her adopted grandmother's house, but twice, the second time for her room at her family's new home. Then there's *The Jennifer Gift*'s title character, who scrimps and saves to buy a lamp with a frosted globe and painted flowers as a Christmas gift for her family. The soft glow of my own similar lamp reminded me, at twelve, of the rare but possible miracle of a yearning satisfied.

As I reread, the connections between books and a childhood game and the relationship between favorite stories and my decorating aesthetic quickly became clear, but I found it more difficult to assess the ideological effects of childhood reading. As an adult, I think of reading as a way to enlarge one's world and develop compassion. I wanted to like Judy Blume's *Are You There God? It's Me, Margaret* because my Aunt Shirley gave it to me, but, as my friend Sara puts it, it seemed to "glorify the conventional." But rereading children's books from the 1970s and earlier, which in memory I mostly erroneously associate with human rights, equality, justice, and alignment with the outsider, I wasn't sure that the ones I favored were typically much better. In fact, it sometimes seemed a wonder that they hadn't actually made me a bigot or scared me into permanent feminine submission. Certainly, I realize now, they sometimes instilled and reinforced in me narrow religious beliefs and traditional ideas of female virtue.

Take *Heidi*, which I once loved passionately and was now surprised to find so didactic. The title character is always, to use anachronistic twentieth-century lingo, "witnessing" to others. Suddenly, I understood better a childhood self who memorized Bible verses, earnestly sought to be Christlike, and comforted myself in my diary by writing about the hellfire that my enemies would someday face.

The *Anne* series also has its preachy moments, though they are never as heavy handed as those in *Heidi.* And for their times, neither of these books may have been so bad. But I found myself shuddering on occasion, like when in *Anne of the Island,* some of the judgments on Anne's dying former classmate Ruby Gillis fall just short of smug:

> Heaven could not be what Ruby had been used to. There had been nothing in her gay, frivolous life, her shallow ideals and aspirations, to fit her for that great change, or make the life to come seem to her anything but alien and unreal and undesirable. . . . [Ruby] had laid up her treasures on earth only; she had lived solely for the little things of life.[2]

Montgomery is always walking a fine line here, having created a heroine who takes rampant delight in earthly pleasures, now rushing to reassure us that Anne, in contrast to Ruby, is pure and balanced, someone who, when her ward Davy uses the expression "god knows," quickly scolds him, telling him it "isn't right to take that name in vain or speak it lightly."[3]

Reading books like *Heidi* and *Anne of the Island* and *Little Women* and *Elsie Dinsmore* must have prepared me to find more contemporary novels, like Virginia Sorensen's *Plain Girl,* familiar and relatable. My own daughter likes this book, but to her, the Amish are a foreign culture. In contrast, stern religious practices and girls who longed to be virtuous were a norm for me, even though, unlike *Plain Girl*'s Esther, I neither felt limited by tradition nor shared her sense of belonging to a supportive community.

I was a weird child, brought up in a fundamentalist Christian tradition and steeped in novels that shaped me into a Puritan of sorts. I believed that actions revealed faith rather than words or emotional displays. I saw religion as a personal, private thing, an inducement to individual goodness. But something happened in the mid to late 70s, when I was a young teenager, some change that began around the time that Jimmy Carter was elected, a man who was, according to an approving Sunday school classmate, "a strong Christian."

The atmosphere of my quiet, elderly church had changed completely by the early 80s, transformed to a younger, more dynamic one just in time for the election of Ronald Reagan, the emergence of the Moral Majority, and the increasing preachiness of shows like *Little House on the Prairie.* The youth group I avoided attending seemed infused by evangelical fervor, everyone witnessing to others and being "convicted" by Bible verses. At least we were too reserved and middle class for speaking in tongues or writhing on the floor. My own family even eschewed public singing, so we were the weird ones who stood silently in the back pew while everyone else joined in on hymns. But restraint was not the way to win God's approval, either, according to our earnest youth leader, who deemed private, dignified communion with a higher power to be inadequate. Our leader maintained that two or more Christians had to be gathered in His name to gain an audience with God, and prayers had to end with the phrase "In Jesus' name" if we wanted them to count.

I returned to *Plain Girl* again and again. A book that would provide my daughter a window into another culture offered me novel possibilities for my own religious leanings: that one could form a community around a belief system, rejecting ornamental words in favor of real action, like quilting parties, barn raisings, weddings, and Sunday meetings. I liked being vicariously Amish, at the same time sympathizing with Esther's curiosity about the outside world.

One line in particular stuck with me all the way to adulthood: when Esther's brother Daniel says, "I wonder what harm a button may do a man's soul."[4] From early childhood, I took Biblical injunctions against vanity seriously and had little interest in clothes, jewelry, or makeup. I'd also been heavily influenced by that passage in *Little Women* where Laurie reprimands Meg for getting caught up in "fusses and feathers" when she becomes a guest in a wealthy home and is seduced by "vanity," "powdered and squeezed and frizzled" and made to "look like a fashion plate."[5]

Ornamentation, I believed at eleven or twelve, was a distraction from God. I find this a fairly mysterious position today just as I no longer see alcohol as unambiguously evil. But my beliefs were once so firm that I still find bracelets, rings, and necklaces as well as alcohol somewhat personally foreign, even while I admire friends with beautiful necklaces and jangly bracelets as they matter-of-factly sip their glasses of wine.

In *Plain Girl*, Esther is forced to go to a public school, and there, for the first time, she is described as "pretty" by a girl in a pink dress, Mary. Esther sees herself and her clothes as common and plain, and she thrills at the compliment and rationalizes that it's okay to think about her looks: "Even the Bible said, 'If a woman have long hair, it is a glory to her.'"[6] My friends and I wore our hair long for years; friendships lapsed when I cut mine at fourteen. Our long hair hadn't been so much a glory to God as a way to set ourselves apart from "superficial" peers who aspired to more contemporary lives. We equated being old-fashioned with being deeper, more substantial.

When Mary calls Esther's apron "cute," Esther thinks, "A nice little word— cute! cute! cute! It was like a canary singing."[7] I never heard anyone but small children and animals called "cute" or "pretty" until I was a teenager, when those words were used quite easily and casually by my classmates. That shocked me a little. I believed it was wrong to place value on anyone's appearance. Eventually I did absorb the lingo of the outside world, but until I became a parent, words like "cute" and "pretty" rarely came naturally to me. I understand Esther's surprise and delight at the language she encounters in the non-Amish world.

Esther worries that her friendship with Mary, her desire to try on Mary's pink dress, or her newfound interests in hair and buttons and games of jacks will constitute the First Step Away. She fears that small acts will set in motion irrevocable decisions in her own life, leading her to leave behind her family and community as her brother Dan has done, much to his regret. I imagined what it would mean to take my own First Step Away. It terrified me, as if straying from my family's beliefs might cause me to walk right off the edge of the world into eternal free fall. The outside world felt unsafe, a place dominated by materialism and meanness, and I had every intention of holding it at bay. Sometimes I was struck by a deep embarrassment at my dependence on my parents. But I was also relieved to have more freedom than Esther.

Reading this book at forty made me realize how much, at ten, I resembled a small crotchety old lady, with the qualities my aging mother now valued in her friends. Many of them seemed to me set in their ways, smug in their beliefs, judgmental of difference, and religious in very literal, apparently simplistic, ways. If my mother's friends were also brave and feisty, smart and funny, she didn't let on in her descriptions of them. And so, rereading *Plain Girl* and *Heidi*, I felt a relief at having moved past the simple earnestness of my childhood self into a more complex identity that my mother had never quite understood.

Rereading books I'd once loved sometimes gave me the feeling of having narrowly escaped a terrible fate. It amazes me as an adult to recognize the struggles and messages embedded in childhood favorites. I had no clue the extent to which Laura Ingalls Wilder's *Long Winter* promotes capitalism and free enterprise, as Francis Spufford argues in his *The Child that Books Built.*[8] Who knew that Heidi proselytized rather alarmingly, or that the books of Lois Duncan and Lenora Mattingly Weber had expressed such a startling aversion to nonconformity?

I was often impervious to the intended messages of my favorite books. Take *The Secret Language*, a third grade favorite that introduced me to the boarding school story, with its conventions of morning inspections, midnight feasts, and trunks that start out as luggage and turn into magical repositories for storing secrets. Rereading this book, I realized that the words of the secret language, dormant in my brain, were ones I nevertheless still could have defined today. When I was nine, they were an active part of my vocabulary. My friend Stacey and I described things as "ickenspick," "ankendosh," and "leebossa." This book, I recalled, inspired my longstanding fascination with secret languages and codes.

I happily concurred with the housemother's comment to the best friends who invent this code that "it's fine that in many ways you make up your own minds and do not copy others. The world will always need those who do not try to be like everyone else." I could even agree with her conclusion that "there is a happy medium between the child who wants to be just like everyone else and the child who refuses to do anything the way other children do. I hope, with all my heart, that you girls will be able to find that happy medium in the months and years ahead." But the housemother's final speech made absolutely no mark on my consciousness: "I suppose it is natural for girls your age to want to have secrets. But as you grow up you'll realize, I hope, that it is not thoughtful to say things others cannot understand."[9]

Maybe I skipped that part. Because not only did Stacey and I adopt Victoria and Martha's secret language for ourselves, we also learned the sign alphabet so we could talk across classrooms. All the way through ninth grade, my friends and I developed a variety of codes and secret methods of communicating—right up until we started taking foreign languages in high school, learning to decipher another kind of code. My weirdest invented method of communication was when Jody and I memorized Morse code and sent messages across the dinner table using our noses (a wiggle for a dot, flared nostrils for a dash).

I wonder how many young fans of *The Secret Language* actually paid any mind to the housemother. Her words strike me now as a clever way to reflect the kind of indoctrination that would satisfy parents and teachers and librarians while recognizing full well that children would completely overlook them in favor of the imaginative possibilities that the book suggests.

I was drawn to stories about family bonds, particularly those about alternative families. But my ability to ignore some messages meant that I was untroubled by what I now sometimes find to be more disturbing undertones in the presentation of blood loyalties in books such as Lois Lenski's *Strawberry Girl* or Noel Streatfeild's *Dancing Shoes*. I still find appealing the extended family of the Amish community in *Plain Girl* as well as the ties Heidi creates for herself after she is failed by most of her biological relations. Such self-created networks were once especially necessary due to high mortality rates. Now they've again become fashionable in literature because of the fragmentation and mobility that routinely scatters households.

Strawberry Girl centers on a war between two families, fueled by hostility over class differences. The protagonist's family is considered "biggety" because they own a tablecloth and china. The plot also involves an alcoholic neighbor whose drinking days come to an end when he gets religion. Ultimately the story is about community and reconciliation.

But when I was a child, it never occurred to me to take note of who is excluded from the family and community, and the embedded 1930s Florida racial attitudes in *Strawberry Girl* made little impression on me. At one point, one character admires the name of another, Jefferson Davis Slater. Lenski's foreword itself seems to echo some Hitler-era attitudes: "Many old customs, folk songs, and superstitions have been handed down along with Anglo-Saxon purity of type, shown in their unusual beauty of physical feature."[10] Ultimately, the community of this book finds forgiveness for a once-mean recovering alcoholic, and the narrator critiques the absurdly small variations in situation that can lead to class distinctions. But while characters break down barriers to form communities, race is not one of those barriers.

My counterpoint to this book was Helen Doss's *The Family Nobody Wanted*, a warm memoir filled with anecdotes about the adorable comments and cute antics of a family of adopted mixed-race children originally considered unplaceable by 1940s adoption agencies—hence the title. The message I took from this book was that race didn't matter and adoption could be not just a viable but a highly desirable way to build a family.

On her website, The Adoption History Project, Ellen Herman points out that this book was

> good propaganda at a time of global anti-communism and domestic racial strife. Family harmony among races and nations, however rare, was an answer to the accusation that Cold War policy hypocritically insisted on equality abroad while tolerating inequality at home. The Dosses proved that Americans believed prejudice was irrational and unpatriotic.[11]

Certainly in adulthood, as the parent of an Asian child, I'm much more aware of these complexities. But I owe a debt to this book for setting me on my path toward parenthood, as did many stories that present alternative families in matter-of-fact ways.

Anne of Green Gables was another book that created a positive view of adoption, and, it turns out, was influential in initiating a cultural shift in attitudes toward adoption that are still prevalent today. Before the beginning of the twentieth century, orphans had been regarded as extra workers, additions to their families that brought economic or practical benefits. *Anne* influenced and reflected a new emphasis on the emotional aspects of adoption for parents and children, says Irene Gammel.[12] When Marilla asks, "What good would she be to us?" Matthew replies, "We might be some good to her."[13] By 1924, with the debut of the comic strip "Little Orphan Annie," another red-haired orphan found herself no longer marginal, but, says Gammel, a "cherished status symbol in the center of Daddy Warbucks' millionaire family."[14]

Fortunately, the messages of Doss's and Montgomery's books far overshadowed those of, say, Noel Streatfeild's *Dancing Shoes*. This book's mixed view of adoption and its promotion of the importance of genetics apparently made little impression on me when I was young. When she was five, my daughter asked me to read *Dancing Shoes* aloud. I started it, stalling quickly on its treatment of adoption. We are constantly reminded that pretty, vivacious Hilary is Rachel's "adopted sister." Every reference to Hilary is qualified. Hilary refers to her adoptive mother as "Rachel's mother." Hilary's adoptive mother even says, "I'm not really [Hilary's] mother. She is not Hilary Lennox, though that's what we call her. She's adopted." "You're her sister in a manner of speaking," one character says of Rachel to Hilary.[15]

These days, a potential parent who would hold an adopted child at arm's length and perpetually define her as an outsider would presumably have difficulty being approved by a home study. But then, anyone referring to their children in a subtly self-congratulatory way as "the family nobody wanted" would also raise eyebrows in the adoption community. Being orphaned remains a popular device in children's literature, perhaps reflecting the reality of higher mortality rates during the time period in which it originated but lasting because it allowed young characters to face obstacles without adult intervention, then finally to triumph and experience the completion of finding a new family.

Today, many adoptive parents are disturbed by the high incidence of orphans in children's literature and any negative portrayals of adoption, but no one is disturbed enough, in my mind, by the gooey presentations. Take the way the TV series *Little House on the Prairie* used adoption as a hokey device to bring cute children into an aging show, completely violating historical accuracy. By the time I was a teenager, that kind of manipulation irritated me.

But as a reader, I mostly embraced stories about families, although I was a little skeptical about the size of the family in, say, *Cheaper by the Dozen*, a nonfiction book about motion studies pioneers Frank and Lillian Gilbreth and their twelve children. I especially liked the sequel, *Belles on Their Toes*, in which Lillian is left widowed and, with all of her children pitching in, takes over the family management consulting business and builds a reputation as one of the world's great industrial and management engineers. What a disappointment to take my daughter to the 2003 movie *Cheaper by the Dozen* and find it an oppressive piece of propaganda.[16] The parents are presented as overly invested in their careers (and any passion for their work is, by implication, overinvestment), the children as whiny, spoiled, selfish, and absolutely right in rebuking their parents for ever being unavailable. By the end, the parents have given up their own dreams in order to cater to their children—but the parents are then richly rewarded for their sacrifices by lucrative job offers and a bestselling book. I much preferred the original story about a strong and inspiring career woman, even if the idea of twelve children seemed potentially fun but awfully chaotic.

As a reader, I particularly embraced stories about families with four children, which describes most of my favorite fictional families, starting with *The Boxcar Children*'s quartet of resourceful youngsters whom I first encountered in kindergarten. Later, I wanted to be one of *Little Women*'s four March sisters. In a variation on the theme, one of my mother's favorite childhood books, *Summer at Buckhorn*, featured five siblings with names like Hinkabus, Pinkie, and Bluetie, who spend a summer barefoot on a relatives' farm, and when my mom read the book aloud to me, I imagined being one of them. I was drawn to Nancy Bruce and her three female adopted cousins in *The Golden Name Day* series, Eunice Young Smith's Hill family with two girls and two boys in her *Jennifer* series, and Elizabeth Enright's similar Melendy family configuration. My fascination with families with four children also led me to Lenora Mattingly Weber's Beany *Malone* series, although I was somewhat uneasy with these books.

In her book *Leave Me Alone, I'm Reading*, Maureen Corrigan writes about relating to this series as a Catholic schoolgirl. Brought up decidedly protestant, unsure why anyone would call a girl *Beany* or *Mary Fred*, I, in contrast, found the 1940s and 50s Catholicism of these books alien. Furthermore, the children are all teenagers, which seemed a bit old from my middle reader perspective. And finally, the books felt outmoded when I first encountered them around 1974, thirty years after the publication of the first novel, *Meet the Malones*. Rereading them now, another thirty years later, I found them surprisingly charming, more World War II period pieces than embarrassingly dated stories, their antiquated moments more amusing than anything.

In *Make a Wish for Me*, for instance, Beany's boss, Eve, says, "In my day we called it 'petting.' And it did a girl no good to be labeled a 'petter.' You'll notice, Beany, it's always the girl who is labeled, never the boy. As I say, it's a man's world. What's the word for petting now? I can't keep up with it. Smooching?" Beany replies, "No, that's baroque—meaning old-fashioned. Now it's loving-it-up. Only at Harkness we have a new word—more-thanning. . . ."[17]

Nowadays, more people remember terminology like "petting" and "smooching" than "loving-it-up" and "more-thanning." Most of this slang had largely fallen out of use by the time I encountered these books, replaced by "necking" and then "making out." Today, people hook up rather than loving-it-up. They certainly no longer more-than, as far as I know.

My reserved affection for the first few Malone family books, the only ones I read as a child, must have protected me from what I discovered as an adult are sometimes troubling messages about female sacrifice and conformity. Or maybe I didn't notice them so much because I did only read the first few books; these themes don't become really objectionable until a few novels in. In the first installment of the series, *Meet the Malones*, Mary Fred is the family's "ballast," the one who takes care of everyone and holds things together. Brother Johnny is the "genius," sister Elizabeth "the lovely one," sister Beany the "capable" one, their widowed father a respected newspaper columnist with legendary integrity.

The family is portrayed with a simple timelessness until the outside world intrudes and we enter heavy-duty 1940s slangland. In the chapter "The Hero of Harkness High," a big-shot football player takes an interest in Mary Fred. Dike— yep, that's his name—prefers "smooth little queens" to "mop squeezers" like Mary Fred or to "studes," girls who make good grades.[18]

But suddenly, wisecracking Dike resolves to make Mary Fred his "squaw."[19] Dike is clearly using Mary Fred; his trendy language announces his lack of substance, as does his unfortunate name, probably meant as an ironic reference to a hole in the wall that lets water through rather than any secret lesbian tendencies.

Meet the Malones tells the dark side of the Cinderella story as Mary Fred transforms from down-to-earth worker bee to queenly popular girl. There's even a fairy godmother, step-grandma Nonna, who takes over the household when Father is sent to Hawaii to cover the aftermath of the Pearl Harbor bombing. Nonna buys everyone fancy clothes and new furniture, bans their ragamuffin friends, sells Mary Fred's beloved horse, and makes over Beany's bedroom despite her protests.

Eventually, Nonna is banished and Mary Fred resumes her role as sensitive good-girl caretaker. When I was young, my own moral compass aligned itself with literature that condemned popularity, vanity, and superficiality, and favored independence, self-reliance, and substance. In Weber's world, popularity is equivalent to being mindless, boring, and mean spirited. But as an adult poring over these stories that I once read in plaid Berkeley Highland editions, I gradually realized that the message is far less about nonconformity, far more about reinforcing the social order by creating upstanding citizens.

By the second book, *Beany Malone*, the youngest sister, now has taken over the role of family "ballast." Mary Fred's in college, rushing a sorority, and she continues to face conflicts about fitting in vs. being independent and finding her own power. Her boyfriend Anders, a twenty-one-year-old freshman medical student, is newly returned from the war and uninterested in campus freshman hazing traditions. Mary Fred's association with him jeopardizes her sorority bid.

Mary Fred must fight to stay loyal to what she believes, in the process becoming more powerful and attractive to those who would have previously rejected her. Beany's conflict, in contrast, revolves around protecting her family; she believes that their generosity and concern for others is bringing them down. In the end, though, Beany must reconsider her desire for her family to lock their doors and close down their hearts. The book comes out in favor of community but also of sacrifice, particularly the female kind.

Much of my childhood reading, I would have said before I started rereading the same books, urged readers to shun conformity, to refuse to participate in bigotry or bullying, and to resist pressure to adhere to societal norms that didn't make sense. The cumulative effect of these perceived messages and my childhood religious indoctrination led me to reject sorority life in college, marry young when everyone I knew was waiting, divorce when everyone I knew was married, protest when I disagreed with supervisors, and become a single parent. But now I see that Weber and many other writers had no intention of making their readers threats to the social order. What Weber really conveys is that it's okay to occasionally stray from the pack, if it means renouncing worldliness and pseudo-sophistication in favor of being a good girl making a pleasant home for her family.

In Weber, boys and men are, in keeping with the times, released from any parallel restrictions. Brother Johnny is repeatedly referred to as the "family genius," while Martie, the mostly absent patriarch, takes sanctimonious public positions on traffic laws and prison conditions, earning him worship from the whole community. In a later book, Beany's own rare moment of ambition dissolves into shame at herself for her supposed attention-seeking behavior. She compares herself to a small child calling out, "Look at me!"[20] This is one of many times that double standards prevail. "Like all females, Beany was more interested in her own concerns," Weber tells us, implying that men largely devote their mental energy to contemplating world hunger.

In the many highly readable, lively, and entertaining books in the series—*Beany and the Beckoning Road, Beany Has a Secret Life, Make a Wish for Me*—Weber rapidly dispenses with her male characters, virtuous and otherwise, in order to give center stage to her self-preoccupied but sacrificing females. As each book opens, Martie Malone goes on assignment for his newspaper or travels to Arizona to recuperate from pneumonia. Also at the beginning of each book, Beany has a dramatic falling out with her moody, difficult boyfriend, Norbett. Then she can proceed, a girl whose worth is secure because she is linked to a father and a boyfriend, but whose independence makes for a more interesting story. I zipped along pleasantly, pulled into each carefully constructed plot. I was mildly disgusted that Beany keeps making up with Norbett in the end. I was horrified and amused at the way people used to drive (fast, with lots of fender benders, no seat belts, and regular breakdowns by the side of the highway). I was finding the books compelling and entertaining.

But then things took a really ugly turn. *Meet the Malones*, published in 1943, may be concerned with the dangers of mindless conformity, but as we swing to *Beany Has a Secret Life*, published in 1955, it is purposeful nonconformity that has become dangerous. In the Malone family chronology, it's still 1946, but the characters are embedded in 50s issues. In this novel, written around the same time as the McCarthy hearings, these characters are first and foremost determined not to be seen as un-American.

Beany and her friend Kay agree to form a secret organization with six other classmates. They all vow to be loyal to one another and tell no one about their club. But burgeoning Catholic families cannot be contained and Beany's keeps crashing the club meetings held at her house. Furthermore, "loyalty" turns out to mean helping other members cheat on tests, coerce teachers, and lie to parents. And then Harkness High cracks down on secret clubs—organizations formed without school approval and faculty sponsors—because such secrecy is "un-American." Beany and her friends are hugely distressed; they would never deliberately participate in anything un-American.

At the end, Father says, "You all read the papers. You've seen how many people join 'the Party' thoughtlessly and then regret it."[21] So this is what America stands for—schools dictating what sorts of groups students are allowed to create outside of the classroom? This book seems to be intended as a vehicle for disavowing the Communist party lest Weber's own views be questioned.

Then things get even weirder. *Make a Wish for Me* pushes Weber's increasing emphasis on conformity and female compliance to its horrifyingly inevitable conclusion—horrifying to me, at least, if not to the characters. Urged by those around her to forgive him, Beany has repeatedly returned to her tortured and inconsiderate boyfriend Norbett. "No, Beany, don't be through with Norbett," says her friend Andy, a boy who remains sadistically flirtatious even when he decides to enter the priesthood. "[He] needs someone like you for a ballast."[22] But in *Wish*, Beany finally dumps Norbett—yay! Then she takes up with a college boy who is ten times worse. He physically restrains her, threatens her with violence, and shakes her so hard he leaves finger bruises on her shoulders. Yet she's the one who finally apologizes. He responds that he should have paddled her.[23]

It was something of a relief to return to the more comfortable ground of other four-children family stories, like the out-of-print Nancy Bruce books by Jennie Lindquist, *The Golden Name Day*, *The Little Silver House*, and *The Crystal Tree*, all as infused with light as their titles suggest. Without light, silver is gray, gold is yellow, and crystal is just glass, but Nancy is a character whose vision transforms everything around her to beauty. Nancy's favorite color is yellow, the color associated with sunshine, and it is sunshine and rest and Nancy's capacity for happiness and a developing bond with her three adopted Swedish cousins that will heal the desperately homesick protagonist.

The most vivid moments involve light: reading on the stairs below a stained-glass window, rainbows playing on the page; going to a blossoming apple orchard in moonlight; rising early with the extended family to watch a sunrise; hearing about a crystal tree that sparkles in candlelight and sunlight. These are the books' quiet highlights, the small turning point moments on the journeys to the larger shifts: Nancy finding a way to have her own Swedish name day celebration after much angst because "Nancy" is not a Swedish name; Nancy discovering that she and her parents will be living together in the gray house that appears silver in the moonlight; Nancy reunited with her family and the crystal tree in the silver house.

While Eunice Young Smith's *Jennifer* series spotlights an entire family, as does Elizabeth Enright's *Melendy* series to an even greater degree, the heart of each belongs to a female character: Smith's Jennifer Hill and Enright's Randy Melendy. In memory, I keep mixing the Hills up with the Melendys, since each series features a family of four lively children, a brief subplot about gypsies, a live-in servant, a move to the country, a cupola, important relationships formed with neighbors, and days exploring woods and streams.

The *Jennifer* books take place in the very early part of the twentieth century and were published starting in the late 1940s. The *Melendy* books, also published in the 1940s, are set before and during World War II. Born in the latter half of the twentieth century, I discovered in the 1970s these books about children who lived around the same time that my grandparents were children, in the case of the Hills, and the time that my parents were young, in the case of the Melendys.

Now, rereading the adventures of the Melendy family, who are always writing, singing, composing, playing instruments, reciting, exploring, and putting on shows and carnivals, I realize that these are books that not only gripped my imagination but helped form it. I wanted to be Randy, the younger daughter who dreams of being a dancer. I wished for a wisecracking older brother like Rush, who composes his own music, an older sister who quotes Shakespeare and is an actress on the radio like Mona, a scientific, earnest little brother like Oliver, and a sprawling house with a hidden room, secret basement chambers, and a cupola like the Melendys'.

Or maybe I'd join the Hill family, whose servant Emma speaks with an Irish brogue, oldest son Kevin always talks with his mouth full, and youngest daughter Holly tends to massacre words—"Isn't school just too cadaverous for anything!" she exclaims on her first day of first grade.[24] Jennifer herself loves superlative slang: "spiffy," "spondolix," and "scrumptious." Their mother keeps admonishing the children to say "surely" instead of "sure," "goodness" instead of "gosh." While not quite the artistic prodigies that the Melendy children are, the Hills remain creative and busy, stringing popcorn for Christmas trees and making all their gifts—a pincushion, a butterfly tray, a pen wiper, tie rack, doll clothes, scrapbook, and sachet.

While I was rereading the *Jennifer* books, my daughter, then eight, sped in from outside and begged to be allowed to go visit a neighbor's shallow fish pond. I said okay, then paced restlessly, torn between a desire to let her explore her world and visions of child molesters and drowning. Somehow, I survived a childhood roaming free and playing in the creek. Why wouldn't she, on a dead-end street in a much smaller town with a much lower crime rate? Soon, though, the pond owner walked her back home. He expressed concern about such a small child being out on her own. And although my daughter was small but mature for her age, I could hardly blame him, especially in today's world, for worrying about accidents and liability. He gave me a look that felt like a rebuke.

My own upbringing, fifty years after Jennifer's, resembles hers and those of my own grandmothers far more than it does my daughter's, who is, paradoxically, growing up with the greatest freedom ever accorded women and girls in our society—and the most physical restrictions on children in recent times. For Jennifer, it's the opposite. Despite enviable freedoms, she chafes at the limitations on girls—being excluded from a hike, having to enter a school through a separate door, earning a smaller cut of the profits than the boys after taking produce to market, being told that she'll someday be a fine housewife. Interestingly, girls and boys are not treated differently in Enright's series, and aside from the politics, ultimately, for various literary reasons, I find them to be better books. But as a child, I identified more intensely with sensitive Jennifer Hill, whom her mother worries will become too "shy and introspective," than the balanced and tremendously likeable Randy Melendy.

So it surprises me how much *The Jennifer Wish* and *The Jennifer Gift*, in particular, are, like the Beany books, about the value of female sacrifice. Jennifer gives up her wishing well wish for the sake of her brother, but is eventually unexpectedly rewarded. She works all one fall to earn the money to buy a beautiful lamp to give her family for Christmas, the lamp like the one I bought for my own room, and for a while, basks in happiness and anticipation. But then, due to a misunderstanding, Jennifer is forced to give the lamp to her friend Sarabeth. I still recall the raw sense of loss I felt, reading this book, the sadness of a character who has to relinquish what has come to be more than an object, something that represents a dream.

When I first picked up *Heidi* after thirty years, what I remembered was a book with a happily-ever-after ending in which a child finds a home in the romanticized Alps. I remembered descriptions of nature and Heidi's intense homesickness when she goes to live with Klara. But what I recalled incorrectly was a portrayal of Klara as petulant and manipulative, an image that comes from movies where, like *The Secret Garden*'s Colin, she is surly and spoiled. In the novel, in fact, in the manner of most disabled nineteenth-century children's book characters, Klara is quite saintly, generous and understanding. The goatherd Peter's mother and grandmother are poor, sick, and struggling, but they remain strong and dignified. Klara's grandmother crosses class lines to bond with Peter's grandmother, and sends welcome gifts, though no gift can quite match up to the healing power of Heidi herself. In contrast, both Peter and the grandfather are complex, good at heart but with dark sides. Peter is angry, jealous, and lazy, dismissed, criticized, and ignored by others, but treated with affection by Spyri, who presents him as flawed by immaturity, not evil.

Ultimately, *Heidi* is a pious story about a heroine who is beloved by all and brings solace to everyone with whom she comes in contact. What I never really noticed as a child was how much this characterization had become a girl-story paradigm: female protagonist heals from her losses, often assisted by nature, so that she can take her place as a healer/nurturer to others. This pattern holds true in *Anne of Green Gables*, *Pollyanna*, *A Little Princess*, and *The Secret Garden*, in which Mary starts out sullen but her disposition is improved by nature. The pattern echoes as well through the *Golden Name Day* and *Jennifer* series.

Often orphaned, mostly literally but sometimes figuratively by parents who have been called away, our heroine must achieve physical and emotional health so that she can work miracles with others. Nancy Bruce helps her lame friend Alex walk again. Mary Lennox helps her lame cousin Colin walk again. Heidi helps her lame friend Klara walk again. Jennifer helps her lame friend Sarabeth—whose name evokes both Heidi's wheelchair-bound friend Klara and the sickly March sister, Beth—to—guess what?—walk again. Many times, the miraculous nurturing powers of these literary heroines come from their very essence, not their effort, not even their touch, that heals all with whom they come in contact. Sara Crewe, Anne Shirley, and Pollyanna simply inspire others through their charm, dignity, imagination, and optimism. The female character who can change others by her very being is surprisingly ubiquitous in pre-1970s girl's books.

Anne Shirley was one of the most influential prototypes of this sort of character. While her accident-prone tendencies and the charm of her outsized imagination dominate the first few books, she has been flattened into a single dimension by the epistolary, comparatively boring *Anne of Windy Poplars*. By now, Anne and Gilbert are safely engaged, her problems therefore magically resolved, her life stable and uneventful. For drama she must turn her gifts to addressing the dilemmas of others: matchmaking, repairing feuds, winning over enemies, extracting apologies, and collecting compliments. "You are always making people happy," one character says. "Why, whenever you come into a room, Miss Shirley, the people in it feel happier." The narrator also makes occasional, similar interjections: "The dullest room sparkled, too . . . *lived* . . . when she came into it. . . . There was always something about Anne that made people tell her their troubles."[25]

The paradigm of the heroine's healing influence is carried to absurd lengths in such books as the *Donna Parker* series, which first appeared in print between 1957 and 1964. In the first book, *Donna Parker at Cherrydale*, Donna is supposed to be thirteen, notes blogger Linda on her website Flying Dreams, but sounds at least sixteen.[26] The book speeds young Donna right into faux motherhood as she serves as a counselor at what now seems to me a strange, even sinister, camp. Children as young as four spend their summers at this converted farmhouse owned by a pediatrician, an elaborate daycare that takes children off their parents' hands for weeks at a time. Today this would be a setup for a horror novel or thriller involving cult leaders and child molestation. But the setting proves to be instead a sunny, pleasant opportunity for Donna to learn lessons in nurturing.

Donna's mother is the ultimate female role model, ensuring that her daughter eats a three-course breakfast every morning. But the other side of the coin is the supposedly smothering mother of a nine-year-old camper who falls ill. Other characters heap scorn on this overprotective, overindulgent mother who won't let go and insists on staying at the camp until her child recovers. The staff tolerates her presence but does not allow her to sleep on the same floor as her daughter. The mixed message is bewildering: one mother who plies her healthy teenager with unwanted food is held up as a paragon; the other mother is expected to allow a sick, scared nine-year-old to buck up and fend for herself.

Donna has inherited the nurturing gene from her mother and from the long line of literary heroines whose mere presence does a world of good. A mute boy talks and a grieving concentration camp survivor finds joy in life again, not because of anything Donna does, but because of what she *is*. The reward that excites Donna most? She gets to take a new sewing machine home to her mother. In later books, Donna became for me a far more appealing character as she transforms into a high school journalist and leader, participates in theatrical productions, and has an exciting spy adventure.

Many heroines have the potential for creative lives, including Donna, who dreams of being a journalist; Anne, who wants to be a writer; and characters like Jennifer Hill and Randy Melendy, who have the talent to be dancers or writers. But with the exception of the more realistic Randy, it is far more important for these heroines to demonstrate their gifts for healing. Jennifer Hill, sort of like Anne, a tiny bit like Pollyanna with her insufferable "glad game," is seen by others as special. She not only has a fertile imagination, but the ability to bring happiness and humor to others. In books of this time, female creativity rarely exists as a route to self-fulfillment or artistic contributions, but is valuable for its ability to please others. Like Anne, Jennifer is "not pretty," but her face lights up when she smiles—the ultimate compliment to girls in books from my childhood. Only uninteresting characters possess unqualified beauty, though Jennifer's starry eyes alone are enough to charm adults.

I loved these books, but talk about impossible standards. Adults were never charmed by me. They scolded me or ignored me. When my eyes got starry, I was deemed spacey by my peers and ordered by teachers to pay attention. I was never told that I had an expressive face, a smile that lit up the room, or a special quality that made others happy. This was a lucky thing, I think now. Unable to imitate or compete with these heroines, I was left to forge my own way.

In the context of this childhood reading, I see how Laura Ingalls Wilder's gentle, episodic family stories, though they did eventually feature four sisters, were a huge departure from typical girls' series fare. Wilder accepts the necessity of compromise and sacrifice for both men and women, and Laura, while always dutiful, cannot fully embrace her family's expectations that she be a teacher, part of the reason that she marries early. Unlike in many series books, marriage is not a form of erasure, but her route to independence and self-definition.

Many of the books of my childhood simply reflected a larger culture and have now become somewhat puzzling artifacts of it. Those books also reflect the staggeringly far-reaching influence of classics like *Little Women*, *Jane Eyre*, and *The Secret Garden*, of stories that recur endlessly in different forms, like Andersen's "Ugly Duckling," the same images, values, and story patterns recycled through book after book. They laid a foundation for my own complex struggle with what it means to be female, for the daily power negotiations faced by wives and mothers and female professionals alike, with the way gender is bound up in the expression of the female artist.

The messages of the books I read were sometimes ambiguous ones. Maybe they shaped me in insidious ways, as millions of years erode soil or carve patterns in stone, in tiny increments that only become noticeable over time. But like many child readers, I largely seem to have listened to what spoke to me and blissfully ignored the rest. If books sent complicated messages about creativity, they also inspired it. I was aware from a young age that maybe female characters tended to chuck ambition in favor of nurturing, but their creators were frequently women who'd somehow managed to marry, have children, and write books. And whatever the choices or circumstances of these heroines, many books took for granted that girls can create. The maturing Laura Ingalls, describing the world for her blind sister, begins to understand the possibilities of language. Nancy Drew delights in curiosity and investigation. Betsy Ray, Jo March, and Anne Shirley act on their passions for writing as a matter of course.

And from so many of these books, I received the gift of small pleasures that outlasted raging hormones and trumped rampant consumerism. For Laura, the strains of Pa's fiddle beside a campfire, the feeling of being tucked cozily inside during the winter, the taste of a piece of peppermint, the glimmer of the stars overhead. For Jennifer, a new bird whistle, butterflies, an ice cream cone, an afternoon matinee, a cherry orchard. For Nancy Bruce, a braided chair seat with yellow rags, a new blue sash for a white Sunday dress, a coffee-drinking cat, birches gathered in spring to make eggbeaters. Creativity is in the cracks and crevices of our lives, as much in the details as in the sweep of a narrative arc. The books I read incited imagination and shaped my notions of girlhood, but they also offered small tools for happiness.

CHAPTER THREE

Pepin, Wisconsin

Little House in the Big Woods

THE CHIEF ATTRACTION OF THE ANDERSON HOUSE, a historic inn in the 180-year-old town of Wabasha, Minnesota, is that you can have a cat in your room. A few weeks ago, the novelty of this appealed to me. We don't have pets, and Sophie really, really wants a dog. I've always preferred cats, and maybe I subconsciously hoped that a night with a cat would win her over to my side.

Instead, I convert to dogs. Ginger the cat lies in wait for our door to open, then streaks along the carpet runner in the upstairs hall. She flies down the staircase and past the lobby's antique floral furniture and hutch displaying baked goods for sale. I flick a casual wave at the front desk guy as if we totally meant to let the cat out. I stroll on after Ginger as if we are playing a game fully under my control. Finally I nab her and head back upstairs, smiling again at the desk clerk like this cat and I just had the most fun ever.

Ginger ignores Sophie's attempts to buddy up. Instead, the cat focuses on gaining the upper hand over the big person snubbing her. She climbs into my lap and swishes her tail while I try to jot down notes. All night she pokes her wet nose into my armpit and ear and kneads my arm with her tickly clawless paws. When I push her off the bed, she runs mad circles around the small room, where all the surfaces are cluttered with rag dolls, antique toys, decorative books, and pots of fake flowers. I have crammed our shampoo and lotion containers, prescription bottles, inhalers, hairbrushes and toothbrushes and toothpaste onto the dresser. There they compete for space with old-fashioned cat toys—a stick with a ball tied to the end, a squeaky mouse, a ball with a bell inside. As the cat runs all night, flicking her tail wildly, decorations and toiletries clank against each other and crash to the floor.

Sophie's knees and elbows jab my back. I wake to find her foot hooked over my ear. The bathroom barely has space to turn around. When I shampoo my hair I bang my elbows against the sides of the minuscule shower stall. Our small room feels uncomfortably crowded, an effect heightened by the busy clashing patterns: floral wallpaper above the wainscoting, a seashell pattern below, a striped chair, a floral patchwork quilt. Later, an illustration from a Maud Hart Lovelace book will remind me of this room, with its carpets and rugs and wallpaper and lamps covered with flowers and swirls and stripes and dots, so apparently this chaos is period appropriate.

A hundred and fifty years ago, this room would have represented luxury for a pioneer family of five. Boy would I have made a lousy pioneer.

I have many friends who credit the *Little House* series for making them readers: Michele and Jan and Lisa and Katy and Sena and Dania and, of course, my cousin Jody. Others liked, but didn't love them, like Sara, and then there's my former student Doodle, who wrote to me, "Laura Ingalls Wilder makes me want to pour gasoline on my head and light a match."

I want to say that Doodle is dead wrong, but I find that I've become something of a fence straddler about the early books. Of course I no longer belong to the age group for which they are intended. Millions have entered the series through *Little House in the Big Woods*, as I did when I was three; throngs of readers have stayed through the whole series, often more than once, including me once upon a time. Clearly, many have found there to be something compelling about even these early novels.

Though almost everyone I talked to had strong opinions about Laura Ingalls Wilder, some reactions to our trip plans had nothing to do with the books. I was surprised at how many friends were impressed that I was going to drive halfway across the country, alone with Sophie. When I was younger, before I'd traveled alone a thousand times, moved alone eight times, or adopted a baby by myself, I would have been terrified to make a journey like this. Now I'm surprised to earn so much admiration and trepidation just because I'm a lone woman embarking on a road trip with a child.

Until then, I hadn't thought to be nervous. But ever since we hit the road, I've carried with me a constant underlying dread, a deep unease about risking crimes, accidents, or natural disasters and spending money to visit places about which I am ambivalent. My route is clearly laid out before me, and yet it feels muddied: I don't know quite why I'm doing this.

Maybe I hope that the pioneer spirit will infect me. Maybe I hope that travel will inspire an in-the-moment awareness of details that distances daily aggravations, forcing me to inhabit my life in a newer, calmer, more grateful way. There is less yearning for adventure in *Little House in the Big Woods* than in the later books.

The dominant themes have to do with the comfort of routine and the joy in daily details.

I was surprised during my rereading a couple of weeks ago to discover how the book, focusing on a year in the life of the Ingalls family, the cycle of seasons and the associated rituals of childhood, revolves around processes. Smoking venison, killing and cooking a pig, churning butter, fashioning hats from straw, making bullets and cheese and maple sugar. I can appreciate these gentle descriptions and the way of life they evoke, but I can also relate to Lizzie Skurnick's affectionate send-up in her book *Shelf Discovery* of Wilder's delight in meticulous detail:

> I had forgotten quite how much of the Big Woods is devoted to animals and the disambiguation thereof. That is, my friend, the pig's bladder. That Mary and Laura are bat about. Because, when you were eight, could you think of anything more fun than playing with the bladder of a freshly slaughtered pig? Why, that might be even more fun than getting to watch Ma skim off cracklings from the drained fat, then boil a whole hog's head and chop the meat to make headcheese. But you know what it could never be more fun than? ROASTING A PIG'S TAIL. That would be, and mark the quotes, "Such fun that it was hard to play fair, taking turns."[1]

As a child, I skimmed some of Wilder's long descriptions of processes and skipped whole paragraphs in the chapters in which Pa narrates tales from his own past. In her book *Constructing the Little House*, Ann Romines calls those chapters in Pa's voice "inset stories."[2] Romines's analysis of these helps clarify my own childhood detachment from parts of *Woods* and most of *Farmer Boy*, a book I read once and subsequently ignored, not so interested in Almanzo. When my daughter read *Farmer Boy* in the fourth grade, her assessment was, "Wow, they eat a lot." Skurnick echoes this comment, but views *Farmer Boy* from a different perspective than I did, as an enormous tribute to Wilder's love for Almanzo.[3]

In fact, the existence of the second book in the series, the only one that isn't about Laura and doesn't take place in the Midwest, may have far more to do with Wilder's daughter Rose Wilder Lane's love for her father. Many fans of the Wilder books remain surprisingly unaware of what critics have long acknowledged, that the books were a collaboration between Wilder and Lane. The only real controversy is how much of a role Lane actually played. On one end of the spectrum, when confronted with this information, die-hard Wilder fans from less literary mindsets like my own family members tend to dismiss Lane's role as merely that of an encourager and editor. Biographer William Holtz exists on the other end of the spectrum, contending that Lane completely rewrote Wilder's books from her sketchy drafts and offering some proof that I find convincing, although many Wilder specialists feel that he overstates Lane's role.

Whatever the case, Ann Romines points out that the first two novels attributed to Wilder embody male narratives, Laura Ingalls Wilder and Rose Wilder Lane's stories of their fathers. Like me, Romines found less interesting the stories in *Big Woods* that Charles Ingalls tells about his father's grandfather and himself as a child. Those narratives, along with Almanzo Wilder's in *Farmer Boy*, center on "themes of traditional male initiation," Romines says, developed through conventional linear plots that emphasize conflict, growth, effort, and achievement. In contrast, much of *Woods* is cast in lyric mode rather than narrative, Romines argues, functioning something like a quilt.[4]

I like this metaphor for the way that the book moves from one episode to another, emphasizing imagery and event rather than a narrative arc that builds tension throughout the book and arrives at a climactic event or turning point moment. As a young child, I was drawn to this sort of episodic story, like the early Wilder books or Carolyn Haywood's *Betsy* series or Eunice Young Smith's *Jennifer* books. In Smith's *The Jennifer Wish*, published in 1949, it's not until page 82 that the title character's family manages to set forth to the country, the book's main setting. Rather than having overarching plots, many of these books are, as my friend Sara put it, like a bunch of vignettes strung together.

Today, even younger readers consider speed and efficiency to be a right, in fiction as in life, and Jennifer's family's departure would be expected to take place on the first page. Now we expect tight cause and effect, every detail planted eventually blooming, plots accumulating suspense as they roll ever more swiftly forward, ideally toward some great change or profound revelation. The fact that *Big Woods* comes from a somewhat different tradition may account for my daughter's initial lack of interest in the books, my former student Doodle's impatience, and my own drifting attention as an adult. And even if the stories-within-the-story about Pa or his great-grandfather follow more conventional patterns, they are still cast within a larger episodic structure.

Maybe this sort of plot development is ultimately truer to the experience of childhood than seemingly more sophisticated, more tightly plotted stories. Even memoirs and fiction for adults have trouble formulating early childhood according to the cause-and-effect patterns favored by Aristotle, who deplored the episodic plot as unsophisticated and lacking in artistry, maybe because such structures are literally infantile. They mirror the way babies and small children experience the world, as a series of events without narrative connections. As a young child, if I'd described a recent year, I would have mentioned unrelated events: Valentine's Day, Easter, my cousin's visits, the Fourth of July, the start of school, my birthday, Christmas. First this happened, then that happened, just like in *Little House in the Big Woods*.

As a child, this is what attracted me to *Woods*—this, and Laura herself. I didn't care if the story was sequential or circular or altogether absent, and I was perfectly content with skipping Pa's tales and Wilder's lengthy descriptions of processes. I just wanted to know about Laura, and I skimmed until I found her again. Romines recalls being troubled by the "obscured centrality" of Laura, who inhabits the book less palpably than in the series' later installments.[5] But now, viewing the narrative arc of the entire series, I'm fascinated by the way language and point of view carefully mimic the emergence of self, of Laura's consciousness. In *Woods*, Laura is too young to have much sense of her individuality, instead functioning as a compass around which a rich world spins. Gradually, as she comes of age and as the books' authors document the making of a writer, she will develop a much firmer sense of her own unique vision.

Across the river from Pepin, Wisconsin, Sophie and I pack up and head over to Kellogg, Minnesota, to check out the toy museum and carousel. I saw an ad for it on a restaurant placemat last night, and since it's right down the road, it seemed like a good place to start our day, diffusing what is bound to be for her a Laura Ingalls Wilder overload. Or maybe I'm just procrastinating going to Pepin because I'm so afraid it will be a disappointment.

As we drive, Sophie marvels aloud at the wide open spaces of the Plains states, though this part of Minnesota and Wisconsin is hillier and curvier than most of the prairie. But I'm focused on more mundane subjects: specifically, the omission of bathrooms in the *Little House* books, something that, amazingly, just occurred to me.

Once Sophie and I checked out from the library audio versions of a contemporary series, *Katie Kazoo Switcheroo*, to listen to in the car. The *Freaky Friday* premise of this series seemed rife with promise: Katie tends to inadvertently enter others' bodies and briefly experience their lives. But Katie is heavily focused on privacy concerns. When she finds herself in the body of a friend's baby sister in *Oh Baby*, her main worry is whether her friend will change her diaper, an apparently horrifying prospect that must be avoided at all costs, even though the private parts in question are not strictly Katie's own. In the next we borrowed, *Girls Don't Have Cooties*, Katie finds herself swept into the body of her male best friend and consumed by anxiety about what she's going to do if she has to go to the bathroom. Her most pressing dilemma revolves around the horror of coming into such intimate contact with her friend's body—even though she is inside it.

These books are popular enough to suggest that they capture a real concern of children. I was amused, when I was seven or eight, at Ramona Quimby's query about the title character of *Mike Mulligan and His Steam Shovel*: When he was working as fast as he could all day to dig the basement of the town hall, where did he go to the bathroom?[6] I'd never thought to wonder about this question, but when Beverly Cleary's Ramona does, I recognized it as a good one. Still, not until now have I thought to wonder where the Ingalls family went to the bathroom. Nowhere among the painstakingly detailed descriptions of roofing houses and digging wells and constructing chimneys and building barns is there any mention of the Little Outhouse in the Big Woods or the Little Outhouse on the Prairie. This now strikes me as somewhat peculiar—not just the absence of that information, but my failure, ever, to wonder about it.

The toy museum in Kellogg turns out to be an elaborate shopping mall containing a bookstore, puzzle store, nostalgic toy shop, and candy store. Though she is too old to be all that excited, Sophie rides a hand-carved horse around the carousel, and then, finally, we settle in to cross the Mississippi River over to Pepin.

Originally, Aunt Shirley meant to include this site on our long-ago trip, but her health was so poor and Pepin was so far, she finally decided to forego it. So now, I'm going there for her, too, but wondering if it will, in the end, have been worth all this driving. From what I've read, there's not much there. According to Anita Clair Fellman, in the early 1960s a local librarian located the site of the log house where Wilder had been born a hundred years before. While her efforts led to the naming of a city park after Wilder, it wasn't until the 1970s that a historical society was formed, and not until 1979 that a marker was placed at the wayside at her birthplace.[7]

The two small buildings that constitute the historical society are easy to locate, on the town's Main Street. One of the buildings is dedicated to local history, the other to Wilder. We wander through a crowded re-created bedroom displaying a trundle bed, a sewing machine that belonged to Wilder's cousin, and a red wool petticoat mounted on the wall. Dresses and coats are also splayed against the wall alongside yellowed index cards typed with Wilder quotes describing similar items. In back there's a kitchen crammed with an antique stove, dishes, and a wizened but still fragrant clove apple once used to scent drawers.

The bell on the front door tinkles as another group files in, three women and two children. "Look," says one of the women. "There's Pa's fiddle."

I glance quickly at the caretaker, busy making phone calls and straightening the front counter. She must hear this every day. By now she probably tunes it out, not wasting her breath explaining that most of these things didn't belong to the Ingalls family. *Little House in the Big Woods* was published sixty years after the Ingalls left Pepin; by then, original buildings, not to mention personal possessions, were long gone. Pa's fiddle is in the museum in Mansfield, Missouri.

The new arrivals drift into the half of the front room devoted to a gift shop, all but one woman, who wanders from room to room with a dreamy look in her eyes. Sophie and I survey the stuff for sale: the requisite books, key chains, collectible spoons, china shepherdess replicas, and salt and pepper shakers. I see none of the items that I remember from the Wilder gift shops of my childhood—sunbonnets, cornhusk dolls, Charlotte dolls.

The book section includes the original series but, I note sadly, in new editions without the Garth Williams illustrations that have been part of the books since 1953. Later, I will learn from a *Publisher's Weekly* article that HarperCollins had been losing sales because children had come to view historical novels as old-fashioned. "Using photographs highlights that these are not history but adventure books," says editor Kate Jackson.[8]

The gift shop also displays a slew of spin-offs of the original series: a series of early-reader books based on individual episodes from Wilder's stories; a series about Rose Wilder Lane's childhood; another about the childhood of Ma, Caroline Ingalls; and yet another from the point of view of Laura's great-grandmother. It staggers me that interest in Laura Ingalls Wilder has reached such feverish proportions as to sustain so many dozens of stories. I'm surprised at just how huge an audience there seems to be out there wanting to prolong the experience of the series and devour stories about pioneer life and Wilder's family.

Then there's a rack that holds numerous booklets by William Anderson, the biographer approved by Rose Wilder Lane's estate, a writer who has been accorded rock star status by many Wilder fans. Anderson is a prolific researcher whose first published writing on Ingalls appeared when he was in junior high, according to Fellman.[9] I remember many of these from thirty years ago, but not the merchandising of the Laura Ingalls Wilder experience that has exponentially proliferated in the wake of the TV show, all the years that I wasn't paying attention.

Fellman lists the many available *Little House* "materials for all ages and occasions," making me realize that the little gift shop in Pepin carries only a small fraction: "There are chapter books, 'My First Little House' picture books, pop ups, ABC and counting books, audiobooks, calendars, diaries, paper dolls, sewing books, crafts books, sticker books, scrapbooks, a tour book, and a cookbook and apron set, not to mention the sequels (Laura's daughter's childhood) prequels (Laura's mother's, grandmother's, and great-grandmother's girlhoods) and the supplement (the unrecorded years of Laura's childhood)."[10] Christine Heppermann writes that "these totems of pioneer something-from-nothing resourcefulness now stand at the mouth of a raging merchandise river."[11]

"Is this the same clove apple you had when I was here many years ago?" asks the woman who has been roaming the museum. As the caretaker confirms that it is, that the clove apple has lasted for 150 years, I catch the look in the woman's eyes. She drove all the way from Minneapolis to revisit this source of childhood memories. Since I drove even further, I feel guilty for my lack of reverence or nostalgia. Why am I here? I wonder again.

A few minutes later, the clove-apple woman picks each original book off the shelf, flipping, replacing, flipping, replacing. "A knife in the dark," she says, putting back *These Happy Golden Years*.

Her words take me right back to that chapter of the book, in which Laura, boarding with a family named Brewster while teaching school, is beginning to despair over the cold and tedium and isolation and Mrs. Brewster's sour unfriendliness. Eventually, the woman cracks, going after her husband in the dark in the middle of the night while Laura trembles behind a curtain. Now, a picture flashes through my mind of a savage-looking woman in a long nightgown, knife cocked in her hand. "That illustration always gave me the creeps," I say.

We exchange a quick look. My guilt fades. I forget my uneasiness at how Laura Ingalls Wilder has become a vast consumer industry that has erased Garth Williams's illustrations and replaced cornhusk, apple head, and rag dolls with plastic things. For a second, we're two strangers connecting over a shared memory. For a second, I know viscerally the lasting power of a book. For a second, I know why I'm here.

Although *Big Woods* was not my favorite, I was drawn, in it and throughout the series, to the simple wonder of a childhood stripped of the clutter of our time— all the socks and toys and knickknacks and appliances and electronic equipment that sometimes burden our lives. Fellman describes the book as "that depiction of a Protestant Garden of Eden in which everything the Ingalls family needs is available through the bounty of their land and woods and the labor of their own hands."[12]

As a child, I found fascinating what seemed to me a stripped-down life. I especially liked that Laura didn't watch TV—ever, it turns out, though televisions had become widely available some time before her death. I wasn't a big TV watcher myself, but still I marveled at the notion of a life without the things I took for granted—televisions, indoor plumbing, telephones, cars. I entertained a childhood fantasy of ushering a time-traveling Laura into the early 1970s and experiencing vicariously her wonder and amazement at all the ways the world had changed. I imagined envy and delight as she gradually learned to use the stereo, crank up the air conditioner, and motor off on a bus to school or town.

How startling to learn from writer Wendy McClure, in her book *The Wilder Life: My Adventures in the Lost World of Little House on the Prairie*, that this was not my fantasy alone. "I daydreamed that she'd shown up in the twentieth century and I had to be her guide," McClure writes. "I've discovered from talking to friends that this was a common desire."[13] I have to admit, even now I sometimes imagine Laura appearing in the twenty-first century, confused by overheard conversations: "What is a wee game system?" she asks. "You keep a pet mouse on your desk?"

My imaginings—and apparently those of others—have always involved the child Laura, the fictional character, certainly not the elderly Wilder who preferred the farmhouse that she and Almanzo built to the state-of-the-art stone house Rose designed for them. The elderly Laura had indoor bathrooms and a phone, and she embraced the automobile. Never mind that Almanzo had some difficulty learning to drive, what with a tendency to pull back on the steering wheel and say "Whoa" while accelerating.[14]

So the elderly Laura who re-created the younger, nineteenth-century version of herself was well aware of the developments of the twentieth century if not the twenty-first, but my fantasy was about an old-fashioned girl my age whose vision of my world would make it fresh and new and miraculous. I imagined how she would exclaim over school buses and electric dishwashers and movie theaters. My attraction to Laura's world was also about novelty, about a different way of life where so little can be taken for granted. The characters in the books led lives of greater simplicity than mine (and, it turns out, than the real-life people they were based on), with lower thresholds of satisfaction.

Ma, we are told in *Woods*, was a well-off, fashionable, independent young woman before she married Pa. By the time of *Big Woods*, the family is comfortable in their little house, surrounded by relatives, thriving and self-reliant. But neither Pa nor Ma clings to conventional ideas of success. Pa's wanderlust will cause him to leave everything behind again and again, and it's not poverty or desperation that finally leads the characters, at last, to settle down, but Ma's insistence that her girls gain an education. Reading these books planted firmly in me the belief that there were far more important things than raking in money, climbing corporate ladders, and achieving social prestige. Although often Pa struggles to provide, there's little sense that he regrets the choices that interfere with conventional provision.

Leaving the museum, we drive to the replica site at the Ingalls family's original property, now a wayside seven miles north of Pepin on Highway 183. I pull up along the drive. Across a lawn stands a cabin, constructed in 1976, a replica of a wilderness home built with local materials and simple tools, not necessarily a replica of the Ingalls home. The property doesn't match my mental image of the book's setting; there's a crooked rail fence around the house, a public restroom built of logs, a covered picnic table, and a pump, the lawn bordered on three sides by cornfields.

The forests were cleared long ago. Gone, also, is the tree with spreading branches where Mary and Laura played house. I see no black-eyed Susans or wild red berries suitable for staining cloth to create a rag doll's mouth, no big oak trees where deer can be hung from branches out of the reach of wolves. I don't know where the cellar once was, stuffed with potatoes, carrots, beets, turnips, and cabbages. I see no sign of the hollow tree used to smoke meat. Before us stretches a neatly mowed expanse of land, baking in the hot sun of a July day.

"This is it?" Sophie says, incredulous. We are twenty-first-century tourists. We expect elaborate re-creations of the past. We expect things to do, buy, eat.

Sophie poses in the cabin doorway. I snap her picture against a backdrop of tightly notched logs, shingled roof hanging down low. We trade places. Sophie takes my picture. Wings beat loudly behind me: not bats, as I imagine at first, but swallows that dart back and forth through the cabin rafters.

Our eyes adjust to the dark interior, a narrow common room and two tiny bedrooms, smaller than many of today's typical closets. We crane our necks at the loft above the bedrooms, a platform meant to suggest the attic where Mary and Laura played. Pumpkins served as chairs and tables, and hams and venison hung above in paper wrappings, along with bunches of dried herbs, braided ropes of onions, and wreaths of red peppers. This platform is empty.

We wander around for five minutes, past markers with raised letters explaining the site's significance, over to a shelter with picnic tables and a pump. We pause to pump our own fresh water and take pictures of each other pumping. Then there's nothing left to do but head back to town. I drive two miles an hour. "This is about the speed of a wagon," I tell an unimpressed Sophie.

Back in town, we walk past the Laura Ingalls Wilder Park to the Depot museum, a cute building with a ticket window and restored train car in front. The "museum" consists of a card table displaying bolts, screws, and other metal pieces that have fallen off of old trains, along with a few pictures and books. The rest of the building is a secondhand shop with an adjoining room heaped with comic books.

We cross the Mississippi back into Minnesota. I point out that when the Ingallses left Wisconsin, they probably crossed on ice not far away, at the part of the river that forms Lake Pepin.

"Mmm," Sophie says.

And I drive on, pretending to be cheerful, hoping our whole trip won't feel like a bust.

CHAPTER FOUR

Journeys into Female Imagination

I.

EVEN VISITING PEPIN, WISCONSIN, a place I had never been except through a book, even reading books that I've never read before but that are part of an old favorite series, it often seems as if I'm uneasily returning to a home I left behind long ago. Sometimes I find myself confined by restrictions I didn't know were there, surprised by staircases much shorter, rooms much smaller, and ceilings much lower than I remember, even while I also feel like I'm taking up right where I left off with old, good friends. Reading when I was a child was about the opposite, something that rereading old favorites can never recapture: it was about escaping, traveling while sitting still, expanding outward, watching the world enlarge, discovering possibilities, and feeling my imagination awaken.

What once inspired me now frequently surprises and often amuses and sometimes disturbs and even horrifies me. Lucy Maud Montgomery's *Anne* series and Eunice Young Smith's *Jennifer* stories remind me of just how inadequate my abilities once felt in contrast to these heroines' fanciful creativity. Depth and originality, these books suggested, are mostly demonstrated through idealizing and personifying nature. Clinging to the Romantic tradition, both Anne and her probable literary offspring, the lesser-known Jennifer, are most alive when outside communing with the natural world. Anne delights in giving ornate names to ordinary places; Jennifer fantasizes that she can talk to bumblebees.

I fell short. The serviceable split-level my parents built when I was a toddler stood on three quarters of an acre. This land had been parceled in recent history from a family farm, the portion my parents bought likely once part of a wheat field. There were no trees until my dad planted saplings, their trunks as wide around as my arm, their branches the size of my number two pencils. What seemed to me my own generic landscape with its impoverished natural world could never live up to Anne or Jennifer's lush surroundings.

Because Jennifer likes to lie in a hammock in her backyard, I was overjoyed when my grandparents brought back a macramé hammock from Mexico. Fantasizing about spending hours reading there, I stretched the flimsy pieces of string between a tiny new tree and a swing set pole because there was nothing else. Merely getting in required both a literal jump and a metaphorical one, a huge leap of faith: I had to climb onto the tangled macramé mess and lob myself down into the netting. Miraculously, it held my weight. I felt triumphant for about two seconds. Then I realized that I'd left my book on the ground. I had to overturn the whole hammock in order to free myself of it, then, book in hand, make another terrifying leap back into it. I read two pages. The sun beat on my face in the shadeless yard. I couldn't find a comfortable position and I couldn't reach my lemonade. I retreated to my comfortable room. I was a failure as a storybook heroine.

But I wasn't about to give up so easily. Because Jennifer's whimsy is drawn mostly from fairy stories, particularly the Andrew Lang series published at the turn of the century, I inquired in the Wichita Public Library's children's room about the *Olive* and *Scarlet Fairy* books. They were so fragile they'd been removed from circulation, so I had to read them at a table in the children's room. I found them alarmingly tedious. I concluded sadly that maybe I just wasn't really that imaginative.

Lucy Montgomery inherited many of her ideas from broad reading, then wielded, through the popularity of her books, a powerful influence in perpetuating sometimes precious images of female creativity. *Anne of Green Gables* is deeply concerned with the saving grace of imagination, its glories and limits, yet as Montgomery writes successive sequels, she becomes increasingly hesitant about allowing the creative vision of her heroine to reach its logical conclusion—a life in which her own thoughts, opinions, and production really matter. Instead, her talents are gradually subsumed to those of her husband and children, and transform into a valuable route to love and community, but never her own "selfish" self-actualization, and certainly not recognition in the public sphere.

Back when I first read the early books, I aspired to be Anne, even during scenes I affectionately find ridiculous today. My favorite of this category is the one in *Anne of Avonlea* when she falls through the roof of an old duck house. Stuck hanging there while her friend goes for help, forced to draw on her own inner resources to pass the time, Anne entertains herself by working out a "most interesting dialogue between the asters and the sweet peas and the wild canaries in the lilac bush and the guardian spirit of the garden."[1] As a child, I felt puzzled by this scene; I had trouble finding such an exchange remotely interesting, and decided that I was too literal and realistic, that my own gifts could never live up to Anne's flights of fancy. Feeling obligated to at least give it a try, I lay in the grass of my backyard, trying to imagine a dialogue between the dandelions and my dad's tulips. I couldn't even sustain the attempt. I concluded that I lacked the proper poetic instinct.

Now, I just laugh at the absurdity of the *Anne of Avonlea* scene. It exerts no pressure on me to prove myself by assigning dramatic monologues to flowers. Now I see how this scene and many of Anne's fantasies provide hilariously outdated and often ironic windows into notions of girlhood, offering a subtle critique that Montgomery eventually drops but that enriches the first three books. Or at least I assume that Montgomery's exaggerated presentation of some of Anne's views is meant as commentary on aspects of romanticism such as Edgar Allan Poe's contention that the death of a young woman was the most beautiful of all poetic subjects. For instance, when Anne envisions a young woman who died a tragic death, it's with jealous admiration toward her "timid eyes" and "pale face,"[2] which I take as a somewhat tongue-in-cheek echo of those Romantic and Victorian poets, who, as George P. Landow puts it, "produced sentimentalized depictions of dead and dying women as aesthetic objects."[3]

My daughter does not, as I did, unconsciously accept such outmoded views of women or girls. She hoots when Anne dreams about rushing to her "bosom friend" Diana's bedside to nurse her through a horrible disease, then taking sick and dying herself from her devotion.[4] The word "bosom" is alone sufficient to inspire prolonged hilarity, but my daughter's uncontrollable laughter also has to do with the completely bizarre nature of Anne's masochistic fantasy. My twenty-first-century daughter finds Anne's dreamy rhapsody over the prospect of her own death pretty funny, too. She also has the good sense to roll her eyes at Anne's endless obsession with Elaine the Lily Maid of Astolot, the central figure in many Victorian paintings, illustrations, and poems, floating down the river in a boat, dead and startlingly beautiful.

As a child, I was less immune than my daughter is, demonstrated by the fact that I did at least briefly if unsuccessfully attempt to write little sketches about talking flowers. After she's rescued, Anne jots down the piece she composed in her head during her rooftop tribulations. Later, after she has written several romances featuring larger-than-life characters and plots, a wise neighbor advises that she stop producing such melodramatic tripe and report on "real life." Taking this advice to heart, Anne polishes up her flower dialogue, presumably a more solid piece of "reporting" than her love stories, and gets her first real publication.

Eventually, and debatably more tragic even than the service of a girl's talent to such drivel, Anne ceases to write altogether. As a young reader, I found this too unimaginable to regard it as particularly heartbreaking. But Anne influenced me in more subtle ways, suggesting that a truly virtuous girl is one who gradually abandons her personality. The Anne we first meet in *Green Gables* is a delightful if exhaustingly talkative girl who can't be silenced, and love-interest Gilbert is attracted to her passion, her inaccessibility, her odd way of seeing the world. But maturity for Anne means taming her imagination as well as curbing her prolific speech and her assumption that she has a right to be heard.

By the second book she has turned her efforts toward striving to be an ideal woman, gentle and soft spoken and pure and high minded. In a strange about-face, we are told in *Anne of Avonlea* that this virtue is why Gilbert likes her.[5] By the time I was a teenager, it embarrassed me to be overheard expressing an opinion or a preference, having noted the disapproval of others and the pattern of heroines for whom coming of age meant blandness, passive acceptance, smiles and polite murmurs, uncontroversial conversation, and the ability to placate others.

In *Avonlea*, as Anne becomes more concerned with female virtue, Montgomery must find another character to fill the requisite dreamy, whimsical child role. She chooses Anne's student Paul, a boy who is allowed the option of growing up to be a writer (and does, later, publish volumes of poetry). But Montgomery quickly finds this dreamy boy character even more problematic than she did her ambitious girl character. We are constantly reassured that Paul is imaginative without being "weak or girlish," that he possesses a perfect balance of sensitivity and masculinity.[6] Everyone but Anne finds Paul "queer"—and while the book was written before "queer" became a derogatory and then proudly reclaimed reference to people who are gay, Montgomery remains on the defensive lest readers draw any such conclusions about Paul's orientation.

Whenever Paul spins out elaborate fantasies about "rock people" and fairies, he also is preoccupied, in a way that seems odd for a boy of that age, with assuring Anne that he plans to marry someday. Paul allows the "elderly spinster with snow-white hair," Miss Lavender (she's forty-five) to kiss him only after delivering a manly anti-kissing speech. Boys, he announces with an air of authority, are averse to such expressions of affection. Then he snuggles right up to his future stepmother. Paul understands already his status as a male, referring repeatedly (and here I gag involuntarily) to his dead mother as "my little mother" and to Anne as "my beautiful teacher." "Porridge will be the death of me," he tells Anne, revealing his yearning to transcend routine details, the ones persistently arranged by women, so he can indulge his fantasy life.[7]

His future stepmother Miss Lavender provides the book's most interesting example of creativity and unconventionality, particularly for a woman in 1909. Her idyllic existence in her cottage, Echo Lodge, allows her to construct games of pretend and vow to defy "every known law of diet."[8] She is childlike, but also funny, charming, and independent. One of her favorite activities is blowing a horn and creating echoes around her property. I was sad to eventually discover that these echoes are, metaphorically, less about making her voice heard, more about a past that haunts her. And ultimately, her imaginative life is seen as a stagnant one that can finally advance into maturity upon her reconciliation with an old lover and their subsequent marriage.

Anne herself isn't fully stripped of her imaginative vision until after she marries. In *Anne of the Island*, right before her engagement, we see a glimpse of Anne's quirky vision, presented with affection and humor and the sometimes gentle authorial irony that Montgomery employs so effectively. In these instances, she manages to distance us just enough from Anne to allow us to view her from the perspective of an affectionate friend rather than to fully inhabit her point of view.

As a result, a passage that could come off as purple and smarmy instead becomes charming: "The year is a book, isn't it, Marilla?" Anne asks. "Spring's pages are written in mayflowers and violets, summer's in roses, autumns in red maple leaves, and winter in holly and evergreen." It is Marilla's matter-of-fact practicality in response that counterbalances Anne and saves this passage. Though she never suspends her fondness for her character, Montgomery herself becomes positively wicked at times in her assessment of Anne, as when in the wake of a broken heart, Anne is "straightway much comforted by the romance in the idea of the world being denuded of romance!"[9]

It is the fifth book, *Anne's House of Dreams*, where we find that she has relinquished all expectations about her own artistic work. When Paul, now a successful, insistently heterosexual poet, suggests that Anne might be famous someday, she replies, "No. I know what I can do. I can write pretty, fanciful little sketches that children love and editors send welcome cheques for. But I can do nothing big. My only chance for earthly immortality is a corner in your Memoirs."[10] My adult reaction is another not-so-involuntary gag. But as a child, I was fortunately suspicious rather than crushed. Why was it necessary for Anne to give up her dreams when Montgomery didn't? Because I recognized that there were autobiographical connections between the child writer and the adult author, I never really believed this ending, or Jo March's decision to run a school rather than write, for that matter.

It probably was a mercy that I never believed, unlike my favorite heroines, that there was anything special about my own busy but comparatively mundane imagination. My childhood landscape was flat and straightforward. The image of the hardy pioneer and the terrain of the prairie did not promote the same sort of myth of organic creative genius that arose from haunting moors, wild oceans, babbling brooks, or towering snow-covered Alps. Before me spread a continuous plain, blank ground that required hard work. Our metaphors were all about planting seeds and tilling soil and tough rows to hoe. How could anyone keep secrets when the clean earth before us stretched uninterrupted to the horizon, without nooks or crannies, without undulation or sudden drops, without hiding places?

My family's home had been built in 1965. There were no hidden rooms or secret cupboards or underground passageways. My neighborhood was boring and brown, without wishing wells, caves, ponds, gypsies, or woods. The neighborhood kids acquired our knowledge of nature and the land's history from an old dump in the back of a field, an abandoned storm cellar in the middle of another, a pathetic, usually dry creek behind my house, and a network of drainage tunnels under the nearby turnpike and highway. The dump was our opportunity for archeological excavation; the cellar and creek and tunnels were our cliffs and rivers and streams and caves. I pretended to be interested in nature, rescuing stranded fish washed through the tunnels during heavy rainstorms, now floundering in puddles that shrank in the sun. I carried the flopping creatures in my bare hands, not really liking the slimy feel of them, to drop them in a pond on private property where children were forbidden to go. On other occasions, I helped catch frogs and nursed an injured bird. My friends, the masterminds of these projects, were curious about the natural world. I went along because participating made me feel like a heroine in a book.

I certainly appreciated nature and the landscape of my childhood much more because of the books I read. But I dismissed my own imaginative play, often in partnership with my cousin Jody, as merely silly, focused as it was on life indoors, on wordplay and human behavior and relationships.

Many of our activities, I didn't realize till many years later, probably originated with *Little Women*, a book that our mothers and aunt loved. Most of our games, I realize now, were imitations of the March sisters': the plays they put on, the newspapers they produce, the will that Amy writes, which I imitated, creating my own Last Will and Testament. *Little Women* was one of the reasons that writing and acting out plays and experimenting with improvisations that had roundabout plots absorbed many summer days, as did our newspapers and magazines modeled after the *Pickwick Portfolio*, though with less literary names: *The Daily Dandy News* and *Smile-a-While* magazine.

Little Women is probably the reason that whenever Jody and I got together, we wrote. Jody was a year and a half older than me. I envied her vocabulary. Her characters didn't go to the bathroom; they went to the "latrine" and would have found discussion of such matters "vulgar." Jody came up with great character names, like Coquette, Quebec, and Delaine.

At nine, I wrote a story about a boy dog. I told my mother that it was the best thing I'd ever produced. She wisely disagreed, probably more out of her pathological aversion to animals than any feminist impulse or literary expertise. She liked my stories about girls, even if the plots, heavily influenced by the small episodes of many chapter books, were somewhat lacking. My characters got to walk to school instead of taking the bus. They moved into houses with balconies. This was the sum total of the action in stories that were pure wish fulfillment: I longed to walk to school and live in a house with a balcony. In the dog story, my protagonist had adventures. Really exciting stuff, like getting lost or digging underneath a fence. It surprised me that my mother didn't prefer it.

This example suggests that I'd absorbed the idea that girls should be passive recipients of life events while boys, even boy dogs, get to be active participants. Fortunately, those prevalent social attitudes were supplemented in books by many positive examples of female creativity. I was particularly drawn to the details of Maud Hart Lovelace's Betsy's writing life—the old trunk she makes into a desk, her pile of sharpened pencils, the contests she enters in high school, her world travel—and saw her eventual marriage to Joe as simply another part of a busy, interesting life, not as a capitulation or sacrifice. I refused to read *Little Men* or *Jo's Boys* because Jo March's writing dreams appeared to have become replaced by the care and education of a bunch of lisping boys, but from *Little Women* and Jo, I nevertheless absorbed many lessons about writing. When I got tired of my characters, I took a cue from her and killed them all off; the lesson was lost on me that this meant that she couldn't write any sequels, nor did I, until I was much older, appreciate Alcott's ironic humor toward Jo's revision process, which consisted of "putting in many exclamation points." Jo's love of reading also validated, if not encouraged, mine. She hates to leave the "paradise" of reading "to wind yarn, wash the poodle, or read Belsham's Essays by the hour together." She is initially drawn to the neighbor boy, Laurie, through a conversation about books, in which, "to Jo's delight, she found that Laurie loved them as well as she did. . . . " And I related to Jo's ability to enjoy experiences more when she imagines telling stories about them when she gets home.[11]

Many of the books I read clearly owe a large debt to more famous heroines with writing ambitions like Anne Shirley and Jo March. *Little Women* is set during the Civil War and Anne and Betsy inhabit stories taking place fifty years later, but all three heroines share a fascination with melodramas. In addition, Anne and Betsy share similar standards of beauty; Lovelace describes a beautiful girl in *Downtown* in a manner reminiscent of Anne: "She had long black ringlets and big black eyes, and a dead-white skin with lips as red as blood."[12] Like Anne, Betsy considers the idea of her funeral to be "quite romantic" and, while watching a gondola in Venice, thinks of the Lily Maid of Astolat floating downstream, that image that has recurred numerous times throughout the *Anne* books.[13] Betsy is prone to being caught up in her own drama, just like Anne: "On such occasions she often cried a little; never much, for it always occurred to her how romantic it was to be crying about her trunk, and then she stopped, and couldn't start again."[14]

But Betsy's imagination is generally far less sappy, and she takes her writing more seriously than Anne if not Jo. Like Anne and Jo, she discovers the importance of writing about what she knows, and like them, she sends her work out for publication. But as Anna Quindlen points out, Anne and Jo "are implicitly made to pay" because they don't conform to expectations for girls. By contrast, she says, Betsy "never has to pay for the sin of being herself, in fact, she only finds herself under a cloud when she is less than herself. At base, she is a charmed soul . . . because she can laugh at herself and take herself seriously at the same time, because she is serious but never a prig, and interested in boys but never a flirt."[15]

A couple of years before I first discovered Betsy, my very favorite book when I was six or seven was Betty Brock's *No Flying in the House.* I was surprised to discover in adulthood that it, like so many of my later favorites, is centered on versions of female power and imagination accompanied by irresistible fantasies once again heavily influenced by the natural world. Returning to this novel, I again found it creepy and charming and magical, part *Bewitched*, part *Little Mermaid*, a classic fairy tale about female agency, mysterious spells, great sacrifice, and the recovery of long-lost families. I still find it haunting when the tiny maternal talking dog Gloria sacrifices herself for the sake of her charge Annabel and turns into a wind-up toy. I'm still deliciously creeped out by the tiny broken cat figurine with emerald eyes that is reassembled and possessed by the evil fairy Belinda, who appears before Annabel to try to convince her to choose the life of a fairy over that of a mortal.

Belinda the villain is the most lyrical character, teaching Annabel to fly so it feels "as if her insides had turned to liquid honey floating syrupy down a golden river, and as they flowed away she became lighter and lighter until she felt light enough to ride on a butterfly's wing." The cat tempts her with descriptions of "hovering over a white capped sea without wetting your feet, or following a rabbit's trail up a cliff thick with bayberry without getting a scratch." Belinda promises to teach Annabel to turn herself into a gull or a butterfly, ride on camels or elephants, or swing with monkeys. "We can explore the oceans with the flying fish, make snowballs on the tops of the highest peak, and ride with the wind to the stars," she says.[16]

The illustration of Belinda screeching and bristling when a resourceful Annabel traps her in the cookie jar still inspires a thrill of fear. When Annabel discovers the birthmark on her shoulder and the name of her mother inside Gloria's collar, I still feel a jolt of discovery. When Annabel realizes that she can kiss her elbow, the mark of a fairy, I remember suddenly how Jody and I twisted and turned our arms in futile attempts to kiss our elbows.

Now when I read this book, with all its nature imagery, sacrifices, and coincidences, it seems a fable about girls' lives, about Anne's and Jo's and Betsy's and maybe even Laura's as much as mine: do they choose to relinquish power in favor of intact families and the certainty of mortality, or do they choose to fly and be free and indestructible? The latter is the choice identified with evil, the one that will separate them forever from love. Do they identify with the steady loyal motherly plainspoken dog, Gloria, or the poetic savage beast of a fairy cat, Belinda, who can be destroyed by any contact with sugar? This not only aligns her with the Wicked Witch of the West who is destroyed by water, but also positions her far from sugar, spice, or anything nice. Annabel makes the proper good girl choice, the one that will reunite her with her exiled parents but rob her of magic, yet what choice does she really have? Isn't love, "the power of the heart,"[17] powerful enough?

While this choice may seem the traditional one, while I wonder why our culture remains so insistent that women can have love or success but never both, the book's end offers an array of female creativity and power. As far as we know, Annabel's mother Princess Felicia is still a fairy, Annabel's guardian who turns out to be her grandmother remains "like a queen bestowing favors," and best of all, Gloria the fairy dog intends to visit soon, "before she begins her stage career."[18] This was one of the first books I read that defined for me so specifically the tensions between love and work, public and private, families and creativity that were supposed to become one and the same in women's lives, love marketed to girls far more than to boys as the most powerful form of creative expression beyond which none other is necessary.

One of the other books that entranced me when I was in the second or third grade, Eva Moore's *The Fairy Tale Life of Hans Christian Andersen*, presented a somewhat different cultural conception of the creative genius, one that can be interpreted as a cautionary tale to children of both genders. The gifted creator is, in this book, one who can't master the real world and whose peculiar talents prevent him from being good at anything else. Perhaps borrowing her basic framework from Andersen's own autobiography, Moore presents Hans as fundamentally odd and pathetic. He's ugly, his father is a failure, and he has unrealistic, even ridiculous, dreams about becoming an actor and a dancer. Then he aspires to be a singer but his voice changes. At school, he's the biggest kid in class, and, persistently humiliated by the cruel schoolmaster, he becomes convinced that he's stupid. He cries in school. He can't make enough money to get his mother out of the poorhouse. He never marries or has children.

But this is framed as a story of triumph: in the end, Hans Christian Andersen, like the ugly duckling in his story, becomes a swan, in his case, a famous writer. Still, his level of success is inversely proportionate to his happiness. While as a young reader I found it vindicating when the citizens of Andersen's hometown raise their torches to him, the book still led me to feel constitutionally doomed to be poor and alone in a deeply scary world. I can imagine how a boy encountering this book would flee even more vehemently from any artistic dreams.

Later reading recast this image for me but continued to promote stereotypes about the sacrifice, suffering, and ostracism inevitable for creative artists. While *The Fairy Tale Life of Hans Christian Andersen* certainly suggests that these notions cross gender lines, such images became most ingrained in me through high school fascinations with the Brontë sisters and Emily Dickinson. The popular view of Emily Brontë held that she was utterly indifferent to society, lost in a dream world, and hopelessly impractical; Charlotte Brontë was seen as more affected by her history of failure. Her first novel was rejected while her sisters' were taken, the collaborative poetry collection she spearheaded sold only three copies, the school she started enrolled no students, and her greatest love was unrequited. Emily Dickinson was typically presented as an either disturbed or heartbroken spinster and recluse, an odd woman in white who lowered baskets of treats to neighborhood children. None of these writers' popular images include athletic ability, gardening talent, or whizbang math skills, much less a capacity for managing ordinary daily life.

This was all very frightening if sort of romantic. The notion of the starving artist beset by failure and suffering figured heavily in my imagination alongside the obligation of women to put aside art for the sake of others. Lois Duncan's *Down a Dark Hall*, my childhood favorite of all of her compelling, if extremely conservative, children's horror stories, lends even more terrifying dimensions to creative ability and artistic production. *Hall*'s premise is intriguingly spooky: what would happen if all the geniuses who died before their time could find young, unformed girls to serve as mediums, channeling unfinished work and recording it for posterity?

At Blackwood School, a place as gothic as its name suggests, four girls discover that they're being held prisoner for that very purpose—to paint, discover mathematical equations, produce poetry, and compose the music of dead geniuses. One girl creates Thomas Cole landscapes before moving on to horrible torture scenes. Another begins with gentle Schubert music before more violent composers start vying for her soul. Originally channeling Emily Brontë, a third writes sweet poetry about the moors before a new dead writer forces her to shift to ugly, disgusting verse (content never specified).

I reread this novel on the heels of Lucasta Miller's *The Brontë Myth*, which traces the changing popular images of the Brontë sisters over the last century and a half. Duncan's Emily is the mythic one, the mystical, wild, passionate Brontë sister, divorced from any reality, and through her and other noted artists, Duncan raises disturbing questions: what sacrifices should be made for art? Is it worth saving at the cost of human lives? But I wonder now, why so much emphasis on the way creative impulses can consume people? Why so little acknowledgment of the possibility that art and knowledge can save them? The real Brontë sisters were far more complex than their mythic counterparts, their passions and successes as vital as their tragedies and failures.

Through her very matter-of-fact presentation, Noel Streatfeild's many novels about the performing arts do celebrate creative lives, avoiding extremes by steering clear of accounts of grueling day-to-day schedules while also never glamorizing the hard-earned successes of her child characters. I loved her books—*Dancing Shoes, Ballet Shoes, Theater Shoes, Thursday's Child*—and dreamed of being a dancer or actor although like Hans Christian Andersen I had no talent in either direction. For a while, these books were out of print, but are now once again widely available and somehow timely in an age of *American Idol* and its imitations. It's ironic that Streatfeild's books have seen a resurgence in popularity because of a phenomenon I imagine she would have deplored, preoccupied as she was with the distinction between serious art that endures and that which is "frivolous" or merely popular. To pile on the ironies, I've always found it a little odd that I learned about high and low art from a popular book in the then-much-scorned genre of children's literature, a book that when I read it was on the brink of going out of print.

In *Dancing Shoes*, Streatfeild conveys the importance of discriminating between the trivial and the profound through the pairing of two sisters. Rachel is the "ugly" one seemingly without talent, serious, dull, plodding and academic, preferring to memorize soliloquies than learn to tap dance, the one whose ambition for her sister is perpetually misunderstood. She is quiet, often mistaken as sullen, withdrawn, and "sulky." She has sallow skin and high cheekbones, the latter being the universal literary code for an ugly duckling destined to become a swan, an underestimated child who will transform to a classic, enduring beauty far surpassing fleeting cuteness. Rachel is the one I wanted to be—not the shallow and silly if charming sister, not the spoiled, arrogant horror of a cousin, but Rachel, whose quiet persistence will eventually pay off.

This is a book that takes art seriously, but if it upped my ambition, it also sent a somewhat discouraging message about genetic heritage and the artist. As the daughter of a famous actor, Rachel, it turns out, has no choice but to pursue an acting career herself, leaving me to wonder, when I was ten or eleven, if any of my own ancestors had been writers. Was there any hope for me? Not especially familiar with the range of surnames on my family tree, I searched the library for writers named McCabe and found none. The majority of my predecessors were probably illiterate, I came to realize; education in some branches of my family remains intimidating and suspect. I felt like a mutation, the family anomaly, with no birthright entitling me to be a writer, and I wondered whether I should aspire to something that wasn't in my blood.

This was one of the ways in which Laura Ingalls Wilder and her books were a great gift. She wrote about girls in books that were huge departures from what was available, and the myth that she wrote them with no background or training, only a mysteriously acquired raw talent, inspired a young self that older would find this idea more oppressive. The myth gave me hope, as did my sense of being related to Wilder in a roundabout way.

Rereading helped me to see the many ambivalent messages I absorbed in childhood about the written word and other forms of art—valuable messages, in many cases, raising essential questions when they didn't present art as a dangerous force and the life of an artist as one to be leery of if not avoided altogether. Despite these messages, I somehow also absorbed in a far more influential way the notion of human creativity as a healing, sustaining force.

In the third grade, if anyone asked me my favorite book, my answer was *Trumpet of the Swan*. I only read it once, though. So now, in adulthood, unlike with the books I used to return to more regularly, coming back to E. B. White's novel created none of the duality I'd often experienced, as if I were reading as an adult and a child at the same time. I wonder if I professed to love this book because it was about animals, since I believed that if I were truly imaginative I would find books about animals appealing.

I hope that, instead, I loved this book because my child self found it as beautiful, funny, graceful and lyrical, humane and clever and gently satirical, as my adult self does. I hope that my fondness for this book vouches for a greater openness than I remember, turning on its head my memory that I responded most forcefully to stories with darker visions but happy endings, to injustice and misunderstanding rather than the miracle of life and creativity that are at the core of this book. But it also turns out that *Trumpet of the Swan*, which I'd always thought of as a huge departure from my usual fare, is only ostensibly different. Thematically, it's closely connected to almost every other book that I loved as a child.

The pompous but good-hearted father swan is the primary spokesperson for the novel's underlying philosophies. A flawed but loving and protective parent, the cob admires his offspring, an "egg of supreme beauty and perfect proportions," and exults in using language to heighten experience, to hilariously overblown effect. "Here I glide, swanlike," he says, "while earth is bathed in wonder and beauty. . . . I glide, I glide, swanlike . . . still I glide, ceaselessly, like a swan." He is initially alarmed at having a "defective" son, Louis, the main character, who cannot speak. Nevertheless, the cob will go to the ends of the earth, commit a crime and compromise his reputation, to help his son. The cob rhapsodizes about how "swans feel exalted" in the air "as though you had conquered life and had a high purpose." He describes "the rapture of the deep," how easy it is to feel so "peaceful and enchanted" deep down in the water that you never want to surface.[19]

Even more obviously than with Rachel in *Dancing Shoes*, this book offers another twist on "the Ugly Duckling" as it celebrates the joy, exaltation, and rapture of life and music. Instead of being born "ugly," the cygnet is born mute, and his voiceless future appears dim. Like the ugly duckling, Louis is out of place among his peers and straddles two worlds. Similarly, Andersen's duckling is really a cygnet who falls in with a bunch of ducks and thus appears different, and his upbringing leads him to be not quite a duck at heart but not quite a swan, either.

Louis's dilemma is even greater. He attends a first grade class at a school with pricelessly unconventional classrooms, where he learns to write, enabling him to communicate with humans by jotting messages on the slate around his neck. But the other swans can't read. Louis resorts to the universal language of music and through his talent triumphs over his disability, clears his father's reputation, and gets the girl. He does have to cut the webbing between his toes to play the trumpet properly, impeding his swimming ability and making him more humanlike. He partially lives in a human world, playing in nightclubs, even staying at the Ritz-Carlton sometimes. But he refuses to be pinioned and prefers to be free, in the wild, even though the cost of this is that he has to regularly donate one of his children to the Philadelphia Zoo, where that child must be pinioned. Despite that disturbing concession, the book is breathtaking in its reverence for life and its delight in the continuing cycle, much as in White's more famous book about a spider who is also a writer, *Charlotte's Web*. In the end, I can come up with few books that I read as a child that do not deal in some way with creative development and production, its costs and joys.

2.

Many of my favorite characters didn't overtly aspire to literary or artistic achievement, including Laura Ingalls and Nancy Drew. It seems odd to include these two in the same sentence: one a real pioneer girl born more than half a century before the other, a girl detective who is purely fictional; one the center of gentle, organic, autobiographical family stories; the other, though now iconic and much beloved, more plastic and manufactured, created as a consumer product.

But Laura and Nancy have some things in common. They first appeared as characters in stories around the same time, Nancy in 1930, Laura in 1932, products of values and expectations of the 1930s while also both breaking type for female heroines, offering adventure and positive messages about possibilities available to girls. May Hill Arbuthnot considers the publication of *Little House in the Big Woods* the milestone of 1932 in children's literature. She writes, "Stories about the west were a staple of the abhorred series books; the *Little House* books benefitted from children's fascination with the setting, but turned the west into more than a backdrop for predictable dramas of good and evil."[20]

Many, many readers and critics saw Nancy Drew as groundbreaking as well, a feminist heroine who transformed the visions of countless girls, providing a model of independence and freedom. A Wikipedia entry cites biographies and articles in which prominent women claim Nancy Drew as an influence, including former child fans such as Supreme Court justices Sandra Day O'Connor and Sonia Sotomayor, Secretary of State Hillary Rodham Clinton, and former first lady Laura Bush.

Both the *Little House* and Nancy Drew series were, it turns out, products of sometimes difficult collaborations, in both cases between writers whose values were often at odds. By the time of my childhood, it was widely known that the Nancy Drew books had been produced by the Stratemeyer Syndicate, headed by Edward Stratemeyer, a children's book mogul who created characters, series, and outlines and then farmed out the actual writing to a variety of authors. The early Nancy Drews, as documented in Melanie Rehak's 2006 book *Girl Sleuth: Nancy Drew and the Women Who Created Her*, were produced by two women. Rehak portrays in fascinating detail the reluctant collaboration of Mildred Wirt Benson and series editor Harriet Stratemeyer Adams. While until recently Benson's contribution had been downplayed, the role of Laura Ingalls Wilder's daughter Rose Wilder Lane in writing the *Little House* series has long been acknowledged by scholars but completely ignored by fans. Many regard Rose's participation as a shameful secret if not an outright lie in the creation of Laura Ingalls Wilder's deservedly canonical books.

As a child, I knew little about the genesis of either series, but I developed ambivalence toward both. I sensed that the Nancy Drews were less artistically written and constructed, so my profoundly mixed feelings toward their heroine made more sense to me. I first started reading Nancy Drew because my cousin Jody did. I was always trying, mostly unsuccessfully, to keep up with Jody, and by the time

I cracked open my first Nancy Drew, she had moved on to Agatha Christie. It annoyed me the way she regularly talked about Miss Marple and Hercule Poirot as if they were real people. I felt left behind now that she had crossed an invisible line from the mild thefts, scams, and lost inheritances of children's mysteries to the gritty murders and sly deceptions of adult books.

But Nancy Drew was all I could handle. I found the stories so vivid, tense, and claustrophobic that I had nightmares. Yet I continued to read them, sucked into their alluring details: mansions, prisoners in towers, buried treasure chests, orphans of unknown parentage, doubles, phantom ships and horses, frightful howls and bloodcurdling screams. I was lured by bats, dust, cobwebs, old diaries and lockets and moldering wardrobes, tunnels and secret cupboards and compartments, loose bricks and panels and floorboards, whatever could hold secrets. In climactic moments, Nancy is tied up on a sinking ship and left to drown, bound and gagged and tossed into a hidden underground room à la Edgar Allan Poe, threatened with confinement in closets, caves, tunnels. "You'll never see daylight again," the villains like to declare.

I spent most of my allowance at KMart on the yellow-spined hardcovers, what I later found out were Nancy's second incarnation, because I couldn't find the books at the library. When I finally inquired why not, a librarian gently told me that Nancy Drews were not good literature. There was no actual Carolyn Keene; the books had no real author. They were produced by a syndicate, a sort of book factory, where the boss wrote an outline according to a formula, and then an employee fleshed out the story. Then another one edited it so it would sound like all the others, and ta-da, a book was born. A book with no real imagination, no art, no vision—just a collaboration for the sake of money.

My family regularly visited Henry's candy factory in Dexter, Kansas. There, we watched workers stirring, pouring, turning, peeling, and cutting the hard candy, cleanly, expertly, relaxed but efficient, perfectly in sync. When I tried to picture a writing factory, Henry's was my only frame of reference. I envisioned a huge room full of metal tables, some filled with writers madly scribbling Hardy Boys stories, others frowning thoughtfully as they edited new Bobbsey Twins books.

In the Nancy Drew row of my imagination, the boss finished dashing off an outline and passed it to the detail filler. Titian hair, check. Blue convertible, check. On down the line to a researcher: a lesser-known name for lilacs is blue pipes. Insert paragraph. On to another writer: suspenseful climax involving confinement. Finally, to the writer who produced the last page, which always alluded to the next mystery: "During the discussion, Nancy was wondering what her next mystery would be. It was a puzzling one, which was called Password to Larkspur Lake."

My image of assembly-line book creation secretly inspired me. I pictured how, at the end of the day, all the writers would throw down their pens in satisfaction, yawning and stretching and buzzing about the recent plot developments. I envied the imagined camaraderie between syndicate writers. I wanted a job like that someday. I even had my part picked out—I'd be the one who wrote the cover description, what I later found out was called the blurb. That meant that I'd get to read all day in order to distill each book into a succinct paragraph.

I didn't need to believe in Carolyn Keene to love Nancy Drew any more than I needed to believe in Betty Crocker to enjoy cake. But the librarian's words planted a seed of doubt. I generally liked to picture the authors of my favorite books as real people, grown up versions of Harriett, Heidi, Anne, Laura. But Nancy had never seemed real enough for me to envision her as Carolyn Keene's thinly disguised younger self. I never once imagined a grown woman giving up a leisurely, adventurous, and fashionable life of sleuthing to sit typing all day in her olive green knit with matching shoes and beige accessories. And I hadn't yet internalized the expectation that a single author should function as the center of authority. Nor did I have any notion that ghostwriters or collaborative processes might be regarded as violations of public trust or compromises of artistic integrity.

Still, my niggling doubt took hold and I began to find fault with Nancy Drew. I noticed that her hair was sometimes blond, sometimes "titian," which my dad said was more reddish, strawberry blond, after the favorite models of a famous painter. The inconsistency made me wonder if the syndicate was always on its toes. And then *The Clue of the Broken Locket* described a boy and girl as "identical twins," a sentence on which I heaped all of my twelve-year-old scorn.[21] Even I knew that a boy and girl could only be fraternal twins.

And now the floodgates opened. I became more and more annoyed by Nancy's perfection, something for which other readers admired her. The healing powers of girls' book heroines, the dazzling competence of Pa Ingalls, combined anew in the character of Nancy Drew. Nothing fazed her. If someone at a neighboring table choked on raw steak, she paused from tracing clues to administer the Heimlich, add a delicious marinade to the meat, and fire up her portable grill to ensure that it was fully cooked. If Nancy's boyfriend Ned discovered a message in hieroglyphics, Nancy darted over to translate it—into French by way of Swahili. If her car overheated, Nancy purchased a new thermostat and installed it herself, substituting roadside sticks and rocks for more conventional tools. If Nancy's slacks ripped while she was camping on a mountainside, she whipped out her sewing kit and stitched up a pair of new pants from tent cloth. So maybe these are exaggerations of Nancy's prowess—but not by much.

Nancy was the original Barbie, thin and stylish and endlessly versatile, capable of assuming a new role with each new outfit, a short cultural leap to Newborn Baby Doctor Barbie, Aerospace Engineer Barbie, Sea World Trainer Barbie, and Beach Party Barbie. But just as I never got into Barbie, Nancy was too relentlessly competent for my taste. She was effortlessly attractive, kind, and skillful, and we were repeatedly told how modest she was, even though she was always introducing herself by saying things like, "I'm Nancy Drew. My father is Carson Drew, the attorney." Those words smacked to me of privilege and entitlement, an expectation that everyone should have heard of and been impressed by her father.

Sharing her first name called attention to all that I could not live up to. In contrast to the young sleuth, I was shy and awkward, and my world felt out of my control. In real life, modesty and shyness came down to the same thing, rendering me invisible. Nancy got away with so much; it wasn't fair. She observed the faint sound of crickets on a pirated recording and concluded that it had been made at Pudding Stone Lodge because you could hear crickets there at night. I railed at this ludicrous deduction: where couldn't you hear crickets at night?

My concept of how the world worked, with God in his heaven, the righteous vindicated, and truth and justice prevailing, was beginning to erode.

"I'm getting tired of Nancy Drew," I told my mother. "The books are all the same." Once I'd become attuned to the pattern of each plot, it became glaringly obvious how alike they were.

Mom nodded sagely. "You've discovered the difference between good literature and trash," she said.

I felt vaguely duped, as if Nancy Drew were my own personal emblem of receding innocence. I went overboard, trying to get back at what? A fictional character? A fictional author? A publishing industry that had tricked me? I started writing my own Nancy Drew stories full of absurdities, meant to be acerbically witty.

Santa Claus is a central figure in my first Nancy Drew story, "Mystery at the North Pole," in which the girl detective heads off to assist the "jolly old elf" with an unspecified problem. I mostly included Santa Claus because it seemed so ridiculous, but now I realize that he's Carolyn Keene multiplied exponentially, the ultimate cultural deception, the elemental representative of mystical childhood belief debunked.

Furthermore, he's a benign figure on the surface, but beneath it all, not so different from your average creepy criminal. His methodology involves peeping and stalking—he sees you when you're sleeping? He knows when you're awake?—and breaking and entering. Granted, he leaves stuff instead of taking it, but still embedded in the whole Santa Claus myth is an acceptance of violation and intrusion if performed by the right well-intentioned cultural construction.

So there you have it, my twelve-year-old disillusionment in a nutshell: Santa Claus didn't exist, Carolyn Keene didn't exist, crime isn't always punished, there is evil in us all. And so I went for the jugular as best I knew how, attacking the weaknesses of plot and character in the books that stood for all that had betrayed me.

Eventually, after five or so ruthlessly ridiculous but unfinished Nancy Drew stories of my own, I spent my rage. But it was a long time before I would grudgingly give her credit for being a paradigm of independence and daring who may not have consciously recast femininity for me but who did, in a roundabout way, help make me a writer. And sometimes what kept me going in grad school was feeling like Nancy Drew in a land of meanings to be uncovered, processes and influences to be discovered.

Critics have reconsidered once widely accepted stances on collaboration and literary authority, and public libraries no longer disdain popular fiction; in fact, they embrace it. And I no longer feel as divided as I did in my late teens and early twenties. Maybe Nancy Drew was an early feminist, I used to think, but I still couldn't quite get past the formula aspects of the books. Now, I feel more able to appreciate the books for what they are.

When I returned to Nancy Drew after a hiatus of many years, I found myself sucked right back in. My daughter and I started playing Nancy Drew computer games when she was eight, and eventually solved twelve of them, albeit only on the junior level. In these games, we became Nancy Drew, questioning suspects, solving puzzles, completing tasks. My rage toward Nancy mellowed; I'd softened; or maybe I was just less resentful because the game required me to be the competent one. Besides, if Nancy got too annoying, we could have her poison the horses and get her kicked off of Shadow Ranch, blow up the boiler room and have her thrown from River Heights High School, or feed her to a man-eating plant in Blackmoor Manor. There was a mechanism for second chances, and third, and fourth, and fifth, so we could kill off Nancy repeatedly, then revive her and re-enter the game.

It was very satisfying. Now I was the powerful one.

3.

Nancy Drew is a confident, sunny character who is not herself an aspiring artist but who demonstrates time and again a creative process full of danger but free of angst, always with a happy ending. My own reality felt a lot more complicated. It was around the fifth grade when my mother explained to me that my aunt had a disease that would grow worse with time, a disease that someday would kill her. Between that knowledge and the increasingly elaborate social codes of the upper grades of elementary schools, Louise Fitzhugh's *Harriet the Spy* was a book that drew me powerfully. I related to its dark side, even when it crossed over to being creepy, even grotesque.

It was in one of the Children's Book-of-the-Month Club packages that arrived in the mail. Every month, I eagerly tore open a package to find a new book: *The Wind in the Willows*, *Heidi*, *Freaky Friday*, *Anne of Green Gables*, *The Cricket in Times Square*, and *Harriet the Spy*. I promptly plopped right down in the living room rocker and read each new book from cover to cover.

My other favorite book that year became *The Cricket in Times Square*. But though I connected passionately to both *Harriet* and *Cricket*, I never re-read either novel, never searched for more books by George Selden or Louise Fitzhugh as was my usual habit when I found something I loved. Both books came to me at moments that I needed them. Maybe I just never needed them again. So I didn't return to them until recently.

Both take place in New York City, a place I'd never been, the first in the Times Square subway station, the second in and around Harriet's home on East Eighty-Seventh Street in Manhattan. Both books, like almost everything I seem to have been drawn to, are about artistic development, though *Cricket*'s exploration of the subject is much simpler and sweeter than *Harriet*'s. But the two protagonists would have understood each other. Chester the Cricket is, down to the bones in his delicate wings, a musician; Harriet Welch is a born writer.

This is undoubtedly what I related to in *Cricket*, that and my belief that it was more sophisticated to like books about animals and boys than about girls. Chester the Cricket, like Louis the Trumpeter Swan, has a phenomenal musical talent, outshining, according to his friend Harry the Cat, even the accomplished violinist at an outdoor chamber music concert. Despite the unconditional love and ready defense of the boy who adopts Chester and fixes him a matchbox home, Chester's mishaps nearly cause the boy's family to cast him out. Chester dreams a two-dollar bill is a leaf and eats it; then, while partying with his animal friends, he accidentally sets the family's newsstand on fire. The mother scoffs at the notion that crickets are good luck. Chester, she concludes, is a common firebug. "He eats money—he commits arson!" she says.[22]

But Chester wins them over and saves their business by chirping the Grand March from "Aïda," "The Blue Danube," "Rock of Ages," songs from musical comedies, movements from symphonies, and solo sections of violin concertos. *Cricket* ends up being a sweet parable about the power of music, the price of fame, the tensions of straddling two worlds, and the need for artistic expression.

Show business demands a punishing schedule, Chester discovers, and he also has to worry about the dangers of cricketnappers. So even though his singing has redeemed him in the eyes of his human family and saved their business, even though his final concert brings Times Square to a complete standstill, he must follow his nature. He doesn't want to eat dollar bills; he craves leaves. An audience of crickets and wild animals in the country is just as valuable as an audience of humans. There are no predators or prey here (a cat and mouse are, in fact, best friends), and no overt longing for a mate though that may be an unstated part of Chester's homesickness. In this story, the best creation arises out of love, a message similar to that of the *Anne* books—but it is understood that even though Chester is moving to the country, perhaps to find a mate and have a family, he won't give up his music.

In *Harriet the Spy*, Harriet's nanny, Ole Golly, contends that the point of writing is to put love in the world.[23] But Harriet learns that lesson only gradually, and I have always recalled her journey as much darker. So why did I love the book so much? Rereading it convinced me that it was more than worthy of my childhood enthusiasm, this story of a girl who is driven to write, who simply can't process the world without a notebook. With it, she feels a glow of happiness, a thrum of excitement, a surge of self-sufficiency. Harriet experiences tremendous loss and is ostracized because of her writing, her insistence on telling her truth, and yet she can't give it up because it's such a part of who she is.

As an adult, I'm bowled over by the anger in this kid, the way she regularly records mean-spirited observations about others and engages in violent fantasies about poisoning her enemies, blowing them up, and seeing them run over by trucks. I'm startled at how passionately I once identified with Harriet, since I don't recall harboring ill will toward my own adversaries; maybe Harriet expressed it for me so that I could remain a peace-loving child with compassion and a deeper understanding toward others' anger.

Harriet's first thought, when her former friends conspire against her, is that they are planning to drive nails through her head. Harriet's friends and the objects of her voyeurism are disconnected, neglected, sad, lonely, needy, desperate. Her best friend smiles only when she's angry, a big, scary smile. Another classmate smiles all the time because she's so shy, terrified of everyone, Harriet concludes.[24] In Harriet's world, even smiles are menacing, hiding anger and terror.

The novel's plot is set in motion by Harriet's realization that the woman who has raised her, the only person in the world who truly "gets" her, has a life outside of Harriet. This shift happens in the first chapter, when Harriet meets the mother of her nanny, Ole Golly. The mother is a toothless, overweight, simpleminded woman living a confined life, and Harriet begins to gain insight about others, understanding that reacting against her mother's life is Ole Golly's incentive to make a different one for herself.

It would be easy to blame all of Harriet's own difficulties on her parents, who demonstrate complete cluelessness when they're not absent altogether. We never know quite what Harriet's own mother does all day. She seems to shop quite a bit, and once she is (grumpily) called out from a hairdresser's appointment to deal with Harriet. The parents are rarely home, often leaving her with the cook when Ole Golly is away, and when Harriet is distraught, it's her nanny, not her parents, for whom she cries.

Despite their evident flaws and neglect, the parents can be oddly endearing, concerned about Harriet if helpless to know what to do for their increasingly troubled child. Eventually, they discover that their daughter is extremely intellectually gifted, and their emotional neglect takes on new proportions in a world that patronizes and fails to accommodate a bright and complicated child. In one of the book's most amusing passages, Harriet is assigned the role of an onion in the Christmas pageant, and together with her parents, struggles to figure out how an onion would dance. An onion is an ideal metaphor for Harriet, whose layers of defenses and complications must be peeled back one by one.

As a child, I saw advantages to the inattention of Harriet's parents. She values her independence; going where she wants when she wants enables her to develop as a "spy," in her case a code word for "writer." Positioning herself as a voyeur to the private moments of others, as intrusive and creepy as it is, allows her to hone her eye for detail and her ability to decipher human motives while also avoiding having to turn a critical eye back on herself.

My own mother was home full time until I was nine. My own home in a small suburban neighborhood precluded establishing a spy route of my own, though I planned out one I never had the guts to execute. Although my circumstances were vastly different from Harriet's, I recognized my own relationship with my mother in Harriet's with hers. Mrs. Welch doesn't understand what makes her daughter tick, doesn't see that her writing is an essential outlet. The notebook is valuable as a medium for creative expression and a conduit for her anger that allows her to function socially—that is, until her classmates read what she's written about them. It was a tossup for me whose actions are worse—her meanness, or their invasion of privacy. Nevertheless, at this juncture, her writing becomes problematic, and when her parents confiscate her notebooks, she is lost; she becomes outright vicious and uses her insights about others to identify what will most hurt them.

The lesson for me wasn't to stop writing, but to guard my thoughts carefully. I kept my own journals under lock and key in a cabinet in my bedroom, and I generally didn't write gratuitously mean things although when I was angry I could certainly be wildly unkind. I also never threw away anything I wrote without first tearing it up into little pieces.

Harriet the Spy was, to me, a powerful cautionary tale about privacy. I didn't take from it any negative feelings about the act of writing itself. In fact, today what I most like about the book is that despite Harriet's mistakes, even while portraying the power of words to do damage, the story celebrates rather than denigrates the roles of writing and literature. Harriet draws from poetry for strength. She and Ole Golly quote from "The Walrus and the Carpenter" in a wonderful bonding moment as Ole Golly prepares to say goodbye, and when her classmates pick on her, Harriet hangs tough with the aid of lines from Kipling's "If." Harrison Withers, an eccentric man on her spy route with a roomful of cats, has given a number of them literary names, including Faulkner and Dostoyevsky. When Harriet is caught spying in a dumbwaiter and hauled out of a house by the scruff of her neck, "Even though her feet were dangling helplessly and her mind was racing with fear, Harriet took a few mental notes of the interiors as they descended."[25]

Writing is embedded in Harriet's genes, and by the end, she's moving toward using it to gain compassion and insight. This is where Ole Golly tells her in a letter that writing is to put love in the world, not use against her friends. Harriet, in response, clings tenaciously to her honesty even while seeking to avoid intentionally hurting others. When Harrison Withers loses his cats, presumably through action by the health department, Harriet connects to his loss. Harrison's name demarcates him as a sort of double for Harriet; both might be expected to wither at their losses —the confiscation of his cats and of her journal as well as Ole Golly's seeming desertion of Harriet. But the human spirit is far more resilient than Harriet expected, and far less willing to abide by any rules that will kill it. Harrison eats healthier meals and starts adopting new cats, a survivor after all.

When adults light on the wisdom to help Harriet find her way *through* her writing, she doesn't magically start recording falsely pleasant observations about others —after all, she's still human, still eleven, and still constitutionally honest. But she does change, focusing in her writing more on her own feelings and surroundings instead of sticking to her previous thoughtless cruelty, though she does report overheard adult gossip and sometimes vicious comments by classmates. But at the end, as her two best friends finally approach her for a reconciliation, she is for the first time able to imagine herself in their shoes, their skin.

Harriet's giddy joy at having her writing back resonated tremendously with me. When I kept up a silent running narration of my life, when I was set on coming up with a slogan for a breakfast cereal contest or a rhyme for a poem about snow, everything shimmered and shone. My thoughts raced, my fingers itched for a pen, and I felt sorry for anyone who didn't experience the world with that resounding, occasionally manic pulse of creativity. I lived for those interludes where colors were brighter, when music was more poignant, when the crack of a stick underfoot, the smell of air conditioning on the first hot day, or the salty taste of play dough conducted a thousand memories.

Harriet gave me permission to look beyond the natural world for my understanding of imagination's possibilities. Harriet cared about human behavior; Harriet cared about words; Harriet made valid my own interests and creative expression. Although I may have initially been drawn to *Harriet the Spy* by a sense of shared suffering with an unconventional heroine, in the end, the book may have taught me more than any other of my childhood about transcendence and survival.

CHAPTER FIVE

Independence, Kansas

Little House on the Prairie

THE *LITTLE HOUSE* SERIES is all about transcendence and survival and building cozy little homes against each new set of obstacles and harsh conditions. Blizzards, fires, plagues of grasshoppers, and the absence of loved ones always give way
to evenings together by a snug fire, Pa playing his fiddle, as he does at the conclusion of all the books but the last. Maybe since I wasn't in any hurry to grow up and
embrace adult obligations, I related to the free spirits of Laura and Pa. I understood
their longings to live beyond the strictures of civilization. I related to the war between desire and duty that Laura perpetually fought.

But I also identified with Ma and Mary's fantasies of a settled life, a serene refuge of a home, the comfort of routine. If I'd been an army brat or a child of divorce,
maybe my sense of connection to Ma and Mary would have made more sense. In
fact, I lived in one house from the time I was three until I was twenty, and my home
was relatively stable and secure. But from a young age I was terrified that I would
never master the skills necessary for adult independence—talking to strangers, performing boring, repetitive tasks, learning to drive, satisfying customers or bosses.

Anxiety fogged around my teenage years. At fourteen, I was a candy striper who
kept getting lost in the hospital while pushing wheelchairs of elderly patients. I was
in a perpetual panic during my brief stint working at Orange Julius at sixteen. It
was the Christmas rush, and demanding crowds of customers stormed the counter. My hands and my polyester uniform were constantly sticky with orange juice.
A year later, I worked for a while in a factory that packaged screwdrivers. I could
keep up with the other workers when slow music played on the radio and everyone
fell into a languid haze. Then a fast tune kicked everyone into high gear and I fell
behind. Conversation was impossible. Books were irrelevant. My life was an endless
repetition of frantically sorting screwdrivers into the correct molded plastic slots.
I felt bleak, imagining that all jobs would be like these, that this was my future.

In my twenties, I gradually grew more confident, moving ten times in as many years. During those years, it was a home I yearned for, not excitement, adventure, or travel. "You didn't inherit my gypsy blood," my mother used to lament. She dreamed of a footloose and fancy-free retirement in a Winnebago, touring the US and wintering in Mexico the way my grandparents did. But she had been liberated to entertain such dreams, I thought, by always having a home base, a place to return to.

In my childhood, we referred to Laura Ingalls Wilder's work as "the Laura and Mary books." Now they are commonly referred to by critics as the *Little House* series, since there are little houses in the titles of two of the books and in the texts of all of them. But the influence of the TV show means that popularly, they now tend to be labeled "the *Little House on the Prairie* books." And so the accidental honor of being the most prominent has been conferred onto this third book in the series, the only one set in my home state of Kansas. Never mind that the TV series that forced this book to its position of distinction is actually set in the Minnesota town portrayed in *On the Banks of Plum Creek* and not on the Kansas prairie at all.

I feel a special affinity for *Little House on the Prairie*, partly because it takes place in my native state, partly because, it turns out, it taps even more into the tensions of my middle age than my childhood. Now I am on the one hand more settled than ever, on the other, more torn, more tempted to chuck it all and go somewhere else, anywhere. *Little House on the Prairie* and *On the Banks of Plum Creek* follow Ma and Pa's efforts to create a home and continuity in the face of natural disasters and unpredictable historical events. The family is dogged by bad luck, first building a house supposedly inadvertently in Indian territory, later facing endless pests and bad weather that destroy their crops and challenge their fortitude. And yet through it all, Ma and Pa remain competent and creative, ballasts against the outside world. When I was a kid, I thought that that was how adults were supposed to be. That's how I expected to be.

Instead I am driving my daughter across Kansas, haunted by my old terror about my own competence. We are headed to Independence, an aptly named town to be associated with these preternaturally self-reliant pioneers. During all the years I lived in this state, I never went in search of Laura's prairie. My mother or aunts would undoubtedly have undertaken the trip if anyone had known quite where the little house on the prairie had been. But Charles Ingalls had never filed on the land, and the process of locating the site was made even more complicated, Anita Fellman writes, because estimates of the distance of the cabin from town later made by Wilder and her daughter Rose Wilder Lane were so exaggerated and inaccurate.[1]

According to the *Little House on the Prairie*'s tourist site's website, in the 1970s two women from the Kansas State Historical Society finally meticulously examined 1870s census records, eventually discovering the foundation of the Ingalls family's cabin and well. For some time, there was nothing more here than a marker near Independence for the site, but once the location of the Ingallses' home had been identified, volunteers built a replica cabin on it according to descriptions from the book.[2]

I was distracted by the way the website still presents the prairie experience entirely through the point of view of white settlers, explaining that the Ingalls family "mistakenly settled on the Osage Indian Diminished Reserve[;] . . . the Ingalls didn't know it, but six months later, the Osages were moved to Oklahoma and they would have been able to homestead the land." What a shame, this seems to imply, that the Ingallses had to leave their cabin when the Osages were about to be kicked off the land anyway. Later those lines will be removed from the website, but I will remember them because they echoed the casual views toward the Indians that seeped into my own uncritical childhood mythology of Laura Ingalls Wilder, along with a host of other notions that have gradually been revealed as either misconceptions or matters of interpretation. The image of Pa as a giant of a man, dazzlingly competent. The notion that Wilder was simply telling a true story without any political agenda, more fact than fiction. The prevalent belief, encouraged by Wilder herself, that everything in the books really happened and in just that way. The widespread assumption that Wilder, an untutored farmer's wife, picked up a pencil one day and, all alone, just wrote these lovely books in tablets, perfect on the first try. And the commonly accepted interpretation that the Ingalls family built their Kansas home in complete innocence three miles over the line demarcating the Osage Diminished Reserve. It seemed to many to be a terrible injustice when the Ingalls family had to abandon their lovingly constructed home and a terrible irony that they could not have foreseen that the US government would end up moving the Indians rather than the white settlers—or, more accurately, squatters, as Fran Kaye points out.[3]

I come back to the books as an adult knowing better, seeing all of the myths I embraced in childhood in much more complicated ways. But although I have a more uneasy relationship with some aspects of Wilder's work, I am still compelled by conflicts between the yearning to be wild and free or settled and domesticated, between wanting to explore the outside world while still always being able to return to the safety of home.

I remember feeling disillusioned as a kid when I found out that some readers regard Pa as a failure, not as the courageous, adventurous pioneer standing up to hard luck that I'd always imagined. But so what if Pa's abilities are partly fictional? They still awe me. At the beginning of *Prairie*, the family doesn't even bother to take along their furniture when they leave Wisconsin. They can't lug heavy possessions across the ice, and anyway, Pa can always make new ones. And sure enough, on days when he can't work on building the house or barn and planting and tending crops, he relaxes by whipping up a rocking chair for Ma or fashioning doors, a fireplace, a roof, a floor, a bedstead.

When Laura has jitters about teaching in *These Happy Golden Years*, Pa reminds her that she's never failed at anything and that success is a habit.[4] He doesn't mention his own string of failures. By then, though he has largely given up on farming and lives on his claim only part of every year, he's a community leader with admirable achievements. Because of that, it didn't occur to me as a young reader to question his wisdom about success. But many other readers have challenged the popular image of Pa that confers on him hero status. Journalist Dennis McAuliffe Jr., who wrote a book investigating his own family's Osage roots, says that

> The actor Michael Landon was horribly miscast as Pa in the television series *Little House on the Prairie*. Landon was too sweet-faced, clean-shaven—and focused. The real Charles Ingalls wore a two-foot-long vinery of beard. His dark, narrow, hard, glassy, chilly, creepy eyes would, a century later, stare out of photos of Charles Manson, the Hollywood murderer. Pa's resume reads like that of a surfer bum in search of the perfect amber wave of grain.[5]

Along the same lines, Eric Ringham writes in an editorial for the *Phoenix Gazette*, "American folklore reveres a man like Pa, the classic pioneer. He's so independent, so rugged, so true to his own ideals that if he were alive today he'd be holed up in Montana somewhere, surrounded by federal agents."[6]

Hardcore Wilder fans like my mom and aunts and cousin would have found such less-than-flattering takes on Pa to be sacrilege. But since adult reality rarely supports childhood hero-worship, I see Pa as a myth just waiting to be debunked. What surprises me more is how other popular conceptions of Wilder and her work evolved regardless of evidence to the contrary.

Take the idea promoted by my own relatives and many other fans that the *Little House* series constitutes objective truths about the settlement of the west, when, in fact, it was never a secret that Wilder's conception of the books was politically motivated. She wrote that they were her response to the New Deal, which, she felt, was stunting the American "can-do" spirit by allowing too much government interference in citizens' lives.

Some readers feel that acknowledging Wilder's conservative agenda diminishes the "objective truths" presented by the books and is a short step away from an attack on conservatism. This was especially exemplified in pre-publication Amazon.com customer reactions to Anita Clair Fellman's book *Little House, Long Shadow*. Fellman's work, a thoroughly researched discussion of the evolution of the relationship between Wilder's influential work and conservative American thought, examines how the individualist ethic of the *Little House* series laid ground for 1980s Reagan neo-conservatism.

Before Fellman's book was even released, an Amazon customer reviewed it, apparently basing her opinions on a publisher's description. "Prairie Mom" claimed that *Little House, Long Shadow* was "an obvious slam against conservatism." She was soon thanked by another customer called "Furry Ears," who also backed up "Prairie Mom's" contention that the Wilder books are fact, not fiction; after all, Wilder insisted repeatedly that everything in them "really happened." In the end, the supposed factuality of the series is another myth that contributes to the notion that Wilder's work represents universal truths about western expansion rather than a single subjective point of view.

Wilder produced the books in her sixties, and, given the faultiness of memory, her claim that everything in them "really happened" has to be taken with a grain of salt. But more importantly, the deliberate, highly artistic shaping of sentences and story that makes these books so accomplished suggests that they are far more than real life events slapped onto the page. Nor are these books the products of an inexperienced writer with amazing stores of raw talent, as my own mother and aunts were determined to believe. Not only had Wilder done a good bit of professional writing herself by the time she wrote the series, but scholars have long accepted that the books were produced collaboratively by Wilder and her daughter Rose Wilder Lane. It wasn't until the early 90s, when newspapers around the country picked up a story about the controversy surrounding William Holtz's *Ghost in the Little House*, that those studies became more widely known outside of the scholarly community.

Dedicated fans balked. My mother and Aunt Gena considered Holtz's claims a travesty; my aunt Shirley undoubtedly turned over in her grave. I felt like I was betraying them when I read his book. I felt like I was crossing over to the other side, embracing corruption and evil, when I found myself convinced by Holtz's evidence of Rose's significant role. There are plenty of critics who find Holtz's claims too extreme, disagreeing with his assessment of Wilder as an amateur and Rose as the real force behind the books, not just as an assistant but as her ghostwriter. I don't know how much credit Lane ultimately deserves, but I admit that I was relieved to find out that the writing of these books hadn't been as effortless as I'd once believed. I'd just graduated from my MFA program where everyone had pretended that the often very polished and accomplished work that they submitted was "just a rough draft." Holtz's book seemed a more honest portrayal of the writing process, reminding me that things rarely came out perfect the first time, that effortless-sounding writing was often the result of hard work.

If toppling the Laura Ingalls Wilder myths was a little disillusioning, it was also freeing to discover that the Ingallses, these paragons of pioneer competence, were actually human and imperfect and complicated. I'm less certain what to make of the most troubling myths of the series, the ones that the Wilder books perpetuate about the Osage Indians, the way they are treated as dismissible, less than human, a threat and an inconvenience to well-meaning and more deserving white settlers. Michael Dorris writes about loving the *Little House* books as a child only to give up on reading them to his own children. He couldn't get past his adult perception of the portrayal of the Indians, the way that they are erased in Wilder's descriptions of the lonely landscape and conflated with wild prairie animals when she does mention them. It was just too difficult to explain to his children the embedded assumptions of the books, particularly the white man's sense of entitlement in assuming that the land would inevitably be his to settle.

In his far harsher assessment, Dennis McAuliffe Jr. complains that Wilder compares the Indians "to reptiles, to garbage or scum" using adjectives "that connote barbarism, brutality, and bloodthirstiness."[7] No wonder that, like Dorris, and like Kimberly Meyer, who describes a similar experience,[8] I stumbled when reading aloud *Little House on the Prairie* to my Chinese American daughter. Like Dorris, I didn't know quite what to say about Ma. I halted regularly.

"I don't like the things that Ma says," I told my three-year-old. "I don't think that the author likes them, either." Wilder doesn't seem to be endorsing Ma's bigoted views such as her fondness for saying, "The only good Indian is a dead Indian" or her insistence that her daughters wear sunbonnets lest they become "brown as Indians." But how to explain this? Preschool was teaching my daughter to respect authority figures, and I was already urging her to question them. I found myself actually appreciating TV versions of the book that sanitize Ma's appalling attitudes and her perception of the Indians as dirty, smelly, and uncivilized.

"Wasn't Ma's comment stupid?" I found myself asking, cringing because at preschool my daughter was not allowed to use the word "stupid." I floundered for a more acceptable word that would make sense to her. "She hasn't been around many different kinds of people, has she?" I tried again. "But do Pa and Laura agree with her?"

The answer appears to be no. Pa and the girls defend the Indians and seem dismayed by Ma's disdain. Ann Romines points out in a gentler way than McAuliffe does the ways that dehumanizing views of Indians are embedded in the language, as when Laura sees men who have invaded her home as having eyes that are "black and still and glittering, like snake's eyes."[9] This, says Romines, "indicates how frighteningly alien to her humanity these men seem."[10] Later, the Ingallses are grateful when an Indian kills a panther to protect his papoose. Charles Ingalls earlier determined to shoot that same panther to protect his own family, but couldn't bring himself to do it. Finally, the Indians and the Ingalls parents have something in common that doesn't go unacknowledged. Is the Indian ultimately the more heroic of the two, for keeping his family safe from a wild animal? Or is it Pa who is more virtuous, more humane, for being unable to shoot it?

The child Laura does sometimes exoticize the Indians through envy of their supposed freedom. The adult narrator seems to have been influenced by romantic primitivism and the notion of the "noble savage." But what strikes me as way more dangerous than these familiar, easily recognizable pitfalls are the book's more subtle and therefore potentially more harmful entrenched assumptions of entitlement.

Michael Dorris finds that it is these underlying attitudes that create more subconscious tacit acceptance of atrocity than the overt racism of Ma, which I do not find to be generally excused or defended by the text. In fact, Laura offers a puzzled corrective, saying, "What did we come to this country for, if you don't like them?"[11] Writing this book after the death of the real-life Caroline Ingalls, Wilder seems determined to disavow her mother's unenlightened views. And though generations of readers may not have questioned Pa's presumption that whites have an automatic right to the land, critics like Romines have found within the text a complex critique of such attitudes. The child Laura asks her parents questions that they fail to answer, admonishing her to be quiet and go to sleep. Such moments lead Romines to suggest that this book provides Wilder and Lane an opportunity to "give voice to those forbidden questions about the relation of the 'Little House' story of Great Plains settlement and the story of the removals of the Great Plains Indians."[12] So actually, Romines implies, this book criticizes more than it accepts, an argument that I'm struggling to decide if I buy.

By the time we arrive in the town of Independence, we're starved, so we stop at a Taco Bell along our route. The restaurant is packed. We wait more than thirty minutes for our food. Waiting reminds me how in Little House on the Prairie, every acquisition of food is an event often worthy of its own chapter: blackberries, Christmas oranges, beef, milk. Back in the car, we drive some more to find the junction of Highways 160 and 75. We pass field after field of hay bales, none of the rectangular stacks, bound by wire, that I used to sit on at the occasional square dance or hay ride. These are round bundles of hay, like sleeping bags rolled sloppily.

I grew up in a city, not on a farm as is generally assumed when I say I'm from Kansas. And now that I live on the edge of the lush Allegheny National Forest, I can see why some view the Midwest as flat and barren, especially when, from the air, it appears neatly organized into rectangles, from the road tamed into perfect rows of corn and wheat. As an adult, I've always been drawn to the ocean. I can stand on a beach staring out to sea for hours while friends say knowingly, "She's from Kansas," as if childhood deprivation explains my fascination and wonder. As I drive through Kansas, though, I think that I'm more soothed by the similarity between the landscapes of the Midwest and the ocean than aware of their contrasts. The ocean feels like the essence of my home landscape, the wild vastness of it beyond human attempts at order.

In Barcelona recently, Sophie and I went to a *National Geographic* IMAX movie translated into Spanish. I was tired, and instantly forgot the movie's title, though I enjoyed listening to the language while wearing funny glasses and watching fish float dreamily past our heads or stab out like little shoots of light. Excavators reached around the soil next to us to brush away dirt that covered fossil remains. Sharks bulleted toward us, small sharp teeth snapping threateningly. We fast-forwarded through geological history, watching rocks erupt and oceans subside. During one segment I gathered, from onscreen labels, visuals, and my barely proficient Spanish, that in 1918, archeologists discovered fossil remains of sea creatures in Kansas, which had once been an ocean floor.

I cringed, perhaps unfairly, because the images being shown throughout Europe and the US seemed lifted right out of a Hollywood Western, or maybe a J. Crew catalogue in the case of the scientists in their broad-brimmed hats and khaki shorts with multiple cool pockets. They shaded their eyes as they gazed across the barren desert of western Kansas, where no prairie grass grew and no trees had been planted on a landscape of shadeless stretches of dust. The land had been cleared of all vegetation except, maybe, Sophie said later, a cactus.

I was indignant. I couldn't remember Kansas ever looking like that. But I was far more familiar with the middle and eastern parts of the state, so what did I know? Maybe I was just possessive and defensive and overly suspicious after a lifetime of battling one-dimensional stereotypes of my native land.

This film was made by *National Geographic*, after all, and it's even likely that they filmed on location, unlike recent moviemakers who've shot fake footage of Kansas in Missouri and even Massachusetts. One expects this from early movies like 1939's *Wizard of Oz*, for many non-natives the iconic view of Kansas despite the fact that it was filmed on an MGM studio lot.[13] But in more recent times, when at least some authentic scenes from real-life settings are more common, John Hughes, director of 1987's *Planes, Trains, and Automobiles*, claimed that Missouri just looked "more like Kansas than Kansas," according to now-defunct blogger "Echoes 1971." A film called *Wichita* was later shot near Boston. (Before its title was changed to *Knight and Day*, critics kept spelling the name of the city "Witchita.")

Though others assume that I'm drawn to the sea because of its novelty in contrast to my landlocked childhood, I like to imagine that the tug that I feel is more primal. I like to imagine that the ocean calls to me because it reminds me of my formative landscape: the plains states that are so flat precisely because they were once an ocean floor. This feels almost like part of my memory even if that ocean floor has been gone eighty million years by the time I drive through on a warm summer day, fields of grain rippling just like waves. You can tame this land, block it into right angles and plant straight lines of crops, but no matter what you do, it feels like a place that may be disciplined but is not docile, that may be subdued but is not submissive, always something fierce and wild remaining.

Rereading *Little House on the Prairie*, I was struck by how frequently the word "wild" appears and how intensely Pa and Laura align themselves with wildness. Pa talks about the Indians, the "wild men," enthusiastically. He befriends Mr. Edwards, the "wildcat from Tennessee." He regularly runs his hand through his hair so it stands up "wildly." The boundaries between what is wild and what is "civilized" frequently blur. Jack the Bulldog is not allowed in the wagon when crossing the Verdigris River; he may be domesticated, but he's still an animal. A pack of wolves look like dogs, and an illustration shows them in a half circle, at once scary and lovely, a human-like configuration that makes these wild animals briefly appear tame, social, civilized.

The emphasis on the harshness of the frontier may contain truth, but it also serves to maintain the mythic glory of western expansion and its larger-than-life participants. Fellman argues compellingly in *Little House, Long Shadow* that Wilder carefully selects details to create a vision of the frontier "as a place of conquest, escape to freedom, lawlessness, individualism, and concern for autonomy."[14] Fellman compares the series to Wilder's earlier memoir manuscript titled "Pioneer Girl," noting how the material was revised "to strengthen the impression of the family's geographical isolation and the distinctive western spirit they shared with other pioneers."[15] Not only have distances from town been exaggerated, but neighbors and relatives have been eradicated, numbers of trips to and from town are underestimated, and community events have been completely erased, Fellman argues, to emphasize the isolation and self-sufficiency of the family unit.

Dennis McAuliffe has an even more insidious interpretation of why it took Pa four days to go to town for supplies and then return. Town, McAuliffe points out, was ten miles away. McAuliffe doesn't explicitly link Pa to the actions of white men who burned Osage fields, forced Indians at gunpoint from their homes, stole their food and horses, and robbed their graves. But McAuliffe does imply that a man with no compunctions about stealing others' land may have been capable of further atrocities.[16]

While we can never know for sure whether Pa was really gone for four days at a time, the repeated allusions to the land's wildness certainly add to the sense of the family's isolation and vulnerability. It seems to me that in her fear of the Indians, Ma is primarily threatened by what she imagines that they represent: the part of her husband that is a free spirit, preferring to live outside of "civilization." Ma is the one who imposes routine, who reins in his spirit that left to its own devices would merely drift to the rhythm of seasons. It's her ingrained obedience to the rules of civilization that causes her to follow her husband and participate fully in their partnership even while she wishes for a more settled life and an education for her girls.

Now that the conversation cannot exclude the humanity of the Osage Indians, many readers confine their disapproval to Ma without flinching at Pa's blithe belief that he can just waltz into Kansas territory, build a house, and claim ownership of the land. "When white settlers come into a country, the Indians have to move on . . . that's why we're here, Laura," Pa says. "White people are going to settle all this country, and we get the best land because we get here first and take our pick."[17] Louise Erdrich, who wrote her own children's book *The Birch Bark House* partly in response to this attitude of white entitlement and the erasure of Indians, says, "I get crazy when I read about pioneers moving forward into 'empty' territory. They were moving into someone else's house, home, hearth, and beloved yard."[18] And Laura, too, questions this, saying "But, Pa, I thought this was Indian territory. Won't it make the Indians mad to—" at which point she is, as usual, silenced by Pa, who tells her to go to sleep.[19]

Ma appears to follow Pa unquestioningly, but often it is clear that she has more at stake and therefore a more instinctive awareness of the danger that might result from intruding on the homes of others. One scene always haunted me, the extremely tense one called "Indians in the House" in which "naked wild men" show up when Ma is alone at the cabin with the girls. She commands the children to stay outside, and Laura watches Ma and the Indians enter the house. Uneasily, Laura wonders, "What are they doing to Ma!"[20] As a child, I found this scene frightening. As an adult, I recognize more fully the implicit sexual threat. Ann Romines places this episode in a larger historical and cultural context, describing the Indians' state of near starvation as a direct result of the white settlers' incursions. It was this hunger that prompted the Indians' "visit."[21]

I am somewhat troubled, however, when Romines attributes Ma's and the girls' fears to "hysteria about the possibility of interracial rape of white women." In this way, Romines keeps the emphasis on the race issue: "The girls are shaken with amorphous fear of what could happen in the house between Indian men and a white woman."[22] The fact is, though, that nearly naked men are ordering around a smaller woman with less physical strength. By attributing the fear of pioneer girls and women to hysteria and racism, Romines ignores the clear potential for violence that underlies the dynamics in this scene. No matter what the race or situation of the men involved, they have invaded the home of a woman who is helpless to protect herself and her children and must do what they say. For me, this scene cuts to the heart of ignorance and prejudice, showing how it originates in legitimate fear that becomes misplaced or generalized.

Even though Laura is very young in this book and the real-life Laura was actually even younger, we see her struggling between the safety and comfort of adhering to rules and the questions and longings that if, acted upon, would constitute disobedience. She yearns, as Romines puts it, "for a life of expansion and inclusion."[23] Yet she also frequently takes refuge in rules that I considered gospel as a child but that now strike me as absurd. Over and over, we hear that Laura must wear a red ribbon in her brown hair, Mary a blue ribbon in her blond, a principle to which Ma rigidly adheres until it becomes a law of nature along with the oft-cited prohibition against children speaking "at table." "All's well that ends well," the Ingalls parents are fond of saying. "Pa said they were clean as a hound's tooth, and Ma told them they were bright as new pins," the narrator tells us, blanketing the girls in the consolation of aphorisms and clichés.[24] But if Wilder had truly accepted those responses, I wonder, would she have written this book? The more I think about it, the more I agree with Romines: if Wilder had embraced pat answers, would she have raised this book's inevitable questions?

I park alongside a split rail fence made of logs, behind one other car, on the side of a desolate highway. The grass rustles around us, whispering in a voice I have forgotten. I grew up in Wichita, home of four aircraft manufacturers and an air force base, a city once called the Air Capital of the World because of the airplane industry that was drawn there by level ground and scarce fog. I didn't know the difference between a wheat field and a cornfield. They were all just fields to me. But when I was little the wild prairie grass swished and sighed as we passed between it and the neat rows of crops, down long straight highways where I never got carsick, on the way to visit cousins and grandparents.

So standing here on the Osage's prairie and Laura's prairie, one of her first homes, I too am home. A place with a complicated legacy in its attitudes toward slavery and Indians, attitudes downplayed in my childhood textbooks, a place where I haven't lived in more than twenty years, but still, somehow, home. It's nearly one hundred degrees, hot and dry, at this remote site. The emptiness, even if it's not quite historically accurate, echoes the isolation presented by the book, making it more like its fictional counterpart than the typical tourist site flooded with visitors.

Sophie doesn't want to get out of the car. "Then you can wait here," I say.

"I don't want to wait here," she says. She's tired and cranky from all the driving.

"Stand by the sign so I can take your picture," I say.

"No," she says, and goes to stand by the sign.

We make our way up the path, the only humans as far as the eye can see. A little bit later a couple drifts past us, back to their car, and drives away. I practically have to bribe Sophie to climb up into an old wooden wagon so I can take a picture of her sitting there, fields of short green stubble spreading out behind her, a telephone pole and hay roll in the distance along with an isolated stand of trees.

None of the buildings were actually here during Wilder's time, not the original turn-of-the-century post office or the transplanted one-room schoolhouse, the former Sunnyside School, including desks from the 1870s and 1880s. There were no post offices or schools in Wilder's book, and the examples here date from a bit later. "This is boring. I want to go," Sophie says as we glance into the first building with its iron post office boxes and barred counter, and then pop into the schoolhouse with its wooden desks and wide-bellied stove and pump organ that we observe behind a wooden railing.

Like most of the Wilder sites, this one goes to some effort to re-create a sense of the pioneer experience for fans of the books and, in particular, of the TV show. The Independence, Kansas, *Little House on the Prairie* website raved that the show was "still being aired daily." Something about the wording caused me a moment of confusion, wondering why the proprietors were so eager to reassure me that the cabin was being aired daily. Were they trying to lure visitors who typically shun smelly old buildings, or what? But, I am happy to discover, the log cabin replica isn't at all smelly. It's tiny, rough hewn and low ceilinged, with wide spaces between the floor boards. A red checked cloth covers a long table with a small vase of orange and yellow flowers and a framed request for visitors to sign the guestbook. A quilt has been draped over a bench, a China shepherdess set on the mantel, cooking utensils arranged in the fireplace. Sophie perks up as we admire the chairs honed out of tree trunks, clever but not very comfortable.

The website says that places referred to in the book can be found within a short distance of the cabin, like the Indian camp along Onion Creek and the high prairie where the girls played, but I'm wilting in the heat and Sophie is clearly headed toward a total meltdown. We don't go looking.

The creeping unease that has dogged me on this trip is still here, in this lovingly created tribute filtered through fiction and sparse historical records. Other than directions to the Indian camp, there is no mention of the Osage Indians, no recreation of their homes although they were a presence in the book while the Sunnyside School and the post office were not. This place is, my friend Tracee will later put it succinctly, a physical manifestation of the dominant reading. It represents the way I read the book as a child, as a simple evocation of a simple life, one that I now know overlooked many realities. Now, aware of the bigger picture, I want something more.

At least now I can say that I've been to the Laura Ingalls Wilder site in Independence. This visit gives me a good old Midwestern feeling of completion, of finishing what I started. But I'm really tired as I drive on, past Half Pint's restaurant, away from town, and Sophie nods off in the back seat. As we go by rows of crops once again, I think of the end of *Little House on the Prairie*, how the family is safe and cozy under the stars. Laura, more excited about new adventures than lamenting a lost home, feels "her eyelids closing. She began to drift over endless waves of prairie grasses, and Pa's voice went with her, singing."[25]

Chapter Six

Mankato, Minnesota, and Maud Hart Lovelace's *Betsy* Books

MANKATO, MINNESOTA, WAS THE HOME of another of my favorite children's authors, Maud Hart Lovelace, and it's right along the Laura Ingalls Wilder highway, a good place to take a break right before lunch and the drive to Walnut Grove. But the houses where Lovelace and her best friend grew up, the houses that served as models for those occupied by fictional best friends Betsy and Tacy, prove to be much more difficult to find than sites related to Laura. Wilder's books are pretty much the only reason that some of the tiny towns where she once lived still exist, and blue signs along the highway tend to direct us straight to her homes and museums. Mankato is much larger, and there are none of those blue signs pointing the way to Lovelace sites.

Fortunately I had the last-minute foresight to print out directions in a hotel business office. It turns out that the childhood homes of Lovelace and her best friend are tucked away at the end of Center Street near the downtown of the small city, two unassuming houses across the street from each other at the top of a hill alongside a road grinding with machinery. "It ran straight up into a green hill and stopped," Lovelace writes in each of the first three books of the series.[1] She's describing Hill Street, modeled after Center Street. Lewis, the side street that intersects Center, has no name in the books, and now buzzes with yellow road graders that push their blades uphill and down, dust rising around them.

"As you set out to explore Mankato," Lovelace once wrote, " . . . you must remember that years have passed since Betsy, Tacy, and Tib (to use story names) were children here. To find Deep Valley in this bustling modern city, you have to close your eyes to the airport, to the streams of automobiles, and to many beautiful new homes and schools and shops. You have to imagine horses and carriages, ladies with trailing skirts and ruffled parasols and children in long black stockings."[2]

On this day in 2007, I'm skeptical that anyone but me has even heard of the

Betsy books despite the obvious evidence to the contrary that stands before me, the preservation of these houses. Still, I doubt that the guys in hard hats, focusing on the dirt road in front of them, have read them, and otherwise, this residential street is deserted, the two houses at the top looking like all of their neighbors. I park by the curb, in between them: on my left, the house that belonged to the Hart family, described repeatedly in the books as the Rays' "small yellow cottage"; on my right, the house that belonged to the Kenneys, immortalized throughout the books as Tacy Kelly's "rambling white house."

Sophie and I walk up the manicured lawn to the Tacy house, but it's locked up tight, further reinforcing my illusion that I am the world's only Maud Hart Lovelace fan. As a child, I hesitated to admit aloud how much I loved her girls' series, ten books that follow Betsy from the age of four into her mid-twenties. There were circles in which it was cool to be a Laura Ingalls Wilder fan, but no one I knew had ever heard of Lovelace. Her name was embarrassing to say aloud, sounding like the bad pseudonym of a romance writer, like someone trying to be "mod" while at heart she was just a fuzzy, frilly valentine, a chocolate all soft in the center, oozing with goodwill and happy thoughts and upbeat endings.

It turns out that Maud Hart Lovelace was, in fact, her real name. And I no longer think that her name or the name of her fictional town based on Mankato, Deep Valley, make her sound like a romance novelist. Now I think that they make her sound like a 1950s porn star.

I had briefly entertained the notion of following the Betsy-Tacy walking tour I found online. I'd imagined climbing the big hill that I remembered from the first four books. But with Lewis Street completely torn up and crawling with machinery, I'd be in the way. Asphalt is heaped along the side, and under the hot sun, it emits a burning tar smell. Somewhere in the town below must be Mankato High School, on which Deep Valley High was based. Somewhere down there is Betsy and Tacy's friend Tib's—actually Maud and Bick's friend Midge's—"chocolate colored house" with "front stairs and back stairs and a tower and panes of colored glass in the front door."[3]

There has never been a movie or TV show based on the *Betsy* series, and at the time of my visit, many of the books are out of print. No multimillion-dollar industry has sprung up around the Betsy phenomenon, no spinoff books or floods of merchandise or frenzy of biographical or critical writing. Mankato doesn't rely on Betsy tourist dollars to stay alive. I speculate that occasional people—okay, women—come here because they loved these books, pausing to stroll around and take a few pictures, maybe, to try to explain to patient spouses and children eager to get back on the road what this series meant to them. Then these ghostly fans climb back in their cars and drive away without signing a guestbook, leaving as silently and invisibly as they came. There is no hype, no fanfare, and because of this, the houses on the top of the hill seem ordinary, kind of sad, almost forgotten by the city that goes on around them.

Sophie and I wander up to the porch of "Tacy's house," the "rambling" white one. It appears to be in far better shape than "Betsy's house" across the street. I try to explain to Sophie, who has never read the books, why I loved them so much. Lovelace was very decidedly not a writer of porn, and a recent description from the *New York Times* jarred me: "Think Serena and Blair of Gossip Girl with lower hemlines and smaller budgets. And okay, no Lady Gaga cameos or gay men or fornication. But otherwise the same!"[4] Well, okay, but none of the jealousy, pettiness, and backstabbing of such contemporary books and TV series, either, as Sadie Stein points out on the Jezebel website, the kind of competition now de rigueur for girls' books, as if contemporary females are obliged to spend all their time and energy jockeying for meaningless power over and seeking revenge against each other—and all of their money on makeup and fashion.[5]

Betsy, in fact, could not be more wholesome, although that makes her sound far more boring than she is. It is true that the books are full of goodwill, happy thoughts, and upbeat endings, but I loved the stories even as a cynical youth because Betsy is a complex character, good hearted and smart and funny, sometimes flighty and often prone to error, her mistakes and scrapes and passions making her human and relatable. Best of all, she is an imaginative and ambitious girl who loves words and wants to understand people. There is nary a fairy or talking flower or romanticized description of nature to be found in these books.

My niece will exasperate me when, the summer she is fifteen, she'll arrive by train for a visit, then spend two days reading *Twilight* and transforming to Bella before my very eyes, seeming increasingly passive, antisocial, and self-absorbed. She'll walk around with a hood over her head, complaining that everyone is staring at her. She'll wear vampire fangs in public and complain that everyone is staring at her. She'll sit under a tree reading a book on the campus where I teach and then come into my office, complaining that everyone is staring at her. I'll be puzzled by this self-consciousness until I read the first few chapters of *Twilight* and discover that one of Bella's most pronounced characteristics is a conviction that everyone is always staring at her. Aha, I'll think. My niece was being Bella.

What a shock to reread the *Betsy* books and realize that, when I was a teenager, I had been just as susceptible to imitating Betsy as Sidney was to becoming Bella. I still can't help thinking that the turn-of-the-century heroine of these books published in the 1940s was a much more forward-thinking role model than the insipid Bella. Peggy Orenstein makes the astute point that perhaps Bella's appeal is that she represents an escape from the current pressure on girls to be perfect, to make straight A's, excel in all extracurricular activities, and be beautiful and fit.[6] Betsy's imperfections certainly appealed to me; she was known to fail math, to mess up, to get carried away. Yes, she was sunny, outgoing, and flirty in ways I could never pull off, but even if I couldn't exactly be Betsy, she still shaped me in memorable ways.

Like Betsy, who is drawn from early on to the orphaned Joe Willard, I was attracted to a boy who was an outsider, a kid who had to fend for himself from a young age and found school functions comparatively silly next to the adult responsibilities he faced early. Like Betsy, I cultivated a high school "crowd," although we were never so much a crowd as a "group," a word that felt to me like we were a pathetic counterfeit version of Betsy's robust circle of friends. Like Betsy, but due to the influence of my Joe Willard, I considered becoming an Episcopalian, and like Betsy, I attended football games, identifying with her lack of any "real and burning" interest in the game. My friends and I did our contemporary equivalent to making fudge and popcorn and singing all the songs from the Broadway musical comedy "The Time, the Place, and the Girl" around the piano: we got together to make pizza and watch *Saturday Night Live* and listen to music and patiently endure the guys who frequently broke into re-enactments of Monty Python sketches. In college, my friends and I once even held a mock wedding, which I realize was partially inspired by this favorite Deep Valley preoccupation.

Sophie and I prowl around, looking in the windows of the Tacy house, which serves as headquarters for the Betsy-Tacy society and is staffed by volunteers. The front rooms appear to be occupied by a well-stocked gift shop. We check the hours of operation. The house is only open for two hours on Saturdays, and today is Thursday. I kind of want to go in and I kind of don't. This place seems so impersonal, so detached from the Betsy who still lives in my imagination, who is still mine.

Another family, two parents and three little girls, wander by, cupping their hands to peer through windows. I hear the woman gush about how much she loved the books. She climbs the steps to the porch while the man and children stand by, waiting. Sophie points out a phone number on the door, and I punch it into my cell. I leave a message: I'm passing through and would really like to see these houses.

Now it's up to fate. When my fellow mom-tourist finishes looking in the windows and comes over to read the information posted on the door, I tell her that I just called the number and am hoping that someone will be able to give us a tour. The woman looks anxious, torn. She squints through the window one more time, then sends another glance toward her patiently bored family. "I can't make them wait," she says. Soon they all drive away.

We cross the street and look in the windows of the Betsy house. Unlike the fully furnished Tacy house, it's empty. I can see clean walls and dusty floorboards, but that's it. I decide to head down the hill to find the Maud Hart Lovelace wing of the public library.

At nine, Sophie despairs of making me a good citizen. I am always doing subversive things like walking down the left side of her elementary school halls when signs clearly direct me to walk to the right. As we enter the Minnesota Valley Regional Library, Sophie points to a sign and hisses at me, "Turn off your cell phone." I usually obey such injunctions, but this time I ignore her and all the posted requests.

This library is so quiet, though. The one we frequent in Olean, New York, is usually buzzing with activity. Children play, even shouting at each other, in an area with games and toys and a treehouse. Adults talk in normal inside voices. Here in Mankato, this library still follows the old-fashioned rules: I feel like I should walk on tiptoe and whisper, and much as I want to see the Betsy-Tacy houses, I certainly should not risk disrupting the atmosphere by leaving my cell phone on. I keep my hand on it, ready to answer the second it rings.

Near the entrance of the Maud Hart Lovelace wing is a huge portrait of the author by Marian Anderson. It shows Lovelace in the 1970s looking grandmotherly in her plastic-frame glasses and clip-on earrings and collared shirt and necklace of small stones. She's got the same direct look and open, friendly smile as in all of her photos, but lacks the glamour of the pretty teenage girl and young writer with hair piled on her head, teased into a pompadour or pulled back sleekly.

Further inside the Lovelace wing, though, there is a wall-sized mural by the same artist. In the middle smiles a younger, rounder-cheeked Lovelace, a tree growing out of one side of her head as if borne from her dreams, shading the buildings and the scenes from the books that unfold around it. A girl plays a piano while other girls sing. A young woman in a small-waisted, flowing dress and hat strolls in front of a downtown building. On the other side of Lovelace's head float the three disembodied faces of Betsy, Tacy, and Tib, who are pictured in yet smaller versions leaning together to tell secrets and picnicking on a blanket.

I move on to the reproduction of illustrator Lois Lenski's map of "Deep Valley" with its undulating hills and tall trees and cozy little houses. I remember this map from the endpapers of the library copies of the first four books in the Betsy series, the ones about her early childhood. I loved this map, all the hills and trees and houses and curving roads. There are more framed Lenski illustrations, scrapbooks and documents that belonged to Lovelace, and first editions of books. On display is the little glass pitcher with the gold-plated rim that "Tacy" gives "Betsy" for her fifth birthday, except that it was actually Bick who gave it to Maud, and the gold plating has since worn off.

I will encounter blurred boundaries between what is real and what is fictional often as I visit writer houses. Before I left for this trip, the only critical work that I could find on the Betsy books was Sharla Scannell Whalen's *The Betsy-Tacy Companion: A Biography of Maud Hart Lovelace.* It focuses on tracing all of Lovelace's real-life sources, which is fascinating though it sometimes mixes the names of characters with real names. "When Maud's experiences are the same as her fictional counterparts, the name 'Betsy' is most often used," Whalen writes. "Maud and her best friend Bick (the real-life Tacy) called each other 'Betsy' and 'Tacy' at times, so it seems fair for us to interchange the names, too! . . . the confusion between fiction and reality arises because the Betsy-Tacy books are so very autobiographical."[7]

To Whalen, this autobiographical aspect is essential for enjoying the books. "The reader's sensation that the books represent genuine experience is increased by the knowledge that Betsy and her friends have not only an interesting present but an interesting past," she writes, often pointing out that the fictional names that Lovelace used rhyme with the names of real-life counterparts: Carney for Marney, Cab for Jab. She asserts that if an incident is mentioned in several books rather than just once, it is more likely to have really happened, and insists that the character Tony's closeness to the Ray family "does not feel manufactured" because it was based closely on the Harts' relationship with a boy named Mike Parker.[8] Whalen's tendency to closely correlate real life and Lovelace's writing sets the stage for others' treatment of Lovelace's books. The only other critical or autobiographical work currently in print is a guidebook to real-life settings and sources by Julie Schrader. Later I will find references such as an online one to a theater production that mentions "Betsy Ray (who is Maud herself!)"[9] and a line in the *LA Times* that says, "Maud calls herself Betsy."[10]

Whalen's book jolted me into the recognition that I am not the only Betsy fan on earth, that, in fact, I'm not even the most fanatical Betsy fan on earth. But as I wander around the Maud Hart Lovelace wing of the library, I still assume that there aren't really very many of us. I can rationalize that this library room is just an archive, a celebration of a hometown author, a place where locals sometimes drag their children to view evidence that someone from their area was once well known. Maybe I don't really want anyone from the Betsy-Tacy Society to call. That way I can leave Mankato and the quiet houses at the top of the hill and still maintain an illusion that Betsy and Tacy are my own personal discovery. Well, sort of. Mine, and Whalen's, and maybe some local history buffs who purchased the houses and created a society and put together these displays of Lovelace artifacts.

These places and things can't bring alive what I loved about the *Betsy* books, all the details about sailor and gingham dresses and freckle cream, Betsy's Ethel Barrymore droop, Merry Widow hats that are so big that in New York, they cause ladies to get stuck in railway car doors. Lovelace was a historical novelist, and when she set out to write these books, she thoroughly researched the time period of her own childhood, determined to get the facts right. It was this period detail that drew me, and it was Betsy's timelessness that caused me to remain. She has a lively social life, witty friends, and a warm, loving family. She cares about books and writing and fashion and boys and sometimes her schoolwork.

I point out the first editions to Sophie, who is getting hungry and grumpy and is not feeling inspired to rush out and read the *Betsy* books. A few years ago, I bought a copy of *Betsy-Tacy*, published in 1940 and opening when Betsy is four turning five, and read at least part of it aloud, but it apparently made little impression on Sophie.

Betsy is a little girl who is always happy. She has teeth "parted in the middle," and, I will concede to Whalen, so does Lovelace in one of the few pictures I find of her with her mouth open. In this first book, Betsy meets the "bashful" red-haired Tacy, and after a rocky start, the two become inseparable friends who "never quarreled."[11] In fact, they are so inseparable that in the first two titles their names are connected by hyphens. *Betsy-Tacy and Tib*, published in 1941, peeks in at the two girls' lives when they are eight and introduces a new friend to the mix, the tiny, blond, fairy-like, practical and literal Tib who never gets subtexts. In the next book from 1942, they all turn ten and their identities begin to differentiate when Betsy and Tacy go "Over the Big Hill." Actually, that book was originally titled simply *Over the Big Hill*, with Betsy and Tacy's names later added by the publisher. These three books were illustrated by Lois Lenski, whose framed originals on the wall of the library are simple, almost like a child's sketches of houses, trees, flowers, and two girls with short dresses and stumpy legs.

The illustrations are perfect for these books, which are largely about creative play and storytelling. A scene reminiscent of those in A. A. Milne's *Winnie the Pooh* exemplifies how Betsy inspires imagination and Tib keeps everyone grounded, both presented as valuable traits. Betsy has just taught her friends to "fly," but the literal Tib says, "It feels just like jumping." "Well, it isn't," said Betsy. "It's beginning to be flying."[12] Much of the time, the girls play, then turn their play into stories. Though there are sad events, like the death of Tacy's infant sibling, the books reaffirm the power of friendship and of stories as they portray happy childhoods—the kind of childhoods in which, when everyone seems to have forgotten your birthday, it always turns out that they're actually planning a surprise party. The first three books end with the three girls making plans for adventures they'll have in the future—always followed by the words "And so they did."

One of the groundbreaking features of the series is that, before there were official categories in children's books like early reader, middle reader, and young adult, Lovelace was writing for these different age groups through the progression of language and increasing layers of characters and events in her own stories. Whalen points out that the length of the text increases with each book: *Betsy-Tacy* has 113 pages, *Betsy-Tacy and Tib* 128, *Betsy and Tacy Go Over the Big Hill* 171, and *Betsy and Tacy Go Downtown*, in which the print size decreases dramatically and the vocabulary and sentence structure are noticeably more complex, 180.[13]

Likewise, the first three books are written in simple language that gradually increases in complexity. These three books resemble early reader ones popular today among first and second graders, like the *Junie B. Jones* series or my friend Andrea Cheng's wonderful *Anna Wang* series. As the language becomes more complicated, the world of Lovelace's characters also expands, first from two inseparable friends to three, then past their own small neighborhood over the hill where there's a "colony of Syrians, strange dark people who spoke broken English and came to Hill Street sometimes peddling garden stuff and laces and embroidered cloths."[14]

Betsy and Tacy Go Downtown, originally called just *Downtown*, was one of my favorites as a child. The more complex language transitions the series into the last several books, which are aimed more at middle-grade readers. The girls are twelve and their world now widens even further as they venture downtown to the theater and, in Betsy's case, alone to the library. Although Lenski also illustrated this one, my 35-cent Scholastic paperback copy has a different illustrator, Lisl Weil, so that in my edition the girls look more grown up and realistic, no longer stocky, chubby-kneed children in shifts. By this book, Betsy has transformed from a storyteller to a writer who keeps a cigar box nailed to a tree and stores in it the melodramas that she produces. This was an exciting book in which Betsy discovers a long-lost uncle, appears on stage, publishes her first poem, and acquires her uncle's trunk as a desk.

While the Betsy high school series retains a vocabulary comfortable for middle-graders, it also deals with the concerns of adolescents in ways that I found comforting when I was a young teenager, before young adult literature became the booming category it is today. Each of these books follows Betsy through one year of high school, much like my mother's favorite books from a generation before, the Grace Harlowe series. The *Betsy* high school books are thicker than the series for younger readers and have a new illustrator, Vera Neville, whose drawings reflect the chang-es described in the first high school novel, *Heaven to Betsy*: "At twelve she had been short, straight, and chunky with perky braids and a freckled smiling face. At four-teen she was tall, very slender, with a tendency to stoop."[15]

As a child, Whalen found it startling to discover this new Betsy with "her hair up and her skirts down"[16] but it is quickly evident that our heroine is still the same old Betsy, resisting change, homesick when she visits a family in the country during the summer, and disappointed upon returning home, where she struggles to con-ceal her heartbreak at the surprise her family has prepared so enthusiastically: they are moving to a bigger house. As always, though, Betsy adapts, and soon she begins her freshman year, caught up in competitions between the two school societies, the Philomathians and Zetamathians, the social room in a turret, and her new friend Carney's solitary dimple and tendency to exclaim, "O di immortales!"

Betsy fans will begin to emerge in force during the years after my visit to Mankato, including Anna Quindlen, who sees the high school books as about Betsy learning to be herself—and an integral part of that self is as a writer. Constantly derailed but "never in the same way twice," Betsy is appealingly complicated, terrible at algebra, finding boys too brotherly toward her, romantic but able to shed that and "become in an instant a balanced capable person."[17] In her freshman year, Betsy learns that she can't let her social life take precedence over her writing, because writing is part of who she is. In her sophomore outing, *Betsy in Spite of Herself*, she has to undergo another variation on that lesson when, deciding to become "dramatic and mysteri-ous," she acquires an irritating boyfriend and removes herself from previous activi-ties like debating club and her and Tacy's annual performance of the cat duet. She can't bring herself to turn down a second chance to compete in the school essay contest against Joe Willard, but once again, she's distracted by other events in her life, doesn't prepare properly, and loses.

By *Betsy Was a Junior*, she has resolved to keep writing and to accept that she is not dramatic and mysterious. This time she's thrown off course by her decision to form a sorority, Okto Delta, inspired by her sister's reports about being rushed at college. Many people don't like this new development. Tony criticizes Greek or-ganizations because "they leave too many people out. . . . Do you know what they call the ones who don't join? 'Barbs,' 'barbarians.'" Like Beany Malone in the mid-50s, Betsy learns that secret societies are bad news, but unlike Beany, she learns this in a book published in 1947 and there are no veiled allusions to Communism. She ends up left out of the essay contest because no one likes "this sorority-fraternity business," and the crowd becomes scattered, particularly Tony who drifts away, skipping school and hanging "around a pool hall which had a bad reputation in Deep Valley." He turns to a "fast clique of older boys" because he is no longer restrained by his "scornful, indulgent, deeply loyal fondness for the Crowd." Fortunately for him but most of all for herself, Betsy comes to the realization that "you wanted different kinds of friendships, with different kinds of people" and disbands the sorority.[18]

Betsy and Joe finds her a senior in high school on the brink of entering the adult world but still clinging to childhood. She competes in the essay contest, writing about "Conservation of Our Natural Resources" and finally wins—but does Joe throw the contest? He says, "Somehow I have a notion my essay isn't much good. It seemed to get all mixed up with Betsy. The color of her hair. The way she blushes. The way she sings when she dances. I just couldn't seem to get going."[19] This would have been a natural ending to the series: Betsy and Joe are finally together, and more importantly, she has a firm sense of who she is.

But popular demand brought Lovelace back to the series four years later, to a Betsy who has veered off course again, broken up with Joe, left college, and lost her sense of direction though she hasn't been deterred from her writing. And so her world widens yet again in *Betsy and the Great World*, one of my least favorites as a child because it seemed to me more boring, more of a travelogue, adapted from Maud Hart Lovelace's own travel journals. In college Betsy did join a sorority, but she "soon got tired of pretending that her deepest interests were social" and now she's going to Europe. Her trip is eventually interrupted as armies all over Europe mobilize despite the fact that Betsy finds war "unthinkable" in civilized times.[20] Betsy returns home and marries Joe in *Betsy's Wedding*, a book that ought to be called *Betsy's Marriage*, since the wedding is far from the main focus. By the end of this book, the US has entered the war, Joe is headed off to fight, and Betsy is moving back home, thinking, "War! Women never invented it!"[21] Here, the series ends, and though it leaves us hanging, somehow we know that Joe will return home safely and that these two will have a long and good marriage, signaled by both of their willingness to make sacrifices for each other and for their country.

And at the end of the series, Betsy is still writing.

One of the refreshing things about these books is their explorations of gender roles and attitudes toward marriage and career for women, taking for granted that they can follow their passions. "Could there be better books," Anna Quindlen writes

and could there be a better girl, adolescent, young woman, to teach us all those things about choices. . . . all these different women, who go so many different ways, with false starts and stops, with disappointments and limitations, and yet a sense that they can find a place for themselves in the world.[22]

And it's not only the books that Lovelace referred to as "main-line Betsy Tacy" that celebrate this range of choices, Quindlen points out, but two peripheral books about characters whose lives overlap with Betsy's, *Emily of Deep Valley* and *Carney's House Party*. What Emily, who doesn't have a chance to go to college, wants most is to become a social worker; what Carney, who goes to Vassar, wants most is to marry and have a family. The goals of both of these girls are taken seriously.

From early on, Betsy rejects limiting stereotypes. When, as young children, she and her friends build a house in Tib's basement out of firewood, Betsy and Tacy are surprised that Tib's father concludes that his son Freddie will be an architect but Tib will be a "little housewife." "Betsy and Tacy thought that was strange," Lovelace says, "for Tib had done as much as Freddie toward building the house. But it didn't matter much, for in their hearts they were sure that Tib was going to be a dancer."[23] Older, in *Heaven to Betsy*, Betsy is

appalled, since she started going around with Carney and Bonnie, to discover how fixed and definite their ideas of marriage were. They both had cedar hope chests and took pleasure in embroidering their initials on towels to lay away. . . . when Betsy and Tacy and Tib talked about their future they planned to be writers, dancers, circus acrobats.[24]

Betsy continues to dream in *Betsy in Spite of Herself*: "Most of the girls just plan on getting married but Tacy and I want to see the Taj Mahal by moonlight, and go to the Passion Play, and live in Paris with French maids to draw our baths."[25]

This doesn't mean that Betsy isn't easily distracted by boys or anything but excited when, as a junior, she gets to take Domestic Science in school. When Joe is elected senior class president, she is gloriously happy for him. I fully believed her enthusiastic support for him but not so much his sudden eagerness to participate in school politics and pranks. Up until this final book, Joe has been remote, proud, antisocial even, more grown up than high school students who live comparatively easy lives. Suddenly, in *Betsy and Joe*, "busy as he was, he found time not only for school activities but also for the aimless, carefree loafing of normal high school students."[26] Maybe he really loves Betsy so much that he throws himself into what's important to her, or maybe he's enjoying the chance to finally be a kid. But I found this aspect of the books, and his somewhat idealized character, to be the most unrealistic element and was not surprised to learn that Joe is based on the way

Maud envisioned her husband, Delos Lovelace, as a high school student. Joe is the only character not based on someone who lived in Deep Valley or who attended Mankato High School, and the less convincing portrayal of him may lend credence to Whalen's insistence that Lovelace's best portraits were highly autobiographical.

Tib's challenge is to find a boy who doesn't condescend to her, who recognizes her forthright strength despite her dainty appearance. She, in turn, is impatient with "manly beauty unaccompanied by manly achievements," as Betsy puts it when Tib's football player boyfriend refuses to throw himself into the game and is roundly ridiculed by his classmates.[27] Even here, in what seems one of the most gender-stereotyped episodes of the series, the implication is that courage is required for a boy to be worthy of Tib, that these girls must find their equals. Though Betsy and Tib worry that Tacy will be an "old maid" because she doesn't like boys, "not in the way the other girls did," it just turns out that, once again, she needs to meet her match. Later, while traveling to Europe, Betsy, who in high school was not above provocative statements to Joe like "I read women writers. I think they're the best," has a cheerful argument with the ship's purser, who is scandalized by some of her political views. "You're not a suffragette," he exclaims, to which she replies, "I certainly am." He says:

"I don't believe it . . . But you're not a militant."
     Betsy wasn't sure she was a militant, but she wouldn't back down. "I would be if I had to be."[28]

These references seem pretty blatantly feminist to me, but Whalen takes umbrage at the idea that Betsy or Lovelace promoted feminist views. "Betsy invariably operated with an unconscious, matter-of-fact assumption that girls could essentially do anything boys could," Whalen writes, asserting that, despite the above passage, she "took equality for granted." Whalen adds that "the women in the Betsy-Tacy books were like healthy women of any time: their attitudes and goals were firmly rooted in a basic self-respect."[29] In my mind, Whalen's comments cinch Betsy's place as a feminist role model. What could be more feminist than Lovelace's matter-of-fact assumptions about the abilities of girls and women?

While Betsy's father secretly hopes for his eldest daughter to settle down and have babies, while he is strict about potential husbands first asking him for his daughters' hands, he is also the one who eventually decides to send both of his older daughters to study in Europe and is praised by Joe for being the "finest person" he ever met. Joe sees Mr. Ray as being an unusually happy man not because he keeps his household under control or has great power or intellect, but "because he never thinks of himself. He is always thinking about doing something for some-body else." While I paid little attention to this as a child, I now find refreshing the emphasis on the importance of self-sacrifice for men as well as women, even if it's taken for granted in women while lauded in men.

When Joe finally proposes, he tells Betsy, "I can always talk to you. I can make plans, or puzzle out ideas, or build castles in the air." Betsy's "Rules for Married Life" revert to what one might expect for a woman in the early part of the twen-tieth century: she resolves to handle Joe's money well, keep herself looking nice, and learn to cook. Nevertheless, she and Joe both expect that she will continue to write after marriage, and Tib envies the way that Joe treats Betsy: "He respects you," Tib says. "He confides in you, listens to your opinions, asks your advice. He thinks your work is important. He thinks you are important—as a human being, not just as a girl."[30]

Readers didn't have to be budding writers to appreciate these books, but to me, it was an important dimension that Lovelace takes for granted the importance of reading, writing, and art. In *Betsy and Tacy Go Over the Big Hill*, the children know neighborhood houses by the books their neighbors have loaned them. One is the house where they borrowed Horatio Alger books; another is the one where they borrowed *Little Women*. In *Betsy and Tacy Go Downtown*, the first chapter is about ac-quiring a copy of *Lady Audley's Secret*, and the second portrays Betsy's yearning to see the play *Uncle Tom's Cabin*. It is worth noting that three of these four references are to literature by women, and Lovelace goes on to promote a culture in which the talents and ambitions of girls are as important as those of boys. In *Downtown*, Mrs. Ray tells Betsy, "Your father and I are very proud of your writing. We want you to keep at it."[31] If she wants to be a writer, her parents conclude, she needs to read good books, so they send her on excursions downtown, alone, to spend days at the library.

We know that Joe is meant for Betsy when he first appears in the series read-ing *The Three Musketeers*, but Betsy herself is often conflicted about her passion for literature and writing. On the one hand, her imagination is unabashedly shaped by novels, as in *Heaven to Betsy*, where we learn that she "understood from novels, chief-ly English" that quick cold baths "brought a glow to the cheek and a shine to the eye."[32] Despite this, she is reluctant to admit her love of reading to her friends. At the beginning of *Betsy in Spite of Herself*, she confesses to Joe that she hasn't told her friends that she's already read a school assignment, *Ivanhoe*. Joe "looked at her keen-ly. 'You wouldn't!' he said."[33]

Betsy's compulsion to read and write doesn't translate into higher grades—in fact, quite the opposite. She gets lower marks on her paper about *Ivanhoe* because she retells the story rather than hitting the "high points" as Cab and Tony do after she summarizes the story for them. Betsy is fairly untroubled by a 54 in geometry because writing, not math, is her forte. But she develops an antagonistic relationship with a rhetoric teacher, who marks her down for flowery writing and later mocks her for describing apple blossoms as "rosy." Mr. Gaston condescendingly insists that they're white, leading Joe to rise up in her defense.[34]

Betsy briefly gives up her own writing when she first starts high school, nostalgically visiting her trunk in the attic and reflecting that "writing didn't seem to fit in with the life she was living now. Carney didn't write; Bonnie didn't write. Betsy felt almost ashamed of her ambition. The boys teased her about being a little Poetess." But by the end of the book, Betsy reclaims her trunk and her work and never stops writing again. In the end, Betsy concludes that one of the year's distractions, her crush on Tony, helped her writing, telling Tacy, "I mean, it will when I get around to write. It's good for writers to suffer." Tony continues to drop into the Ray house, "teasing and affectionate as ever, and quite unaware of having improved her art." By the end of the book, Lovelace reflects, "What would life be like without her writing? Writing filled her life with beauty and mystery, gave it purpose . . . and promise."[35] I related to Betsy's struggle to integrate writing into her life even though no one around her shares her passion, and I identified with her maturing realization that that writing is an inextricable part of her identity. Though she knows that she's lost the essay contest toward the end of *Spite*, she reflects, "I'm darned glad I did my best on the essay contest. . . . It belonged to me, not to some person I was pretending to be."[36]

Betsy's sister Julia was one of my favorite characters, as devoted to her music as Betsy is to her writing, often providing the role model Betsy needs although sometimes also creating an example she can't live up to. In *Heaven*, Julia plays *Pagliacci* so often, singing all the parts, that the Rays grow "callous to the sorrows of the strolling players."[37] Julia is so immersed in her music, she barely notices how boys worship her, whereas they tease Betsy, much to Betsy's frustration. Julia turns down a proposal at the end of *Spite*, telling Betsy, "Each of us has to be true to the deepest thing that is in him." Her advice to Betsy is that "You have to be wise as a serpent and harmless as a dove"—something she says while "looking anything but harmless."[38] Julia is passionate and serious and sometimes ruthless in her ambition, never distracted, as Betsy is, by her social life, never anything other than who she is, confessing in *Junior* that she both loves and hates Deep Valley "because it has held me for so long. And it isn't my native heath. Never was."[39]

For a while, Julia is tempted by sororities at college. They shower her with "subtle attentions—sweet notes, wee bouquets, affectionate strolls on the campus." But when she is cut by her first choice, she realizes that all she really wants to do is study music in Germany. She has completely lost interest in sororities by the time her former first choice invites her to join after all. Her parents support her ambitions though Mr. Ray says, "But I'm hoping that she'll meet someone she wants to marry, settle down and use her voice for lullabies."[40] After a year in Germany, Julia comes home changed, "fat as a roll of butter!" according to Mrs. Ray, her weight gain deemed "cute" by Betsy.[41] Their pleasure in the size of their budding opera singer daughter and sister is amusing in light of our culture's current obsession with thinness.

By the end of the series, Julia has married a flutist, "and they planned to pursue their careers together."[42] The girls' ambition, passion for their art, and assumption that they will have careers were radical messages for their time. They may partly reflect women's entry into the workforce in large numbers during World War II, but Lovelace maintains Betsy's ambitions even in the books published in the 1950s, when the social message once again dominated that women's place was in the home. Lovelace's portrayals sometimes seem radical for our time, too, if the popularity of books like *Twilight* are any indication. I don't know if I'll ever convince my daughter to read Lovelace's books, so old-fashioned compared to what she normally reads: books about African American kids by Sharon Draper, novels about Chinese and Indian girls by Gloria Whelan, and yes, the *Gossip Girl* series. In the face of these, I don't know if I'll ever convince her how relevant the *Betsy* books are still. As we walk through the library in Mankato, she just wants lunch.

Just as I decide that we'll go somewhere nearby to eat, giving the Betsy-Tacy Society a little more time to call, my phone rings. Sophie glares at me as the tone echoes through the room, and even my hushed voice sounds loud as I answer, hurrying into the lobby. I speed on into the bathroom where I can talk at a normal volume. A volunteer offers to meet us at the Tacy house at 1:00, in only fifteen minutes. I take one last look at the Maud Hart Lovelace room and then we hasten back up the hill.

There we find two women and four girls, two blond, two Asian, also waiting for the tour to begin. Sophie shoots me a threatening look. I am not to ask where the Asian girls are from. I don't, even though they are the only non-white children other than my daughter that I have seen so far on this trip.

I know it's naïve to judge the past on the standards of today. At the same time, I imagine if I'd been a non-white child I might have been uncomfortable reading about white children who black their faces for a stage production of *Uncle Tom's Cabin* (*Downtown*), or about Betsy's elders' recollection of American Indians "on the warpath" in Deep Valley (*Spite*). Lovelace is very much a historical novelist in these passages, keeping her characters' comments and attitudes true to their period, not endorsing them herself. Still, if I hadn't been a white child, I might have felt more readily alienated by the description of tenor Chauncy Olcott's voice as "so divine that his stoutness and darkness didn't matter at all," which seems to imply that his darkness is a flaw.[43]

Nevertheless, Lovelace was particularly interested in the Lebanese community of Mankato, and the plots of two of her books, *Betsy and Tacy Go Over the Big Hill* and *Emily of Deep Valley*, revolve around the protagonists' friendships with members of the Syrian community who are often called "Dagos" by their neighbors. Young Betsy, Tacy, and Tib befriend a girl named Naifi and find a community full of "gaiety and kindness," defending it when Betsy's sister Julia refers to their talk as "gibberish" and apologizes for making Betsy take refuge in "that awful place." "But Julia!" Betsy says. "It's a lovely place."[44]

In *Emily of Deep Valley*, when the title character can't go to college, she creates a sort of Hull House for the Lebanese community and helps to form Americanization classes for its members. In both books focused on interactions with this immigrant population, Lovelace's title characters point out that the Syrians came to the US seeking religious freedom, wanting to be Christian instead of Muslim. This reassures the fictional townspeople as well as readers who are primarily American born and raised in Judeo-Christian traditions that these characters are, under the surface, like us. While this attitude may seem limiting in our own time, it was progressive for its time and place. In the same way, both books also highlight the patriotism of the foreign-born neighbors. In her sophomore year, Betsy's assigned essay contest topic is "Immigration should be further restricted," reflecting a controversy of the time period without elaborating on Betsy's particular views. However, in *Emily of Deep Valley*, Emily argues that this debate does not even apply to the Syrian neighbors who have already made a home in the US.

In *Hill*, Tib's mother is glad that her daughter stands up for Naifi, even if her dress has been torn in the process. "America is made up of foreign people," Tib's mother says[45]—and she should know, being of German extraction herself. It's not surprising that in these books, written during a time of high patriotism and anti-German sentiment in the US, the many German characters disavow the "old country ways," bringing "a lot of Germany with them, but . . . mostly the good part. Singing societies, and coffee cake, and Christmas trees."[46]

While touring Algiers in *Betsy and the Great World*, Betsy observes people living in "unlighted, evil-smelling, filthy caverns" and wonders briefly why they seem to hate tourists, but immediately concludes that in their position she wouldn't like "well-fed, well-dressed, comfortable looking travelers coming to stare." Later in the same book, a European friend observes that Betsy is reluctant to admit that "anything American is less than perfect"—a comment that offers a light critique of her firmly entrenched patriotism.[47] Through such subtle moves, Lovelace frequently raises questions that would have been controversial in her time, then allows her winsome protagonist to go on with her well-adjusted life so that we're not always sure what hit us.

While we wait, we wander the gift shop, leafing through books laid out on tables, copies of the early-reader volumes that are still in print, nonfiction about children's books and Minnesota travel, sticker books, paper dolls, coloring books, and journals. We glance at bookmarks and pendants and t-shirts and soap made in Minnesota until the volunteer calls us over to convene the tour.

The renovation of the Betsy house, where we finally start, is still in progress. The goal of the Betsy-Tacy Society is to restore these houses so that when visitors enter them, they'll feel "like they've walked back in time and stepped into the pages of the Betsy-Tacy books," according to the society's website. Our tour guide tells us that the work on the Betsy house has been featured by PBS twice, and eventually, I'll watch the DVDs. I have uncles who would be riveted by these episodes of *Hometime*, which mostly focus on discussing the best way to fit windows or plaster walls. I'm less interested in these topics, disappointed that the videos barely touch on Lovelace's life or her books or even the decorating choices involved in re-creating the Hart/Ray house.

Our tour guide tells us that one of the clues that have helped volunteers to reconstruct the Betsy house was a letter that Lovelace wrote to a young fan. In the 1970s, a 17-year-old named Bonnie Gardner lived in this house, and she reported in a letter to Lovelace that the porch steps had rotted, the front porch had been screened, the wooden floors had been painted grey and carpeted, the house had been converted from yellow to light green with dark green trim, and there was a bat problem. Lovelace wrote back to her, describing the house in her own day: the trees on the front lawn, the yellow rose bushes along the wall, the lilacs in the yard, the front parlor with a piano and the back parlor with a comfortable big couch and a stove that warmed the house. The house, Lovelace wrote in another letter, was small "but the sloping lawn was big, with maples and a butternut tree in front of the house, and behind it fruit trees and berry bushes and a garden, and Old Mag's barn, and the shed where the carriage was kept," a quote straight from *Betsy-Tacy*.[48] Such descriptions enable us to imagine what the house will look like when it is fully restored. Our guide tells us that the Betsy-Tacy Society also hopes to eventually purchase a third house, Tib's chocolate brown one.

We walk through empty rooms, the volunteer passing us illustrations of what each once looked like, with couches and rugs and books and sleeping cats. Even though the floorboards are grungy and dusty, loose in places, it is easy to see what a pleasant little house this once was, and though the rooms are small, I suddenly realize that each one is the size of one of the cabins that the Ingalls family occupied. Two childhoods, only thirty years and eighty miles apart, so different. The Hart family was clearly far more prosperous than the Ingalls, so much more settled and part of a community. Laura Ingalls Wilder's books are about the refuge of family in the midst of hardship, almost contemporary in their insular approach to the importance of nuclear ties above all others. The Lovelace books seem comparatively old-fashioned, firmly valuing friendship and community, never presenting the family as an inviolable unit.

I am especially struck by the difference in standards of living between the Hart family and the Ingallses when the tour guide tells us about artifacts found in the ceiling beneath the attic. I will later read more about these on the website: a letter written by Maud's father to her mother, high button shoes, long black stockings, a shirtwaist, a valentine, puzzle pieces, Lincoln Logs, checkers, porcelain doll arms, magazines, and newspapers.[49] What abundance, I think. Even a discarded doll's arm would be more than Laura usually got for Christmas, if those accounts of oranges and pennies in the Ingalls girls' stockings are to be believed.

As we cross the street back to the Tacy house, I ask how many people actually come here each year on Saturdays during the two hours the house is open. Roughly three thousand, the guide says, which staggers me. If three thousand actually make it here each year during those weekly two-hour windows, how many arrive during the other 166 hours in each week, just taking pictures and moving on?

We walk through the rooms of the Tacy house, looking at the brass bowl that Mrs. Ray—or was it Mrs. Hart—bought for herself at Christmas; Mr. Hart's footstool that also, no doubt, was appropriated somewhere in the books for Mr. Ray; a corner cupboard and rocking chair and the Hart family coffee pot that takes center stage throughout the books. We view Maud's typewriter and displays of stories and letters by Maud and her husband, Delos Lovelace. I glance at all of these with mild interest, having learned by now how impossible it is to capture a book through decorating a room but what a labor of love it is to try.

Finally, we walk up to see where the bench normally is, the one donated in honor of the bench where Betsy and Tacy often ate their dinners and made up stories. There's a railing and concrete steps that were not in the books. But there's no bench. It's been vandalized and removed for repairs. I'll read later that it's carved from stone, with a bronze plaque that reads, "To honor Maud Hart Lovelace, who here began the childhood daydreams that one day would be our window to the past."

As we get ready to leave, I glance back up the hill, imagining it as it looks in the fall, covered with goldenrod and asters. Whalen traces the mentions of goldenrod and asters, Lovelace's code that the season is transitioning into autumn, throughout the books. She finds ten references, some also accompanied by sumac and thistles, so it's no wonder that this image of the hill in autumn has stayed with me.

It's still summer now, though, hot and dry and not at all picturesque, clouds of dust hanging above the road while noisy machinery churns and scrapes. Over that hill, maybe there is a brindle cow sleeping under a scrub oak tree, as in *Betsy-Tacy*. But we're starved, and it's time to go on.

Back when I was in college, I used to have to consult bookstore clerks and librarians and page through editions of *Books in Print* to ferret out which of my all-time favorites were still available. I used to have to spend Saturdays sifting through books in dusty used bookstores trying to locate the ones that were no longer being published. Now, it still amazes me that I can just look on the Internet to find so much information and track down copies of the books I loved. And over the next few years, it will be through the Internet that I track the emergence of more and more Betsy-Tacy fans. HarperCollins will issue new paperback editions of the books as a result of what they call "moderate public demand," labeling the books as "modern classics," featuring introductions by Meg Cabot, Anna Quindlen, Laura Lippman, and Mitali Perkins.

I will feel a little possessive twinge the way I did when I discovered that Laura Ingalls Wilder was not really mine after all, but I will also experience the overriding relief of knowing that I'm in good company. More famous fans will come out of the woodwork, raving about Betsy: Bette Midler, Judy Blume, Nora Ephron, Ann M. Martin. The *LA Times* will describe Betsy as "an impish brown-haired girl with an unusual amount of attitude for her day" and the series as "a kind of cult treasure among thousands who have read them." The same article reports the upsurge of interest in Lovelace's work, including a national newsletter with a thousand subscribers, a Betsy-Tacy Internet chat line, and "a plethora of commercial Betsy-Tacy styled items (from lithographs to pewter figurines to cookbooks)."[50]

Soon a quiz on the Internet will invite me to figure out which Betsy-Tacy character I am. Of course I'm Betsy. The Amboy, Minnesota Community Theatre will put on a play called "Deep Valley Vignettes—Betsy-Tacy on Stage." There will be Betsy-Tacy conferences and conventions, where attendees engage in informal debates on Joe vs. Tony and attend dinners in costume, eating food inspired by the books. One website reports on one such gathering: "There was Betsy in her cherry-colored robe having a bath at the pension in Munich when the soldiers are out, women dressed as paper dolls . . . two young girls dressed for the Cat Duet (which they performed). . . . "[51] Soon there will also be a Facebook page, whose status updates will startle me a little. It's as if characters from some shady grove of my youthful imagination have come to life and started sending me messages: "From Deep Valley, happy Thanksgiving to friends of Betsy, Tacy, and Tib!"

I'm happy not to be the only Betsy fan in the world, but with that comfort come mixed feelings toward the appropriation of these books by conservative twenty-first-century values, as exemplified by the Amboy website. The play promotes, the site reassures us, "the timeless themes of family love, loyal friendships, and enduring faith . . . all those things we hold close to our hearts. There's also a good mixture of history, patriotism, humanity, romance, and old-fashioned fun thrown in for good measure."[52] Somehow, even if this description seems basically accurate to me, I chafe at the rhetoric that infuses it, draining some of the life from my memory of the stories. The play begins with Maud returning to Deep Valley and reliving her memories of "the happiest childhood a child could know," words that just don't seem true to me of Maud Hart Lovelace's lively, unsentimental style.

If the books do gain a new generation of readers, the spinoffs, the merchandising, the charm bracelets, the Betsy-Tacy collector dolls, the limited edition plates with scenes from the books, the straight-to-DVD movies, and the cable TV series may not be far behind. The next time I stop in Mankato, I imagine that there will not only be lithographs and pewter figurines and cookbooks; there may also be collectible perfume bottles containing Mrs. Ray's violet scent; kits to assist children in reproducing the bottles of colored sand that Betsy, Tacy, and Tib sell to their neighbors; sheet music for the Cat duet; and a Betsy-Tacy soundtrack including Chauncey Olcott's "My Wild Irish Rose." Maybe, just as little girls wander around Laura Ingalls Wilder sites in long dresses and sunbonnets, Lovelace fans in Mankato will be snapping up Betsy fashions to wear to the *Betsy in Spite of Herself* pageant: Merry Widow hats and Magic Waver curlers and corsets and boudoir caps.

In October 2010 I will finally sit down to revisit all of the books again in their new editions. One autumn night, as a light cold rain falls and leaves skitter across the street, I will drop my daughter off at a school dance and then decide not to follow up on my plan to call a friend to hang out. All I really want to do is drink some spiced cider, eat a glazed doughnut, and read about Betsy. I no longer crave parties and football games. While my daughter is off in a middle school gym navigating a world of kids who casually say "WTF" at every turn, I am content at home with a bunch of teenagers whose favorite slang is "Ain't it awful, Mabel?" And yet somehow, like Laura Lippmann and Meg Cabot, I find these books surprisingly contemporary. As Cabot notes, Betsy has neither "magical powers, a boyfriend who is a vampire, nor a cell phone" but she still feels modern, like one of us.[53]

As I read, I discover that my childhood pictures of these characters and places have been erased. Now I envision the real-life models for the characters. Now I picture the hills and streets of Mankato. As a child, I insistently imagined Betsy and Tacy living in a cozy little valley despite Lovelace's repeated reminders that their homes sit at the top of the street. I pictured the hill with the bench as a high, steep one, sort of like the turnpike hills near my home in Wichita. Now I know what it really looks like, that that low hill requires minimal climbing. I know what the pitcher Tacy gives Betsy looks like, and Mrs. Ray's brass bowl, and Julia's piano.

But in the years since my visit, many things have changed. I'd never heard anyone mention Betsy Ray and Laura Ingalls in the same breath, for instance, until recently. Now, Betsy and Laura have started to cross paths, inevitable, I suppose, given the proximity between the authors' childhood homes, the commonality that both girls grew up in the Midwest in "olden days," and the fact that between them they star in eighteen children's books. Not to mention that just as Laura is never allowed to wear blue and Mary is never allowed to wear red, Tacy often wears navy blue because she has red hair (and like red-headed Anne Shirley, she never, ever wears pink).

In 1930, Lovelace and her husband Delos entertained Rose Wilder Lane in New York, serving her jellied chicken, but this happened before the publication of the first book of either series.[54] Legend has it that Lovelace refused to read the *Little House* books so that she wouldn't be accused of plagiarism. Then, according to one story, when Lovelace was completely finished with the series, she went to the library and said, "NOW I can read the Wilder books."[55] I find this tale a little suspect since Lovelace had vague plans to write yet another volume in the series about Betsy's daughter Bettina, but it also surprises me that as a child it never occurred to me that Betsy and Laura had so much in common.

Meg Cabot warns in a *Wall Street Journal* article that comparisons between the two series may be misleading. "Though visions of Melissa Gilbert bobbing through a flower-strewn field as Laura Ingalls Wilder may be dancing in your head, these books don't contain a single scene about soap-making or Ma stitching a homespun dress," she writes. "Lovelace doesn't weigh down her narrative with the kind of tedious descriptions of rabbit skinning I always skipped over in the Little House books."[56]

Though the coming-of-age experiences of these beloved heroines diverge wildly, in the years after my visit to Mankato, Betsy and Laura will take to mixing and mingling with one another. When Minnesota State University hosts the first "LauraPalooza" conference in 2010 in Mankato, Betsy gets in on the action. The event, described by conference-goers in the *Mankato Free Press* as "a sort of prairie version of Star Trek's Trekkies," features talks by Wilder biographers, paper presentations by academics, panels like "Loving Laura in a Lindsay Lohan World," craft demonstrations by fans, and a chance for "folks to get a taste of Deep Valley!" with a walking tour of "Betsy's neighborhood, with young Betsy escorting her new friend Laura around her town, storytelling, and other surprises." Conference participants dressed as favorite Laura Ingalls Wilder characters are joined by Betsy fans, one in a Mrs. Ray costume; Betsy's mother would have been the same age as Laura. "I think Laura and Betsy complement each other so well," "Mrs. Ray" is quoted as saying.[57]

In 2007, none of this has happened yet, and it feels as if I'm leaving one completely different world for another, these small, cool, pleasant houses for the more rough and rugged pioneer life that Laura represents. It's midafternoon on a hot day, and by now Sophie and I are starved. We wish the car air conditioner would hurry up and cool off as we set off back down Hill Street, out of Mankato, leaving behind civilization to return to small, dusty towns surrounded by farmland. We drive away from happy books about friends and fun to the warmth of a pioneer family in the midst of grim struggle and setbacks. I glance at my gas gauge: almost empty. I will stop for gas and food soon, I think, but for now I just want to get on the road. That's my big mistake.

CHAPTER SEVEN

Walnut Grove, Minnesota, and Burr Oak, Iowa

On the Banks of Plum Creek and the Lost Years

AS WE DRIVE DOWN NARROW, twisting rural roads, past acres and acres of corn, I imagine that I can hear, under the blast of air conditioning and the clicks of our tires, the sound of insects: the whir and clack, the pulse and buzz, the chirp and hiss that forms a static through this otherwise silent, seemingly deserted land. The sounds intensify and subside and make me feel itchy. I picture the grasshoppers in the third book of the *Little House* series, *On the Banks of Plum Creek*, arriving in clouds, filling the air with the sound of their chewing and spitting, covering the land so completely that every pioneer footstep squishes a few.

When we left Mankato, I thought that there would be tons of green signs along the highway promising food, gas, and lodging at the end of a short exit ramp. There had been lots of those on the way in, and in town we'd passed a mall area with every chain restaurant imaginable. But now there is nothing, no green signs, only field after field of green cornstalks. I see one of the Dairy Queens ubiquitous to Midwestern small towns, but I don't think I can stand another lunch at a Dairy Queen. So I keep going.

"I'm hungry," Sophie keeps saying.

"We'll stop soon," I keep replying, expecting to round a bend and see a whole host of inspiring lunch choices.

Instead, we get spilled onto a rural road. We pass a gas station but I don't stop. It will be so much more efficient to kill two birds with one stone when we find a cluster of service stations and restaurants.

But gradually it dawns on me that that one Dairy Queen and that one gas station were it. Now we're passing over miles and miles of isolated country roads populated by the occasional white farmhouse with a long winding drive, empty cars parked askew, and dogs sleeping in the sun. There are no other cars on the road. There are no farmers on tractors in the fields. There are no feed dealers or even cows. Just corn, just green feathered plants as far as the eye can see. No breeze flutters them. They look dry and a little desperate. This is ghost farmland, abandoned in the July heat. Now I'd give anything for yet another fast food hamburger, even.

I drive for nearly an hour with no restaurants in sight. What would pioneers do? I wonder. WWPD? They wouldn't panic just because no rabbit or squirrel presented itself to be skinned and cooked for lunch. They wouldn't freak out at the lack of wild blackberries or blueberries along their path. They'd just light a campfire and cook something from their supply, some bacon or beans or rice, or maybe they'd have a cold lunch, some leftover cornbread or beef jerky. I pull over onto the dusty shoulder and dig through the cooler for our modern-day equivalent: a couple of stale mini-bagels and some small packets of peanut butter and jelly pilfered from the free continental breakfast a couple of hotels ago. Using the car trunk as a table, I assemble some hasty, sloppy sandwiches, and we eat them while sitting on a grassy incline that slopes down into a ditch.

Feeling smugly resourceful, I drive on, my next urgent goal to find gas. Around the next curve, I'm sure, there will be a town, there has to be. Where do these farmers shop? How do they get fuel for their tractors? Don't they buy groceries or go out to eat? But we round each curve to more of the same, vast green fields of dry cornstalks, some red barns. But it's only a few more miles to US 71. It's simply impossible that there won't be a gas station there.

Consulting my Mapquest directions, I set the odometer. Only five miles to the highway, four, three, two. Click. The gas-tank-shaped light on my dashboard starts to glow.

As we tick off the last mile, I strain forward, waiting for civilization to come into focus.

But all that appears is the abrupt end of the road. It dead ends at a cornfield, the asphalt cutting off two inches away from yet more cornstalks. To my right and to my left is Highway 71, which should be a harbinger of hope, of civilization somewhere in my future.

Except that barricades block it off in both directions. The highway is closed.

For long seconds I gape at yellow construction vehicles that inch along, stirring up dust that blows over my car and clouds above the cornfields. Guys bear down on the concrete with their long drills. The drills buzz and whir. The little arrow on my gas gauge points straight at the E for empty. The gas-pump-shaped light continues to beam.

If I go straight, I'll be tooling through a field. The barricades prevent me from turning left or right. My only choice is to turn around and go back to where I came from.

My only choice is to go back many miles on roads where I know that there is no gas station.

My only choice appears to be to run out of gas in rural Minnesota.

But I'm a member of AAA. I can always call them for assistance. As I pat the cell phone in my pocket, it beeps, the signal that the battery is running down.

OK, I think, WWPD? Well, first of all, if their horses were thirsty and the creek bed dry, they wouldn't panic, because they'd have a barrel of water in their wagon. They wouldn't have let themselves end up so unprepared.

And if they ran into a wall of prairie fire blocking their route? They would stop and dig trenches or fight it with burlap sacks or something.

I roll down my window and call to a guy in a hard hat. I explain to him that my directions instruct me to go right on 71. I hope he can suggest an alternate route. A magical one that I somehow missed. One really close by. With a gas station.

"Well, you can drive on the shoulder," the guy says. "Just watch out—we're punching holes in the highway." I follow his gesture to a row of holes down the middle of the road that I meant to travel. I have no idea why they are punching holes in the highway, but I don't ask.

Instead, I swerve around the barricade and wobble along the shoulder, weaving through an obstacle course of machinery, orange cones, holes, tractors, graders, drills, and workers. I feel like a daredevil. I feel like an outlaw. I keep expecting someone to frantically wave me back, but workers ignore me as I hug the shoulder.

My gas light glows on. My cell phone keeps beeping. Soon we leave the construction vehicles behind. Sophie and I are the only human beings left on this apocalyptic highway, maybe on the earth. If I run out of gas, I wonder, will AAA deliver some to me on a closed road? I'm composing and silently rehearsing my desperate plea to a AAA dispatcher when my cell phone beeps again and then powers off.

Sophie is sleeping in the back seat, oblivious to my agitation. Finally, ten miles down the road, I weave around one more barricade and regain an open highway, but there's still nothing but a stretch of gray concrete and fields of green cornstalks.

If my car starts sputtering and coughing, I decide, I will cruise over to the shoulder and park. Somewhere there will be a house, a farmer, a barn, a feed store, a car with kindly people who are not serial killers. I picture us trudging down the side of the road. I can already feel the sunburn, the parched mouth, the rumbling in my stomach. For some reason I envision our clothes turning ragged and muddy and the soles of our shoes flapping loose. I imagine us collapsing into heaps in a cornfield, sleeping there while mosquitoes feast.

And then I see the most profoundly beautiful sight of my life, ahead on the right: a squat little building with two glorious pumps in front of it and a green sign listing gas prices.

Maybe this is the perfect way to arrive in Laura Ingalls Wilder Land. After all, the pattern of *On the Banks of Plum Creek* is one of crisis and rescue: Laura almost drowns but manages to survive; Ma gives away Laura's beloved doll, Charlotte, but Laura is eventually able to reclaim her; Pa gets stranded in a blizzard and keeps from starving by eating the oyster crackers he's bringing home for Christmas. Even those pervasive and horrifying grasshoppers seem to be conquered at the end of the book, when brutal winter weather is seen as a sign that the next year will bring no grasshoppers but instead successful crops and prosperity.

And Sophie and I were nearly stranded in the middle of nowhere, and then, as if it sprouted suddenly from the prairie, a gas station appeared. I pull up to the pump, wrung out with relief, like one of those settlers wandering through a white-out blizzard suddenly bumping into the side of a barn.

After our harrowing journey in which the last hour felt like years, it's startling how quickly five miles fly by. In no time, we are parking in front of a wood-frame farmhouse where the proprietors of the Sod Houses at Sanborn, a tourist attraction that has been featured on the History Channel, live. Signs in front advertise a bed and breakfast, in the farmhouse, I think at first. Gradually it dawns on me that visitors stay in the soddies.

There's a bathroom right off the parking lot, in a small building, past a room full of sunbonnets and long dresses. A sign invites us to dress up, but even if we were the sort of people who liked to wear sweaty hats and extra layers in one hundred degree heat so that we could pretend that we lived 150 years ago, we are way too tired. We skip the photo op and head back out to the gravel parking lot in our twenty-first-century shorts and t-shirts, crossing over to a pathway that leads us toward the soddies. There's a house and an outhouse, a small log cabin, a dugout, and a shed with a sod cutter inside.

I can't imagine walking around in a sunbonnet in this heat, but apparently a lot of guests are excited at the prospect. On the website for the Sod Houses at Sanborn, a page details the fun things there are to do: "Follow the trails. Create your own fun. Bonnets to wear." This last item is accompanied by photos of smiling children in sunbonnets.[1] Rabid fans of the TV show loosely based on Wilder's work, I will learn much later, are known as "bonnetheads."

This all strikes me as a little bizarre, especially since Laura hated wearing her sunbonnet. It no doubt was a pain, restricting her peripheral vision, and it seems to me now that the sunbonnet falls onto a continuum that at one extreme includes foot binding and at the other high heels, its intention largely to limit the awareness of women and girls and thus the freedom of movement that would allow for independence and self-protection. And the additional racist purpose of the sunbonnet is frequently alluded to throughout the Wilder books: it protected against a tan that might cause others to mistake a girl for an Indian (it was apparently not such a travesty for boys to get tan—at least not enough of one to make them wear sunbonnets). My friend Dania writes,

> My dad is from India, and I remember reading that line toward the end of *These Happy Golden Years* when Grace tells Laura something like, "Ma says wear your sunbonnet or you'll turn brown as an Indian" and they all laugh and I felt sort of . . . weird. The line's used to break the tension of Laura leaving home, but it's not funny to me, and wasn't then. . . . at the same time, I so thoroughly identified with Laura that I was like, right, she didn't wear her bonnet and she got tan and I'm already "tan" so—see—I'm Just! Like! Laura![2]

At the Sod Houses at Sanborn, I learn, overnight guests sleep on straw ticks and are enjoined by a laminated manual to fold and lay aside the fragile quilts. I find this manual in a pleasant little house made of brick-shaped chunks of earth, grass growing on top of its roof, a house that would have cost fifty dollars to construct in Laura's time, according to the sign. "The prairie was treeless, yet the ground offered building blocks," says the website from which I printed pages before our trip. At one time, a million of these houses stood on the prairie and now have collapsed back into it. Some find this sad and lament the loss of all of these structures, but I don't quite get that—isn't that the great advantage of a sod house? To make use of natural resources without permanently altering or destroying them?

I sit down in a wooden rocker and peruse the manual's plastic-covered pages. Overnight guests are invited to fetch water in buckets, light the oil lamps, play with the wooden toys scattered around, read the antique books, and follow nature's call to the sod outhouse. Breakfast, the manual hints with sadistic glee, is likely to be mush.

I rock sleepily in the little house, which has a wood ceiling and wood floor, preventing a common problem of sod house inhabitants, according to the website: dirt, grass, and insects tended to fall on occupants' heads. As I remember this, despite this particular house's wood ceiling, I am happier than ever that we have a hotel reservation.

It is so hot. I feel all damp and sticky and gross. I would like to just sit in this chair and rock forever, turning through pages that I printed from the website, while Sophie wanders around, picking up wooden toys, turning through books. The website makes liberal use of phrases like "family togetherness," "simple pleasures," and "make do or do without." Underneath a picture of girls in long flowered dresses and aprons and sunbonnets hoisting a teapot and carrying baskets along trails is the caption, "Chores." An image of a girl staring out over the prairie is labeled "Solitude," a photo of another girl looking thoughtful, "Serenity." "Relive the nostalgia of Little House on the Prairie days," the page concludes. Hmm, I think. Bedbugs, no showers, no antibiotics, no anesthesia, no air conditioning. I'm not really feeling that nostalgic. Or serene, either: Sophie is impatiently tugging on my arm. "Come on, Mom," she says.

I reluctantly leave my chair to follow her outside, where the sun beats down and flies buzz by. I slap mosquitoes away and feel perpetually itchy. Before us stretches a prairie that the owners and sod house proprietors, the McCones, have restored to look like it did in the 1880s, a stretch of tall grasses and wildflowers. Despite the bugs and heat, I have to admit that this place is kind of cool, even if I have no desire to live in the 1880s.

We wander into the log cabin and up the ladder into the loft, decked out with wooden toys. We take a toy tractor for a spin around the loft and then are ready to leave. What would we do if we stayed here overnight? Dress in period costumes and take pictures of each other. Spend fifteen minutes looking at all the buildings. Play with the toys in the loft for a bit, then pick a few wildflowers. Then what? Walk the trails if it weren't quite so hot, maybe.

We walk some more, glancing at the sod shed and the dugout like the one the Ingalls family moves into at the beginning of *Plum Creek*. It's a tiny cave dug into the earth in the side of a hill, like a rabbit hole or a fox den.

Clusters of bugs swarm before our faces. The tall grass rustles with the movement of some invisible small animal. A butterfly lands on the tip of a grass blade. This grass would have been so tall in Laura's time, a marker tells us, that an adult would have had to sit on a horse to see across the prairie. "Celebrate the prairie," the website urges. "Before the plow. Before cornfields. Before fences. The natural prairie was boundless." I can see this as I gaze across the ocean of grass, under a sky that looks exactly the way the website describes it: "Blue skies," it says. "Big skies."

On our way out, we pass a gazebo that puzzled me earlier. "For Guests Only," says a sign in the window. Inside, there's a TV and coffeemaker. Now I get it: overnight guests tired of roughing it can escape to this gazebo and the air-conditioned comforts of modern life.

We wave at the proprietors who take admission fees from their lawn chairs in front of the house. Then we head to our own modern accoutrements: dinner at Perkins, a hotel swimming pool. Sophie fantasizes that she will meet kids there who are more interested in books than Disney World, and she does. Or at least kids whose parents were fans of the TV show and have dragged their kids along with them instead of going to Disney World.

On our drive to Walnut Grove, I experience no déjà vu. No long-suppressed memories rush to the surface. But thirty years ago, I probably had my face buried in a book while my silent, compliant uncle followed the map up to this town. "Do you girls have on your seatbelts?" Aunt Shirley kept asking from the front seat. Jody and I left our seatbelts unfastened and hid our crimes under books opened face down across our laps.

At night in motels, when ordered to bathe, Jody and I locked ourselves in the bathroom. We ran water and perched on the edge of the tub, loudly wringing out washcloths, living out a *Farmer Boy* fantasy of Almanzo Wilder, whose affluent upstate New York family actually does own a bathtub. Young Almanzo realizes that as long as he fills the tub and makes the proper noises, no one will know whether he's taken his Saturday night bath, and inspired by this, we swirled our hands in the water and played catch with the soap and splashed our washcloths and laughed hysterically. Then Jody and I put on our pajamas and emerged, pretending to be clean.

This is my main memory of Walnut Grove—this, and cows with bursting udders lowing in pain in the shallow, muddy water of Plum Creek. It looked nothing like the sparkling stream surrounded by lush vegetation in the TV show. Silver Lake had been drained and was a swamp. I can trace the beginning of my adolescent disappointment to these glimpses of Plum Creek and what was once Silver Lake.

This time, my expectations are, admittedly, low. In our hotel room in Marshall, Minnesota, I lie on my bed basking in the blasting air conditioner and the absence of sun, bugs, straw ticks, high prairie grasses, and endless concrete highways. My gas tank is still pretty full and my cell phone is charging. Sophie channel surfs and I relish the joy of not sleeping in a dugout the size of a twin bed while dirt chunks fall on my head, or in a cornfield by the side of the road while mosquitoes picnic. I am perhaps much easier to please now than when I was thirteen.

The next morning, we hit Walnut Grove, a tiny town now heavily populated by Hmong immigrants. There's not much here but some railroad tracks and a few businesses called things like Oleson's Mercantile and Nellie's Café, and, of course, the complex of buildings related to Laura Ingalls Wilder, where, the Walnut Grove

Laura Ingalls Wilder Museum website promises us, we can recover a past "when life was simple, dreams were plentiful, and family love was for a lifetime."[3]

It's not that I don't want life to be simple. It's just that I don't believe it ever really was. And the plentiful dreams of the *Little House* books were so often unfulfilled ones, defeated by grasshoppers and blizzards and illness and fire, even if the dreamers' spirits remained resilient. And finally—was family love really for a lifetime? Geographical distances made frequent visits impossible, but Wilder had little contact with her family throughout her adult life and never visited them again after Pa died. If I just can't buy into the myths, if I'm going to be such a curmudgeon about them, am I crashing someone else's party just by being here? Is this the source of my constant unease, this feeling that if my thoughts were transparent, the proprietors of these places would boot me out the door? Am I like an unbeliever going to church just to poke holes in others' belief systems, or a sneaky relative visiting the cousins only to pass on vicious gossip about them to the rest of the family?

When I was a child, I believed so firmly that Laura Ingalls Wilder's work belonged to me, had been written for me, was about me, was all mine. How did I turn into an imposter, an appropriator, an interloper, a traitor to my childhood, here in Walnut Grove for some vaguely nefarious purpose? But of course, here in Walnut Grove, fans of the books are far less numerous than fans of the long-running TV show, which seems to me a mouthpiece for the religious right. Michael Landon didn't hide his own conservative political views; Dr. John J. Fry, professor of history at Trinity College in Chicago, concedes in an online interview that Landon may have been responding, through the TV show, to LBJ's Great Society just as Laura Ingalls Wilder was responding to the New Deal. Even more so than the books, if possible, the TV show celebrated the will of the impoverished and downtrodden to help themselves without government intervention.[4]

Whatever the case, my uneasiness is compounded by a growing suspicion that many Laura Ingalls Wilder pilgrimages are motivated by a desire for a homogenous world that doesn't tolerate difference or dissent. In my own love of literature, I have navigated between two worldviews: the wish to find comfort in voices and values like my own, and the need to be unsettled and affirmed by questions, possibilities, and complexities. Wilder offers a Laura who experiences these dualities, these conflicting desires, but the TV show is far less dimensional, with too much self-satisfied flag waving and Bible quoting for my taste, too many safe retreats into clichés.

It's not that Wilder's work is unpatriotic or sacrilegious. It's not that she utterly disavows cliché. It's just that focusing so narrowly on the patriotic or religious sentiments reduces her work to something far less rich than it really is. While religion is central to her characters' lives, the books are not didactic. Wilder herself felt that one's beliefs should be kept private;[5] I can't imagine that she would approve of the TV show's constant allusions to church, Bible verses, and Christianity.

At heart, I'm still a Midwestern child who believed in God and felt pride in the ideals of my country. But now I'm an adult who is far less certain what I believe, far more likely to question the way we sometimes interpret those beliefs and ideals and impose them on others. And I'm the mother of a Chinese American daughter who gets frustrated at the ways that oversimplified patriotism negates her heritage. It amazes me how the binary thinking of our culture sometimes translates my discomfort into anti-American atheism. And, now in Walnut Grove, I have a prickling recollection about the ways that my trip here at thirteen was transformative, watering the seeds of my developing worldview so that I returned to Kansas a more complicated child than I started out.

At least fifty cars pack the lot outside the eight-building complex. We have to enter through the sprawling gift shop, which crawls with little girls in sunbonnets and long dresses purchased here. I see almost no little boys. I see no one who isn't white except for my own child. Dania writes about her childhood uneasiness of knowing that "there wasn't a kid like me, even remotely like me," in the woods or on the prairies and creek banks and towns of the *Little House* series. Still, she says, she related to the continuing theme of Laura negotiating her own sense of being out of place and yet always cycling back to some kind of security.

So the lack of racial diversity here at the Walnut Grove site, despite the population of Hmongs that surrounds it, doesn't surprise me. The fact that there are any children at all does strike me, because there have been no children at the other sites we've visited. It's all about adult nostalgia. But not here, in Walnut Grove. Here, the kids are nostalgic, too.

It takes us a couple of hours to see everything: a museum, dugout display, farmhouse with interactive exhibits, chapel, depot from 1898, covered wagon display, some Walnut Grove jail cells and big cardboard cutouts of Ingalls family members that you can stand behind to have your picture taken. There's a room with memorabilia from the TV show and a building containing a covered wagon display, printing equipment, and farming tools. I vaguely remember some of these things from 1976, but the complex and exhibits have grown significantly since.

We look at artifacts, exhibits, photographs, and storyboards. We both pause, puzzled, before a display of a doll carrying a bucket, her two middle fingers broken off. This is just supposed to be a representation of a pioneer girl fetching water, I guess, but we can't take our eyes off the broken fingers.

"Did she get frostbit?" Sophie asks.

"Maybe," I say dubiously. "Or maybe her fingertips were gnawed by wolves. Or maybe they got caught in farm machinery."

We stand and ponder the many possible tragedies that might have befallen this girl's hand. How odd, I think, that there is no sign reminding us about the hardships of pioneers, about what might happen if they left the house without mittens, about the lack of immediate medical care available if you were to inadvertently chop off your fingertips while cutting firewood.

"Or maybe her fingers just broke by accident and the curators decided to leave it to our imagination," I say. "Maybe they think we won't notice her injury if they don't call attention to it."

Sophie has moved on, grossed out by the furs. There's a buffalo coat like the one Pa wears when he digs a hole in a snowbank to survive a blizzard. There's a hat and muff like the one Laura receives at a church Christmas celebration. These furs are now unattractively ragged, but it's the intact claws hanging from the muff that freak Sophie out.

We move on to displays related to the TV show that I gave up on by the third or fourth season, disgusted at how it got further and further from the books I loved. When we were in the gift shop earlier, I noticed that it sells all eleven seasons, including *Little House: A New Beginning*, in which, apparently, the Ingalls family relocates to the city with their historically inaccurate brood of adorable adopted children, and then, for some mysterious reason, citizens blow up Walnut Grove. I saw a gift shop clerk roll her eyes at this, but the irony is that tourism generated by the TV drama that symbolically destroyed this small community is what in fact guarantees its survival. And so there are displays of photographs and memorabilia related to the show and to the stars who have visited Walnut Grove, including pantyhose worn by the actress who played Nellie Oleson and scale models of the Ingallses' TV series home. Those displays are, however, confined to one room.

Because I feel so out of place, so secretly subversive among nostalgic TV show fans, I will be especially relieved to find out that I'm not alone in my discomfort about the discrepancies between the books and the show—not just in terms of plot, but character, tone, and intention, in the way that beautiful and gentle stories transform to overwrought, sensational aberrations, feeling to me somehow depraved despite their celebration of God and country. My friend Carol admits to watching the show with her daughter until she "couldn't stand another week of tragedy and Michael Landon's tear-stained face." When I went looking several years ago, it turned out that Internet conversations had cropped up like a page on *Mental Floss* where those who had watched the TV show shared their skepticism, and a blog called *WTF Little House on the Prairie*, which described itself as "A 21st century look at a 20th century interpretation of life in the 19th century. The goal is to answer one question: Seriously?"[6]

At *Mental Floss*, participants reminisced about the trauma induced by the TV show, recalling various episodes: the one where the guy in the clown mask molests a young girl, the one in which a girl is forced by her father to bind her breasts so as not to tempt men, the time Ma almost hacks off her own leg when an infection leaves her delirious, and that final episode where citizens blow up the town, it turns out to prevent land swindlers from taking over. Someone named Anthony wrote, "It was as though the director of that episode just decided to step out for that little bit and—ta, da—in stepped, oh, say Quentin Tarantino. The sawmill—BLAMMO! The mercantile—KA-BOOM!!! The Ingalls home—KABLOOEY!!!!" Someone else pointed out that the church and the Ingalls house were actually spared. "One of the most morbid shows ever," another traumatized fan summarized it.

After a quick glance at the exhibits related to the TV show, we move on to "Grandma's house," an old house with nineteenth-century furniture and interactive exhibits. There, we labor to lift a heavy iron, pull the handle of an old washing machine, and play a pump organ before we retreat to the relatively easy activity of viewing scenes through a stereoscope. In the empty chapel, Sophie leaps up to the pulpit taken from an early Walnut Grove church and, with a pounding fist, preaches the only sermon she's ever heard. "I have a dream," she announces.

We try out another pump organ here. It takes a lot of effort to stomp on the pedals hard enough to work the bellows that supply air. I'm convinced that the pump organ should be revived, not as a musical instrument but as a piece of exercise equipment, alongside treadmills and bench presses. How did anyone get fat in pioneer days, pumping pedals, walking miles to town, or hoisting thirty-pound irons to smooth out fabric wrinkles?

And yet people did grow stouter as they got older. When I was thirteen, all of these pictures of thick, middle-aged, stern pioneers depressed me, these images of aging people I'd only previously imagined as young and energetic. The shock may have been even greater when the reality was contrasted against the glamour of the TV stars. But now that I have left behind my rail-thin youth for the stubborn extra pounds deposited on me as I age, a few more each decade, I take comfort in these pictures and in the fact that Wilder's writing career didn't really take off until she was in her sixties.

Every Saturday in July, a nearby park hosts a family festival that advertises acoustic guitar performances, Laura and Nellie look-alike contests, folk music, blacksmiths, woodcarving, weaving, cornhusk dolls, seed art, a craft and vendor show, pony rides, Civil War reenactments, car shows, Native American dances, and art exhibits. But we've apparently come on the wrong Saturday, because there isn't much going on. We buy hot dogs, and Sophie grimaces through a pony ride on a live merry-go-round; she considers herself much too old for any kind of merry-go-round. Then she pets frantic, quivering ducks and bunnies when what she really wants to do is smuggle them away from all of the shouting kids that surround them.

On the edge of the park, we pay for the historic bus tour of Walnut Grove, then line up to board a yellow school bus that seems to have driven into town straight from its regular route through hell. The bus features sticky vinyl seats, no air conditioning, no water, and many confused tourists.

"Why'd she change Nellie Oleson's name?" someone asks the guide as if the books are strict autobiography. I hear a mother explaining to her children that the books were published in the 1960s and 70s. The tour guide mentions all the spelling bees in *On the Banks of Plum Creek*, which came out in the 30s. I'm trying not to be a stickler here, trying not to be an obnoxious thirteen-year-old foremost authority, but there are no spelling bees in *On the Banks of Plum Creek*.

The bus stops so that our tour guide can dash into a church and ring the bell that Pa donated his boot money to help purchase. The bus also stops at a body of water called Lake Laura that I don't remember from the books or my previous visit here. We stop briefly to view Plum Creek, which is prettier than my recollection, overhung by trees, the water clear, if not as beautiful as in the TV show. The climax of the tour is the dugout site.

The driver parks and helps unload wheelchairs and walkers and crutches. All that's left of the dugout is a depression in the earth, and getting to it is a rocky, buggy journey past tall grass and thickets of brush. But like pilgrims seeking healing, people hobble down the bus steps and even the severely disabled laboriously plant their crutches one after the other, shuffle behind walkers, wheel their chairs. At the dugout site, we take turns photographing ourselves and our relatives in front of the marker.

The last stop is the pageant site. There we visit our third dugout replica in two days. This one is smaller than the ten-by-ten model back at the museum complex, and emits a foul odor. By now, we've pretty much had enough. We get off the bus in Walnut Grove parched and drained by the heat, stop for some root beer floats, then drive back to our hotel to swim in the pool.

In the evening, before the pageant, there is a regular community dinner held at a local church. It seems like a nice idea, but we can't get inspired to go. We do attend the pageant, "Fragments of a Dream," sitting on long benches in an outdoor theater, a pageant that, according to our bus tour guide, was begun in 1978 as an effort to portray Wilder's life with more accuracy than the TV show. The whole town seems to come together for this play, which involves sixty volunteers, including a guy who has played Pa for fifteen years. The set and special effects are clever in this pastiche of *On the Banks of Plum Creek*, the Ingalls family's mostly unrecorded move to Burr Oak, Iowa, the opening chapters of *On the Shores of Silver Lake*, and, yes, even the TV show.

Out here as the wide prairie surrounding us grows dark, I remember how the Ingalls family arrive in Minnesota, finally "safe and at rest" in a life without hostile Indians or ravenous wolves. Laura watches as "the peaceful colors went all around the rim of the sky. The willows breathed and the water talked to itself in the dark. The land was dark gray. The sky was light gray and stars prickled through it."[7] It's getting a little chilly, but I like being outdoors on this land I read about over and over. The play is like a dream under floodlights, and I'm caught up in the performance, especially the singing and the dancing.

But there are moments that the play seems to borrow from preachy and misogynous aspects of the TV show. Mr. Oleson, for instance, is portrayed as a weak, timid, good-hearted man with an overbearing shrew of a wife we're all supposed to want to see whacked with a flour sack. The presentation of religion follows the rhetoric of the TV show more closely than the books' more subtle approach; there are many references to the Bible, Jesus, and godliness. I feel that dismay again, that these books have been reduced to appeal largely to white evangelical Christians, alienating others who might connect to more universal aspects of the Ingallses' human struggle.

At the end of the play, when Mary goes blind, the narrator reassures us that she's still determined to follow her dreams. "If you want to be a teacher, you will be a teacher," Pa declares. Mary was never, in reality, a teacher, however much she once dreamed of being one. Mary longed to go to college; she dreamed of writing a book. Although miserably unsuited to it, Laura became a teacher in order to help put Mary through the Iowa College for the Blind. Mary came home afterward and lived with her parents for the rest of her life. She never wrote a book.

After family members who might have remembered things differently were gone, Wilder wrote books in which her likeness, the fictional Laura, became the heroine. Since Laura is at the center of the books, what's with the play's sudden focus on Mary's future achievement and Pa's hollow promises? Wilder gives Laura much of the credit for obtaining an education for Mary, but the pageant shifts the credit to Pa. In fact, her tuition was paid for by government assistance from Dakota territory, a fact never mentioned by the books, while Laura and Pa undoubtedly both contributed to Mary's room and board, supplies and clothing.[8] As I watch the play, I try to decide what my priorities would be if I were the one retelling the story: adherence to the story; historical accuracy, even if it includes the kind of government intervention that Wilder and Lane repudiated; or a retreat into a patriarchal model that asserts the father's position as head of the family and primary provider. And I wonder how Mary would have told it differently—would she, instead of Laura, have become the imaginative, determined one?

The pageant does ultimately rely more on historical fact than either the TV show or the book. But it also aims to stay true to *On the Banks of Plum Creek* by ending on a note of hope. In the novel, though Laura anticipates a year ahead without grasshoppers, in real life the grasshoppers returned and, for a third consecutive year, destroyed Pa's crops. Wilder does not mention this in any of her books, or that her parents gave up on homesteading the land, bought it from the US government and immediately resold it, had a baby boy who died, moved to Burr Oak, Iowa, to run a hotel, and then, when that venture failed, returned to Minnesota. There, a stroke left Mary blind. The hopeful ending of Plum Creek doesn't acknowledge any of the ordeals ahead, and by the time Wilder takes up the narrative in *By the Shores of Silver Lake*, the family is preparing to move on. Those difficult years have been left out of the story altogether.

Although Wilder doesn't write about living with relatives in Spring Hill, Minnesota, or running the Masters Hotel in Burr Oak, Iowa, except in an unpublished memoir, I am curious about these places, both stops on the Laura Ingalls Wilder Highway. I've always wondered why Wilder left both of those places out of her series. One explanation has to do with an editor telling Wilder that no one could remember being three, as she was during the events of *Little House in the Big Woods*, so she aged herself two years and later in the series had to leave out two years to catch up with herself, an explanation that doesn't make much sense to me since there's actually a four-year gap between *Plum Creek* and *Silver Lake*. In a letter, Wilder once said that she didn't write about the family's move to Iowa because she didn't want to introduce new characters. A tour guide tells us that the period may have been just too sad for Wilder to write about, or maybe it was just too shameful to admit that the family had backtracked east. Certainly the defeat that the family experienced during those years would not have provided much inspiration about the self-sufficient life.

While there is no *Little House* book about Burr Oak, writer Cynthia Rylant attempted to fill in the gap with her children's book *Old Town in the Green Grove*, carefully researched and written to capture the spirit of the series without mimicking it stylistically. Rylant follows the Ingalls family through the birth of baby Freddie, the third year of grasshoppers, Pa's decision to give up on farming, the family's summer near Spring Hill, Freddie's death, and the rough months of hotel-keeping in Iowa. Rylant is true to Wilder in many narrative choices: the way she lists the foods in the pantry, the way she brings out the sense of richness in the ordinary and echoes Laura's dislike of town life. There are some subtle correctives as well—whereas in Wilder's story, Laura is the only one regularly called pet names by Pa like "Half Pint" and "Flutterbudget," thus implying a favoritism toward Laura and reaffirming her centrality, Rylant has Pa regularly refer to Mary as "Pumpkin Pie" and younger sister Carrie as "Buttercup."

Although I have been critical of Wilder-related book spinoffs, TV productions, and rampant merchandising, Rylant's work exists for me in a different realm than many of these products. It seems to me that this book is the act of a passionate reader who has absorbed Wilder's books thoroughly, that she finds a way to create what feels like a collaborative work and tribute at the same time.

On our trip, we pass but don't stop in Spring Hill, but we do spend a morning in Burr Oak, which advertises itself as the only site whose original buildings are still standing. The tourist copy I read about Burr Oak beforehand invited us to start our journey in a historic bank building, the site of the first bank robbery in that county. We could then tour the old hotel and stop for ice cream next door at the Mercantile. I imagined charming old buildings, including an ice cream shop with the usual gift shop attached. I figured we would take a tour of Burr Oak, then top it off with lunch at the Mercantile.

We arrive at 10:00 a.m. to find a desolate one-street town with only a few buildings. It reminds me of ghost towns in old westerns, men meeting up for duals at high noon in the middle of the street, dust kicking up, outlaws high-tailing it out of town before sunset. We start at the Information Center, the old bank building which, it turns out, is also a gift shop. I pay for tickets for the tour starting in fifteen minutes, then browse around, looking at postcards, the usual books, and the bank's old vaults and safe deposit boxes. One postcard stands out somewhat startlingly from the many photographs of the hotel's rooms. This one depicts a bizarre collection of artwork, soft sculptures of the Ingalls family made out of pantyhose and posed on living room furniture—a bit of a trick since, lacking stomach muscles, these life-sized rag dolls apparently don't bend in the middle and mostly tilt stiffly in semi-upright positions.

Sophie and I stare, laughing uneasily. I imagine this postcard to be some kind of ironic folk art, a commentary, maybe, on the limp state of hardy pioneers reduced to cooking meals and making beds for transient customers, of brave, adventurous characters cruelly transformed to pantywaists away from their heroic battles against grasshoppers and blizzards. Or maybe the artist wished to parody the stereotypical-ly broad, pasty-faced features of the midwesterner, although even nude pantyhose gives everyone a bit of a tan. "So," Dania says when I tell her about it later, "the Ingalls family were brown as Indians?"

A couple in their fifties with Southern accents comes in to buy tickets. And then we head off, the four of us and our guide, for the Masters Hotel. It's tiny from the front. As we cross the street, the woman says, in an awestruck voice, "It's small-er than it seemed in the book."

The guide smiles politely and refrains from pointing out that there was no book. Or maybe the woman has read Wilder's unpublished autobiography *Pioneer Girl*. Maybe she has read Rylant.

"Why do you suppose that there were two entrances?" asks the guide, pausing on the long porch.

"Oh, I remember this from the books," the woman says. Her skin is prematurely aged, her voice gravelly.

There's a long pause. Finally the guide prompts her: "Well, one was for men and the other was—"

"For women!" the woman finishes her sentence gleefully, as if she has just re-covered a memory. The tour guide smiles and nods.

"I loved the books so much, I built a cabin on my property," the woman confesses. "I'm furnishing it with old stuff." Her husband smiles indulgently, bored but affectionate.

We go in the men's door, the one that used to lead to a tavern but now is a room displaying furniture, clothing, and signs from the era that the Ingalls family lived here. Some of the few items actually connected to Wilder herself are framed letters on the walls, the author's ever-gracious responses to fan mail.

We all pause to read a list of prices for a stay at the Master's Hotel in the late 1870s—25 cents for a bed, 25 cents for a meal. If guests wanted a bath, the tour guide says, it was a 75-cent charge. The 25-cent charge guaranteed not a whole bed but a space on a bed with two other men.

"I love the olden days," the woman says. "Except that." She points to a cham-ber pot. "I would have been whopped before I would have emptied one of those when I was a kid." She chuckles. We all can't help but smile at her enthusiasm for some aspects of pioneer life while she flat out rejects others.

On another wall is a framed government advertisement offering rewards for grasshoppers brought in dead or alive, an apparently lame attempt to gain control over nature. "Do you sell these in the gift shop?" the woman asks. "I want one of these for my cabin."

There are quotes posted on the wall as well, labeled "Laura's virtues"—sayings about courage, hardship, and love. "Families are forever," reads one, and being the wicked, cynical person I am, as with every time this sentiment is evoked by yet another museum, I want to point out that Wilder left home as a teenager and never went back. And I have a further bone to pick with her, the more I think about it: while Wilder portrays some resentment and jealousy, in particular between Mary and Laura, they appear to resolve their lifelong conflicts very quickly in a conversation in *Little Town on the Prarie.* Though by all accounts Wilder quarreled and bickered regularly with Almanzo and Rose, these books are idealized portraits of family life, so unconflicted as to make generations of children feel that their own family dynamics were deeply dysfunctional. Wilder was very rarely around children apart from her own only child, and I can see now what I didn't as a child, how often the ways children behave and relate to each other are simplified if not romanticized.

On we go down to the kitchen to view metal rings used to scrape pots, a butter mold, and brass triangles that were placed in the corners of staircases to collect dust. It's almost impossible for me to imagine how the entire Ingalls family, all five of them, lived in the small bedroom with its adjoining kitchen and dining room where Caroline routinely cooked and served seventy-five guests at a time.

"I remember churning butter when I was a girl on my grandma's farm," the woman says. "Do you sell these butter molds in the gift shop?"

Our tour ends upstairs in the parlor, where it is as if the best has been saved for last: there before us are not only the hotel's original pump organ but also, it turns out, the sculptures from the postcard, the life-sized people made out of pantyhose, stuffed and dressed in authentic pioneer garb, the Ingalls family's ghoulish doubles. Sophie and I carefully do not look at each other. I swallow hard, realizing that I'd got it all wrong when I'd imagined these sculptures as the product of an artist with a charmingly perverse sense of humor and eye for the ironic juxtaposition, perching these muppet-like figures on heavy antique furniture. Now I understand that, examining the postcard, I completely missed the tone. These soft sculptures reclining flaccidly on a couch and in chairs were meant as a loving tribute, not a grotesque commentary.

For a long moment, we all stand and stare, and the woman does not ask how she can purchase one of these for her cabin. If Melissa Gilbert wasn't how you pictured Laura, if those old photographs in museums of lumpy, dumpy middle-aged people just don't jibe with how you envisioned the Ingallses, imagine the disillusionment of finding them here in Burr Oak, Iowa, life-size sock puppets fashioned from someone's discarded pantyhose.

I finally shoot Sophie a glance, and although she had snickered at the postcard, now she doesn't crack a smile. The tour guide asks if the little girl wants to try out the pump organ. Sophie dutifully complies.

And then we escape from the home of the Pantyhose People into fresh air. We're hungry for lunch, so after taking a couple of photos of ourselves in a wagon, we head over to the Mercantile. When we open the door, a sour smell hits us, the dusty, unpleasant odor of an old building crammed floor to ceiling with second-hand stuff for sale, heaps of chipped old dishes and warped paperback romances. Some elderly local men have clustered around a table in the diner area. I decide that we'll eat on the road, and so by noon we are off again, headed toward Owatonna, a chicken and biscuit lunch, and an afternoon at a hotel water park.

CHAPTER EIGHT

Coming of Age
with Literature

TWO AND A HALF YEARS BEFORE I came along, my parents had another daughter. She was born prematurely with an underdeveloped heart, and she lived only three hours.

I grew up with this ghost sister, this sense of absence that was like a presence, this girl in the shadows who would have been smart and funny, beautiful and wise, I always imagined. She's the one who would have taught me to use makeup and flirt and find the good stations on the radio, all skills at which I grew up totally defi-cient. She and I would have cultivated an alliance against our brothers and our par-ents. Instead, I was left alone to fend for myself with a pair of brothers and a pair of parents who stuck up for each other, always leaving me the odd one out.

I refused to entertain the idea that this sister might have been unimaginative or reclusive or rigid or competitive or mean. I simply couldn't believe that she would have struggled with her weight or had acne or smoked pot or stabbed her friends in the back or partnered with my older brother to torture me. I idealized the idea of her, keenly missing the sister of my imagination.

On trips to Mt. Olive Cemetery in Pittsburg, Kansas, my parents always stopped at her tiny grave. There was no name on the small flat gravestone. It just said, "Baby Girl of Bill and Lucille McCabe."

"What would you have named her?" I asked my mother when I was five or six.

"We didn't have time to name her," she answered.

"But weren't you going to name her something?" I asked, and she finally said, offhandedly, "Oh, I don't know, Carol I guess."

My mom spent most of her spare time in the dark, unfinished basement, her sewing machine whirring as she made all of our clothes. While she sewed, her dress-maker's dummy loomed in a corner, a torso made of what appeared to be card-board covered in cloth. I secretly called the dummy Carol. Older, it occurred to me that my mother had come up with the name *Carol* on the spot, that in fact, she was planning to name the baby *Nancy Grace*, and then, with all the possible permutations of fate, I would have been someone else or maybe I would have been nobody at all, never born.

But it was years before I realized this, before I experienced Carol as anything but a vast loss, the first great absence and significant deprivation of my childhood. "After we lost our first baby, I thought I'd never have another daughter," my mother kept saying. Later I learned that she had also had two miscarriages. My mother was always saying to me, mournfully, "You'll never know what it's like to have a sister." She was close to her two sisters, Gena and Shirley, and her sister-in-law Arlene. My parents didn't have friends. Their social life centered on relatives.

My favorite book characters mostly had sisters. Laura had three, Jo had three, Betsy had two. There were two Melendy sisters and two Hill sisters and three Malone girls. Nancy Drew was an only child, but she had her loyal sidekicks Bess and George, and Anne of Green Gables had Diana, her bosom friend, who was like a sister, or so I thought until I came across a whole body of criticism on Anne's homoerotic relationships with other girls. It's true, as Irene Gammel says, that Anne's world is one "of girls holding hands, writing love poetry to each other, and swearing everlasting devotion." Gammel sees this as a way of bringing readers "tantalizingly close to unspoken feelings of sensuality and sexuality, while ingeniously portraying these feelings as universal and innocent."[1]

Some critics have read these patterns more literally, and things really got out of hand when, at an academic humanities and social sciences conference, scholar Laura Robinson presented a paper called "Bosom Friends: Lesbian Desire in L. M. Montgomery's Anne Books." An *Edmonton Journal* article covering the conference singled this paper out from all of the presentations on the program with the headline, "Did Our Anne of Green Gables Nurture Gay Fantasies? Or Has a Professor Had Too Many Sips of Marilla's Cordial?"[2] A newspaper in Halifax proceeded to set up a phone-in hotline inviting callers to vote on whether Anne was gay or not; 45 said no while 2 said yes. Another headline writer couldn't resist punning on "Anne of Green Gay-bles."[3]

It's true that Anne has intense feelings about her friends during a historical period when gender segregation was more rigid, when marriage could feel like a risky venture to women because of the high mortality rate associated with childbirth, and when, as a result, a kind of romantic idealization of female friendship prevailed. Historian Carroll Smith-Rosenberg examined diaries and letters of nineteenth-century women to conclude that there was widespread acceptance of intense relationships between women in the nineteenth century, and that close women friends might be regarded as more important in a woman's life than a husband, since men and women occupied rigidly separated spheres.

But I resist the line of criticism that takes this romance too literally, robbing the novels of one of their appeals, the celebration of female spaces that are free of complicated sexual tension. We have few real models for close female friendships, and, with heterosexual romance and marriage widely given primacy in Western culture as the most central, most essential of all adult relationships, sometimes it seems to me that we only know how to view connections between people through lenses of sexuality and metaphors of couplehood.

Women who deeply value their female friendships, even those whose erotic energy remains focused on men, can seem suspect to outsiders. Why, I've wondered throughout my adult life, are there so few paradigms for friendship? I've often found myself searching for some sort of construct that could accurately explain my relationships with close women friends, and gradually I came to realize how much my mother's ties with her sisters, their bonds and visits and phone calls, their gossip and dramas and laughter, had shaped me. My mom had constantly lamented my lack of a sister, and so from a young age, I had gone looking for one.

My mother had often reminded me that my cousin Jody was the closest thing to a sister I would ever have. As children, our connection was built on books and writing and imagination. But she lived four hours away, and so I kept looking, looking for someone else who loved the same things that I did, engaging in a childhood quest for a best friend that I now understand was really about recruiting sisters, trying to fill Carol's position.

What felt like a tumultuous period of transition started the spring I was twelve and lasted for more than two years. I knew that my aunt was dying; she seemed tired sometimes, cranky at others, but her death didn't seem real to me. Death didn't seem real until a boy named Billy from my Sunday school class died in a fire, someone my own age whom I'd known, though not well, my whole life. Two months later our neighbors' house burned in the middle of a school day. It was evening when the firefighters started carrying smoldering furniture onto the lawn. I remember all of it sitting there, charred dressers and beds and a little table with a fish bowl, three dead goldfish floating on top. I remember walking through the house with my parents, through the rooms with blackened walls and ceilings, the acrid smell almost unbearable.

I had nightmares for weeks, but I thought I was too old to be so affected, so I kept my terror and sleeplessness a secret. I sat up reading night after night, finally sinking into sleep and dreaming of rooms filled with smoke, choking me like the smoke that had choked Billy. I imagined the ghosts of Carol and of Billy and of my grandfather all crowding around me, I dreamed of fires burning underground where no one could see them, and I'd feel the hot ground and try to warn people, but no one believed me. Someday, I knew, those fires would burst through our driveway and our floors and consume us all. Maybe it was really my aunt's death I was dreaming about.

Once I woke up screaming. I heard a door unlatch down the hall and the whir of cold air from a window fan, and then my mother appeared in my doorway as if she had blown into the hall. She smelled like the cold cream that masked her face. She smelled like powder from a pink puff, and Ivory soap, and mint toothpaste. Those scents brought me back to the ordinary world, where shadows were just tricks of light, not ghosts.

"It was just a nightmare," I said, embarrassed, afraid to talk about Billy or ask about my aunt. My mom sat down on the edge of my bed and whisked through the tissue-thin pages of her study Bible, the cold cream making her seem carved in marble. While I lay there miserably, heart pounding, she read to me Bible verses about how only God could make sparrows fall to the ground, about how even the very hairs on my head were numbered. Then she rose and laid the Bible on the nightstand, pushing aside my library books because, she always said, you must never place anything on top of a Bible. "Go to sleep," she said. "I'll leave this here in case you need it."

I lay in bed watching the beams of cars from the turnpike traveling along my wall and worrying: What if God willed me to die the same way he could will a sparrow to drop to the ground in mid-flight?

When I finally plummeted into sleep, it was uneasy, full of dreams about birds falling like rain from the sky.

On the very first day of seventh grade, I found an instant best friend with whom I had a seemingly astonishing number of overlapping interests. Later, this would seem to me the last friendship of my childhood, the last one free of constant awareness of boys and commiseration over periods and uncertainty about the future. At first, at least, my friendship with Marissa was based purely on reading and imagination and creative aspirations.

In the cafeteria on the first day of junior high, we started talking as we tentatively unloaded our lunches, my food sloppily shoved into plastic baggies, hers arranged in appropriate-sized Tupperware containers. It turned out that we both loved the movie *Escape to Witch Mountain*, in which the main characters were from another planet and had psychic powers.[4] Marissa's favorite book was Lois Duncan's

A Gift of Magic and I had just read Zoe Sherburne's *The Girl Who Knew Tomorrow*, both books about ESP. We both loved Noel Streatfeild's novels about kids who danced and sang. Another of her favorites was Elizabeth Enright's *Spiderweb for Two*, and she was beside herself with excitement when I told her that there were more books about the Melendy family.

The first time Marissa came to my house, I was still stunned by my good fortune at having such an accomplished new best friend. She had played "The Entertainer" with the Wichita Symphony, and she demonstrated it for me, a difficult arrangement that she played really fast, without a single mistake, on the piano, her fingers curved delicately in a way that didn't seem at all affected. Marissa regularly participated in beauty pageants, and no one could compete with her in the talent contests. She wanted to be an actress, a dancer, a writer. "Can you imagine writing a *book*?" she asked me.

I was pretty sure that I'd write books someday and didn't see it as quite such a big deal, so I just shrugged. But I was flattered and honored that she'd chosen me to be her best friend.

The first time I went to Marissa's for a sleepover, we ate dinner with her noisy family and afterward, Marissa showed me her diary, where she had sketched a pair of ballet slippers, long ribbons intertwined. We did a few ESP experiments, trying to replicate each other's doodles on a piece of paper from across the room. Then she asked if I'd ever done the Ouija board.

She might as well have asked me if I'd ever smoked crack, I was so shocked. An uncle had given me a Ouija board for Christmas some years before. My mother's lips pursed together and after my uncle left she told me that Ouija boards were against our religious beliefs. They could open our house up to demons, and me, well, I might end up possessed by an evil spirit.

My Ouija board went up on a closet shelf under a heap of folded blankets. Its presence alone gave me nightmares. I didn't quite know what a demon might look like or sound like, but I turned my face away from the closet at night, guilty that I was harboring evil.

I couldn't possibly explain all of this to Marissa. And in the light of day, in the midst of a cheerful household of clattering dishes and slamming doors, my fears seemed kind of silly. I watched Marissa lift the lid from the Ouija board box, trying to ignore the little voice that nagged at me, saying, *That's the way it happens. That's the way people give up their principles and values, a little at a time.*

We swirled the planchette around to warm it up. Marissa said that a few turns would loosen it up like bike gears after a winter of disuse.

"Tell us our names," she ordered the planchette. She drew out her words so they sounded spooky and mysterious.

All of a sudden, Marissa's mom popped into the room, and I jumped. But she didn't flinch or scold when she saw the Ouija board. She didn't get all frowny and tight and tense like my mom. In fact, she barely seemed to notice. She just wanted Marissa to go take her vitamins.

She did, leaving me alone with the board. It seemed perfectly harmless and ordinary and inanimate. I didn't know what I'd expected—a cursing voice to emerge from it? A foul, rotten smell?

"Ouija . . . it's only a game—isn't it?" the box said. It seemed more funny than scary.

I told myself that the Ouija board was less creepy than many sleepover rituals. It was less disturbing than séances or games like Light as a Feather, Stiff as a Board. At birthday parties, I'd always hated it when my friends suggested those games, but we'd never called up any spirits. We'd never managed to float anyone into the air on our fingertips. It was all just pretend.

Marissa returned. "Tell us our names," she told the board again in her low, ominous voice.

The planchette jerked an inch and stopped. "Did you push it?" Marissa and I asked each other. I hadn't. She insisted she hadn't. And we went on waiting, Marissa coaxing it in her spirit-summoning voice, like she was reassuring the ghost of a skittish cat: "Come on. We won't hurt you. Tell us our names."

Eventually, the planchette jerked again and haltingly began spelling. "W-E-N—"

"When?" I guessed as the planchette gained momentum. "D-Y-J-A-C-T-Q."

"Wendy Jactq?" Marissa asked. "Who's that?"

"Y-O-U," the planchette spelled.

And so we sat for hours as a slice of moonlight widened on the floor and the house went still around us, our fingers curved over the planchette as if arched to play a piano piece, while the Ouija board told us a story. Marissa was Wendy Jactq, I was Carla Jactq, and we were sisters from the planet Leshma.

It was the names that convinced me. If either of us were pushing, we'd never choose such ugly names. We'd be Emilia or Krista or Louisa or Gretchen, something pretty or old-fashioned or foreign sounding, not Wendy or Carla.

The planchette picked up speed, skittering around the board like a frantic bug. It barely paused on one letter before racing to the next. Sometimes we raised our hands till they hovered right above the planchette. We weren't even touching it, but it still zipped on.

"This has never happened with anyone else," Marissa breathed. "We really must be sisters."

The small gap between my fingers and the plastic felt hot, electric. It flew on as if of its own accord. It didn't falter unless we completely removed our hands. Our parents were Bene and Gruce Jactq. We, Wendy and Carla, had three more sisters: Abigmxs, Icuagsclsurag, and Mindy, Wendy's twin. Carla/I and Wendy/Marissa had left Leshma behind to find out more about our ancestors, who were originally from Earth. Departing from our home planet, we had to renounce our extrasensory powers.

It made perfect sense to me. I'd never quite felt like I belonged in my family. My parents had brown hair that they had passed on to my brothers but not me. They all liked watching TV and I hated it. I vaguely sensed that our worldviews were different, although I didn't yet define it in terms of political leanings, me more liberal, them more conservative. All I knew is that it did often seem like we'd originated from different planets. Maybe that's why my mother had discouraged me from using the Ouija board: she was afraid of me finding out the truth.

Later, after we crawled into our sleeping bags and Marissa drifted off, I lay awake, shocked with myself for the line that I'd crossed. What if a demon had sunk its teeth into our spirits, and now, slowly, like a snake digesting a mouse, the demon swallowed our souls right up? What if we became nothing but empty shells, all skin and bones, with haunted eyes and straggly hair and incomprehensible speech? What if I woke up and found that I had turned into a beast with filthy words spewing from my mouth? What if the evil energy in the room caused light fixtures to crash to the floor and shatter into a thousand spiky pieces? When I got home, what if the dolls on my shelf contorted their faces and spoke in the voices of my ancestors?

I lay awake, agitated, the same way I did when I slept over at my aunt's house and all I could think about was that she was going to die, that there was a nearly dead person sleeping in the next room. Now, finally, I spun toward sleep, my mind whirling as fast as the planchette. My thoughts skittered from one to another and then into a swirl of black that turned into the blackened room of a burnt house, choking me.

The next week, Marissa came over to my house and we packed a lunch and took an excursion to all of my favorite places in my neighborhood. I didn't yet realize that our subdivision had been built on what had once been Osage Indian land. I only knew that for many decades it had been a large family farm, sold off in lots starting in the late 50s. I could hardly wait to show Marissa all the evidence that remained of the land's past, the storm cellar in the middle of a field, the wooden footholds up a tree trunk to where a treehouse had nested a generation before, the dump where the original farm's family had discarded old toilets, shingles, and a now-rusted car that rested there upside down, making a great playhouse. I was eager to show Marissa the landscape formed when I-35 had been built to pass over our road, creating a hill on otherwise flat land as well as the drainage tunnels that ran under it like caves, leading to a man-made pond. We climbed high up under the turnpike bridge to the slab of concrete where you could sit directly beneath the thundering wheels of cars. Then we walked to the creek, talking about Leshma.

"This really explains why I've always wished so hard to have a sister," I said. "I must have somehow known that you and Abigmxs and Icuagsclsurag and Mindy were out there in the world."

"Having sisters isn't all it's cracked up to be," Marissa said as we waded through the high grass of a vacant lot to where the deepest part of the creek snaked. "My sisters are always getting into my stuff."

It was a windy fall day, the wind flattening the long grass and roaring so loud we had to shout. I'd given up on my hair, tangles of wheat-colored strings, and focused on pushing against the wall of invisible resistance.

"This place is wonderful!" Marissa yelled as we reached the small cliff that plunged twelve feet to the dry creek bed. We slid down the dirt walls into the corridor of creek. It was a relief to be down there, sheltered from the gale.

We settled on the creek floor, unpacking our lunches as blade after blade of tall grass bowed down above, shivering and toppling sideways with each new onslaught of wind. We talked about how incredible it was that we'd gone to the same elementary school and lived on the same road for all of this time and hadn't known each other. How lucky that we'd met in the seventh grade lunchroom, long lost sisters, best friends forever.

Marissa and I made a thousand plans, most of which came straight from Elizabeth Enright's Melendy books. We were going to put on a show, just like in *The Saturdays*. We would hold a carnival in her backyard, with games and booths where we would sell craft items, just like in *And Then There Were Five*. We would create a treasure hunt with rhyming clues, just like in *Spiderweb for Two*.

But we tried out for a school play and were both struck by stage fright. We turned our attention to the carnival we planned to hold in her backyard, which had stone paths and steps that connected three graduated levels and a stone fountain. It made me think of *The Secret Garden* or Stonehenge. I got excited imagining crowds strolling along the quaint paths, colorful balloons bobbing along, purple-mouthed children dripping grape syrup from snow cones and peeling pink fluff from cotton candy sticks, their parents carrying red-striped bags of popcorn. We envisioned a fortuneteller and a talent contest and a merry-go-round, a ring toss and grab bags and fudge and divinity and a craft table with bead necklaces and candles and home-made pillows propped up in rows. We agreed to get started right away making things for the craft sale.

I'd made an A– on a quilt block pillow assignment for home economics. My pillow was a little lumpy and overstuffed, with straining seams, but sewing it had made me feel connected to book characters and the grandmothers and great-grand-mothers I'd never met. I'd started off with the sorts of tiny stitches expected of girls in old books. Then, just like all of my favorite tomboy heroines, I got impatient. My stitches lengthened, slanting sloppily. So my pillow wasn't perfect, but I'd still gotten an A, and I decided to make more to sell at the carnival.

My parents had spent a few years as proprietors of two double-knit polyes-ter fabric shops, and when they'd closed, most of the contents of the shops had ended up in our basement, which was now fully equipped with a cash register and leftover bolts of material. There were cutting and checkout counters and thread and button racks where lost crickets often died, so that our basement felt like a fabric shop for the Addams family, the little plastic windows showing rows of cheerful buttons interrupted by dead bugs: button, button, cricket, button, but-ton, cricket. Teetering on the counter were piles of old folders of color swatch-es and squares of fabric samples. An idea came to me: if I sewed together nine of these pre-cut squares to create a block, I could make a ton of pillows for the carnival really fast.

Unfortunately, the available colors didn't really coordinate. They ranged from mud browns to neon oranges to soft pinks. But I mixed and matched, trying to fig-ure out how to make them work. Then I sat down at the machine to stitch together the pieces, which was much easier than sewing them by hand. I finished two pillows in less than an hour.

When I showed them to Marissa, she went silent. She picked one up and turned it this way and that, fingered the edges, poked and pinched and frowned thought-fully. "We can't sell these," she finally said.

Instantly I saw my pillows through her eyes. They bulged unevenly. The squares were mismatched. The seams were crooked. The colors clashed.

"Oh, no, these were just experiments," I rushed to say, but after that, we never mentioned the carnival again. And as I hemmed the fake-denim skirt that was my current home economics project, I fumed and blinked away tears. Threading my needle, making careful little stitches that could pass for Mary Ingalls's or Beth

March's, I remembered the Bible verse about how much easier it was for a camel to pass through the eye of the needle than for a rich man to enter heaven.

It would be easier to stuff a camel through the eye of a needle than to please Marissa, I thought.

But Marissa was admirably resilient, with a remarkable capacity to let one dream go and move on to another. Right away, she was ready to plan a treasure hunt with rhyming clues, like in *Spiderweb for Two*. After much consideration, we decided to do it for Tanya, who lived down the street from me. She knew our neighborhood thoroughly and her birthday was coming up soon. I was excited. Maybe I was no good at acting or piano playing or pillow making. But writing? That was my thing. I could do this. Marissa would have to be impressed.

I planned to create intricate clues full of double meanings and clever rhymes and riddles that would take a while to figure out. But then I thought about my audience. Tanya was a good-hearted artist and animal lover who would rather tramp through woods or the creek than read or figure out clues, so I couldn't make them too complicated. I wrestled with this task for an entire evening before I brought my drafts to Marissa at lunch the next day. They were all along the lines of my first one:

In a line of trees, fourth tree from the road
Across the field from your abode
In a low branch (there are a lot)
Your next clue is where X marks the spot.

Marissa read it over, frowning. "But I wanted to have clever clues, like the ones in *Spiderweb for Two*," she protested.

"If everything has double meanings like in the book, she might not want to bother trying to figure them out," I said. "She's not really into poetry and stuff." In truth, after working on the clues an entire evening, I wasn't sure that I was that clever. Anyway, the clues in *Spiderweb for Two* had been written by a grownup, the book's author, Elizabeth Enright. And besides, in the book the poems were even attributed to adults, Father and Mrs. Oliphant.

"But the clues in *Spiderweb for Two* make Randy and Oliver figure stuff out— they have riddles about shadows and clocks and jewels and bird names. This is so obvious," Marissa complained.

"If you don't like mine, you can come up with something better," I said.

She backed right down. "Okay, okay," she said.

Tanya knew from the beginning that I was behind the clue left in her locker and the ones scattered around the neighborhood, but she gamely followed each one, from the field beside her house to a drainage tunnel under Highway 54 to the hollow tree at the end of the creek. That clue directed her to the drainage tunnels under the turnpike the day after her birthday where Marissa and I lay in wait with candles and a cake. "Surprise!" we yelled when Tanya appeared. "Happy Birthday." It seemed pretty lame, just the two of us.

I'd imagined this part of the hunt as like the end of a mystery story, where on the last few pages everyone sorts out all of the strange events and cryptic actions of others, making sense of them as the solution comes together like pieces of a puzzle. I loved those pages where everything got explained, cleared up, resolved. But now, as we peppered Tanya with questions, she just shrugged. She was clearly uninterested in rehashing all of the details of the hunt, and in that light, our excitement began to seem to me kind of mean, like we were proud of playing tricks on her. All of a sudden, it didn't feel like Marissa and I had done any of this for Tanya. It felt more like we were in a conspiracy against her, all triumphant because we'd managed to fool her.

Soon after, Marissa's behavior turned inexplicably odd. I caught her whispering with our boy-crazy friend Stacey, who used to talk about nothing but Donny Osmond but had moved on to stalking real boys in the junior high halls. Suddenly, Marissa was always bailing on me when we were walking together to lunch and forgetting to meet me to exchange notes between classes. She hinted around that it was something exciting that was distracting her, but she wouldn't tell me what.

I was hurt, and then I fumed. Marissa promised to tell me what was going on if I guessed, but my imagination was offering little assistance. Did she have some rare disease she was concealing from me? Did she just enjoy torturing me with the mystery? Was she embarrassed to be seen with me in front of some more popular person? Ann Landers said that a huge personality change might signal drug use or mental illness. Had Marissa taken up marijuana or gone off the deep end?

"Maybe you can guess," I said to Ruth across the lunch table, watching Marissa's smug secrecy give way to alarm. She shook her head at me, but I was tired of her telling me what to do, tired of trying to please her to no avail, tired of being excluded. I ignored her, plunging into the story of her inexplicable behavior. Ruth listened intently, then shrugged. "I'd say she likes a boy."

Marissa's face flamed red, and everyone else stared at me, smirking, like they couldn't believe how dumb I was. But I'd thought that Marissa was like me, in no hurry to grow up. Marissa was supposed to be my best friend, tell me everything, share with me private jokes and intimate secrets, care about books, the creek, and the planet Leshma, not leave me behind.

I begged her to tell me who it was. She went silent. I was livid with jealousy that she'd told Stacey and not me, that everyone else had figured it out before me. That's when words spewed out of my mouth like I really was possessed. "If you don't tell me, I'll tell everyone that you like someone. I'll get up on the table and get everyone's attention and say, 'Marissa likes a boy,'" I said. Then I was shocked at myself. I'd had no idea I could be so mean.

Marissa shrank away. After weeks of acting happy and superior, now she just looked small, pale, and scared. I was a horrible person. Evil. And she clamped her lips tight and refused to say any more.

It took another few months for my own hormones to kick in, for me to understand how greetings and exchanged looks in the halls could seem loaded with meaning, for me to experience the thrill of just saying someone's name aloud or writing it on a piece of paper, for me to really get the push and pull of wanting everyone to know and not wanting anyone to know how foolish you've become. Eventually, the boy I loved with a sudden, startling ferocity in junior high became my high school boyfriend.

I would see Marissa for the last time when we were twenty. Stacey had just died in a car wreck. Marissa had a baby. I'd married my rebound college boyfriend once my high school boyfriend finally accepted that he was gay. Marissa came to my house for lunch, and we talked about Stacey, my marriage, her baby, her nursing studies, my writing ambitions. Years later, I heard that she had married a minister, ran a dance studio in her basement, and was a mother of four—her own Melendy quartet.

But at the age of thirteen, unable to imagine the future, I felt as if everyone was passing me up, talking about grown-up things and writing love poems and pursuing romance. I felt like a child among adults, still mired in my world of books and secretly writing poetry about things like snowmen and deodorant cans and the last pickle left in the jar, parables of identity in the voices of inanimate objects.

I also began rereading the *Little House* books for the last time in my childhood, it would turn out, in preparation for the trip my aunt was planning that summer to all the places where Wilder had lived. I loved the series as much as ever but felt uneasy. I knew that Stacey and Marissa would think I was still reading baby books, and I was a little scared of going on a trip with a dying person.

I was sure that Stacey and Marissa didn't wake screaming from childish nightmares about fires or dead boys or grandfathers or pamphlets like the one my mother had left lying around the house, called "Is Lupus Hereditary?" Sometimes at night I imagined a secret code inside my aunt's body, maybe passed on to mine also, instructions to damage tissues and organs. Any minute, I thought, I might start dying, too.

One day I opened a novel by Sonia Levitin, *Journey to America*, which I had found at the library. I lost track of time, reading about a Jewish family escaping from Germany during the Holocaust. The young main character had been temporarily sent to a refugee camp, deprived of food there, and treated cruelly by the director.

I had, amazingly to me now, never heard of the Holocaust. I had barely ever met anyone Jewish; Ruth, who sat at my art and lunch tables, was my first Jewish friend, and she told me how kids sometimes accused her of having killed Jesus. She also complained about the way the world revolved around Christianity. "Even the calendar is based on the life of Christ," she said. I'd never thought about that before. She talked about the ways that the Jews had been persecuted throughout history while another girl at our art table rolled her eyes, and for a while I thought maybe Ruth was being paranoid or overdramatic.

Many years later, my own daughter would read *Number the Stars* in the fourth grade and *The Devil's Arithmetic* in the fifth. She would never have a chance to build up illusions about humanity. Not that my Chinese American daughter in a white community ever had the luxury of believing, even for a brief time, that bigotry and discrimination had been eradicated. She and her classmates, the products of television and movies and September 11, exposed to historical realities in school much earlier, were far less likely to be spared the knowledge of the existence of violence and brutality. My daughter has, as a result, become tough, a realist. I don't know if this is a tragedy or a gift.

Because keeping children innocent was a pervasive value of my parents' generation and because I cultivated such intense ignorance and denial until I entered adolescence, I had a long way to fall from my idealistic heights. It seems weirdly perverse to me now, this construction of childhood that has, since the eighteenth century or so, cast children, at least those on the higher end of socioeconomic privilege, as innocent creatures to be protected from real life at all costs. This idea carried to extremes has spawned a whole literary form, the coming-of-age story, in which sheltered protagonists must lose their innocence and finally see the world as it is.

One of the first steps in my own plummet into reality was reading *Journey to America*. At first I thought it must be made up. I'd always believed that once slavery had been abolished in the US, the world had become a just, gentle place. I knew there had been wars, but I assumed they were all about evil dictators who had to be stopped so that other countries could establish democracies and ensure freedom to all. Wars were, I thought, distant things that didn't really involve ordinary people. Now, I wondered over the idea that in recent times, in the lifetimes of my parents, people could have been driven from their homes, forced to flee, to leave behind beloved pets, friends, jobs, schools, and violins just because of their religion.

After finishing *Journey to America*, I began to page through our 1964 *World Book Encyclopedias*. Under "Hitler," there was only a brief mention of his hatred of Jews: "Hitler saw that some were successful, and they reminded him of his lack of success. He blamed them for his own failure." I looked under "Nazis" and "concentration camps": nothing. Finally, under "Jews," I found a brief paragraph saying that six million people had been slaughtered by the Germans during World War II.

Slaughtered. Not just driven from their homes, but killed, six million? I remembered references to smashed windows in *Journey to America*, a feeling of menace, soldiers singing about the spurting blood of Jews. I hadn't grasped that this reference was anything but metaphorical. How, logistically, was it possible to murder that many people? I scanned a long entry on World War II, but I couldn't find any further information on what had happened to the Jews.

In the middle of the night, I woke, remembering a book I'd bought from a Scholastic order form recently, called *Anne Frank: Diary of a Young Girl*, with a picture on the cover of a girl with dark, haunting eyes. It was 2:00 a.m. when I opened the book and read a few entries, about restrictions and yellow stars on sleeves and mysterious events.

Then I turned to the Afterword and skimmed, with growing horror, the summary of how Jews had been rounded up and sent on trains to concentration camps, where they'd been systematically murdered, herded to die in gas ovens or shot in groups by firing squads.

I read on to the section containing the biographical note, starting with Anne's birth date: June 12, 1929. My mom had been born three months before. My dad had been born the next week. I read about Anne Frank's death at Belsen while the red numbers on my clock clicked over: 3:00 a.m., 3:30. Finally I reluctantly closed the book and turned off the lamp, my mind racing so fast I didn't think I was ever going to sleep.

I awoke panicked from a dream that started to seem funny once I thought about it. In it, I'd been in a refugee camp, sitting on a long bench before a table, like in my elementary school cafeteria. As the director rolled out a cart, she made an announcement.

"There are two kinds of sandwiches," she said. "Tuna and kitten. You are to eat what you are served. Do not look inside your sandwich."

My sandwich felt heavy and warm. The trill of purring vibrated the bread. I slipped the kitten into my pocket and ate the bread, heart kicking into high gear as I watched others around me biting into sandwiches and trying not to gag. *Take the kittens out first*, I wanted to implore them. *Don't eat them. Hide them.* But I was too terrified to speak.

Now, afraid to turn off the light, afraid of rediscovering the terror still lurking there in the darkness, I reached for *Journey to America* and reread the first chapter, bolting up as I lit on a paragraph I didn't remember.

"I had read of wars," it said, " . . . even of people eating their pets in time of great hunger. . . . My mouth went dry with terror. My beautiful cat! What would become of him!"[5]

Reading that gave me chills. Somehow, my subconscious mind had picked up these details and circulated them back to me in my dream.

"Have you ever heard of Anne Frank?" I asked my mom the next morning while I poured my cereal. She shook her head. "She was your age," I said reproachfully. I didn't get how she could not have read Anne Frank's diary, why she showed so little interest in it now.

Everything seemed different to me that morning, as if my vision had shifted overnight. I moved through a strangely artificial world of bright lights, gossip and jokes, long black tables and Bunsen burners, the shocked knowledge of horrible things. I tried to tell Stacey and Marissa and Ruth F. and Ruth Y. and Kim about it but the words wouldn't come out right. "I read this book," I'd say, and their eyes glazed over. So instead, at lunch, I said, "I dreamed that I had to eat a kitten sandwich."

"Ugh," my friends all said. "Fried or baked?"

"Still alive, with all its fur," I said.

"Ugh," everyone said, looking dubiously at their own sandwiches.

I was mad at myself for turning what felt like a profound revelation into a gross story to horrify my friends. All day, I remembered the way I'd heard bones crunching while people in my dream ate their sandwiches. I remembered the kitten that snagged its claws against my pocket, how scared I was that it would meow and give me away, that kitten, something innocent and helpless that I couldn't protect.

Sometime that spring, I tried writing a story based on the time travel fantasy of my childhood, the one in which Laura Ingalls arrives in the 1970s from the 1870s.

She's amazed at cars and TVs. She gazes in wonder upon girls in shorts, at flush toilets and dishwashers. But then I hit a dead end. Taking the story to its logical conclusion was too disheartening, imagining what would happen when the novelty wore off, when my imaginary Laura's initial surprise and fascination and wariness gave way to the human tendency to start taking things for granted. Did I really want to corrupt Laura, to make her less satisfied with oranges and hard candy in her Christmas stocking, to see her trade Pa's fiddle for an eight-track tape player?

I went back to rereading the *Little House* books, anticipating the summer when I would spend a month with my cousin Jody, the closest thing to a sister I had. Ic-uagsclsurag and Abigmxs and Mindy were still somewhere out there in the world, I reassured myself, if only I could find them, and in the meantime, I would travel with Jody and my dying aunt to tourist sites related to Laura Ingalls Wilder. I barely mentioned the trip to my friends because I knew they wouldn't understand, but uneasily I anticipated it, trying not to think about my aunt's illness, vaguely expecting, hoping, that this trip would bring back to me the best parts of my disappearing childhood.

CHAPTER NINE

De Smet, South Dakota, and Mansfield, Missouri

By the Shores of Silver Lake, The Long Winter,
Little Town on the Prairie, These Happy Golden Years,
The First Four Years, and Where the Books
Were Written

I'VE ALWAYS FELT THAT IT WAS VERY WRONG OF ME, but despite my own childhood longing for a sister, I still find Mary extremely irritating, especially in *By the Shores of Silver Lake.* The child reader who buys into Laura's point of view, who identifies with her wholeheartedly as child readers tend to do, is almost inevitably going to feel a little hostility toward Laura's smug and golden older sister, particularly in the earlier books.

But in *Silver Lake,* these manipulations become even more layered and intriguing. I feel far more guilt at disliking Mary—I mean, the poor girl has just lost her sight and all of her life dreams. Two books later, in the opening of *Little Town on the Prairie,* the sisters have a revealing conversation about the tensions between them. Mary has become "light-hearted" and "serene," her "voice so gay that she did not seem to be walking in darkness." Laura admits to her that she used to want to slap her, a sentiment that I have shared. In turn, Mary admits that inside she sometimes still feels "rebellious and mean" and that she was never really "good," just showing off—"showing off to myself, what a good little girl I was, and being vain and proud, and I deserved to be slapped for it."[1]

The sisters' relationship is transformed to something more mature by this conversation; they can now move into a true friendship. And yet, more than forty years later, a subtle sibling rivalry has evidently outlived Mary enough to infuse the text;

the autobiographical nature of the writing, Wilder's lifelong insistence that every-thing in the books "really happened," lends a perpetual circularity to the interac-tion between the text and the life.

The fact is that close identification with Laura keeps pitting us against Mary as we read and reread the series. While this is a testament to Wilder and Lane's skill at bringing readers fully into the highly dimensional world of their protagonist, as an adult reader I can't help but feel that sometimes the deck is stacked against Lau-ra's older sister, that she is portrayed in ways designed to make us side against her, that this casts doubt on the transformation that *Little Town* portrays: does Mary re-ally gain such total peace, are the sisters really so firmly united, how can their ran-cor really be relegated to the past if the author can write about it so convincingly many years later and then it lives on and on in books that readers cycle through over and over again?

That *Little Town* reconciliation scene functions on many levels, mitigating the guilt of both the protagonist and the reader and seemingly representing an elder-ly author's continuing effort to come to terms with her relationship with her sister —and who can blame her? If we are to believe in the literal truth of these books, young Laura was robbed of her own childhood by Mary's disability. It became Laura's job to care for her sister and to be her eyes, describing the world for her, both a taxing duty and an essential part of Laura's training as a writer.

Furthermore, Laura eventually goes against her true nature to teach, work that makes her feel trapped and desperate, in order to raise money to send Mary away to school. Even in her sixties, Wilder portrays Mary with ambivalence, sometimes worshipful, devout in her admiration, yet sneaking in with a hint of vindictive glee Mary's occasional meanness.

And who can begrudge either sister a little passive aggression? Mary will never fulfill her life goal of becoming a teacher, and until the Ingalls family learns about schools for the blind and raises funds to send her to one, it appears that she will have no access to any kind of education, something that she has always valued high-ly. In episodes of the TV show first aired in March 1978, Mary loses her eyesight and rages at everyone, descends into depression, submits to hysteria, and lashes out in anger. I'd been watching the show with indignation for a few years, but this por-trayal of Mary pushed me over the edge, prompting the protest letter that Jody and I wrote to "Micheal" Landon. We scolded him for making Mary human instead of presenting her as a meek saint who passively accepts her fate. After all, Ma says in *Silver Lake*, "Mary has never once repined."[2]

So maybe in real life Mary didn't complain, fall into screaming fits, or cease to bathe or comb her hair. She may have somehow maintained decorum. But when

I read the books as an adult, I grudgingly concede that her anger is very much there, under the surface. Mary beats a hasty, self-protective retreat into a sanctimonious self who values platitudes. Who can blame her for, like Ma, recoiling against roughness, preferring a sheltered existence in contrast to Laura's restlessness? How many of us, if suddenly struck blind, wouldn't prefer the safety of home and family to unattainable notions of freedom and adventure? "It's nicer to be home," Mary says in *Little Town*,[3] and it's easy to understand how hard and isolating it may feel to her to be in crowds or outside on an open prairie where it is more difficult to be guided by landmarks. In contrast, roughness and danger appeal to Laura. "You and I want to fly like the birds," Pa says to Laura.[4] Laura is lonely and scared in the midst of town, feeling confined when the family moves to Pa's store.

As a child clinging to my own desire for safety, on some level I could relate to Mary and even admire the way she reshapes her dreams to accommodate her limitations. But still, like Laura, I sometimes wished to slap her. As Laura embraces her role as Mary's "eyes," describing the world for her, Mary can be ungrateful, frequently admonishing Laura for perceived inaccuracies. For instance, when Laura says, "The road . . . breaks off short," Mary scolds her, because logically, of course, the road continues to the lake no matter how it appears to the naked eye. Laura feels frustrated, thinking, "There were so many ways of seeing things and so many ways of saying them." The differences between the literal, logical older sister and the more imaginative, poetically inclined younger one emerge in stark relief as Laura struggles to interpret the visual world for her sister. "We should always be careful to say exactly what we mean," says Mary in a prissy way that for me as a child called into question her purported saint-like bearing. Earlier in the book, Mary has made Carrie miserable, scolding her for fidgeting, and though I find Mary's pride in her own perceptiveness, despite her lost eyesight, to be touching, I don't always like her at these moments.[5]

Laura is repeatedly reproved by Mary for her uses of language. Laura describes Big Jerry as "riding right into the sun," to which Mary replies, "Laura, you know he couldn't ride into the sun. He's just riding along on the ground like anybody." Again, Laura feels frustrated: "But Laura did not feel that she had told a lie. What she had said was true too." She is likewise scolded for saying that a shanty is "tiger striped,"[6] and that sheep sorrel tastes "like springtime." Mary will have none of this. In the latter example, Mary "gently corrected" her: "It really tastes a little like lemon flavoring, Laura."[7] The verb choice suggests that Wilder in her sixties still found these memories of Mary's jabs to be irritating—why else does she always say "Mary corrected" instead of "Mary said"? Why else does she so often present Mary as a stodgy stick-in-the-mud?

Throughout the books that take place in South Dakota, we see the lines being firmly drawn between Pa and Laura, Ma and Mary. When Laura and Pa agree that the prairie in South Dakota is different from other places they've lived, Ma says that of course it's different: "We're west of Minnesota, and north of Indian Territory, so naturally the flowers and grasses are not the same." "But that was not what Pa and Laura meant," Wilder writes. "There was really almost no difference in the flowers and grasses. But there was something else here that was not anywhere else. It was an enormous stillness that made you feel still. And when you were still, you could feel great stillness coming closer."[8] Ma doesn't get it. Mary doesn't get it. A divide cracks open, widens. Through another subtle trick of language, Laura aligns herself with Pa when she commits the same grammatical transgression as he does, both of them saying, "He don't." Only Laura is scolded for this error. But she is undeterred from choosing Pa's language instead of her mother and sister's.

Through details, Wilder demarcates the emerging factions. For the first time since *Big Woods*, there is a mention of Ma's delaine dress, an emblem of just what she has given up to follow her husband to this wild land. Furthermore, her disapproval of Indians is more virulent in this book than ever before. She refers to them as "howling savages" and makes a disgusted sound at the memory of their skunk skins. Laura refuses to accept Ma's assessment, although Laura's own perception is sometimes highly idealized. For instance, she notices admiringly that when the French-Indian Big Jerry rides, "The horse and the man moved together as if they were one animal."[9]

Sena Jeter Naslund pointed out in a lecture at Spalding University how much these books are about vision, early on occurring in the form of mistakes in vision, such as in *Big Woods* when Pa perceives danger when there is none and thinks a stump is a bear. Inversely, Ma, mistaking a bear for a cow, slaps it. By *Silver Lake*, Laura is struggling with the complications of language and vision, the frustrations of being corrected each time she tries to capture her own sense of the metaphorical, of nuances and underlying meanings. And despite her snippy moments, Mary does acknowledge Laura's gift for interpreting the world. "You make pictures when you talk," Mary says.[10]

The strictures that Ma and Mary place on Laura's grammar and try to impose on her vision are part and parcel of the increasing limitations on other aspects of Laura's behavior. Girls are enjoined "to speak nicely in low voices and have gentle manners and always be ladies." They are told that "a lady never did anything that could attract attention." Laura is forbidden from playing with a boisterous girl cousin who uses "wicked" words like "gosh." Ma may be objecting as much to Lena being a child of divorce as to her wild behavior—but the tidbit that Le-

na's mother is not only divorced but remarried is never explicitly stated, and mostly a speculation based on the circumstances of Wilder's own cousin Lena. Though
Laura is a "good girl," she feels a strong pull toward Lena, who races on ponies and
allows her to ride one: "She and the pony were going too fast but they were going
like music and nothing could happen to her until the music stopped."[11]

   In another episode in which Laura chafes at the restrictions on her freedom,
Mary is, once again, pleased with herself for seeing through Laura's deception when
Laura claims that her sunbonnet is on. In fact, as Mary realizes, Laura is hastily
donning it as she speaks. Meanwhile, I'm thinking *here we go with the sunbonnets again.*
Late in the book, Ma exclaims, "For pity's sake, Laura, put on your sunbonnet!" As
Laura obeys, her vision becomes firmly circumscribed, but this time not in a negative way; what she sees is instead what most matters to her: the sunbonnet's "slatted
sides" shut out her view of the town, so that all that remains in her line of vision is
"the green prairie and blue sky."[12] On the next page, Laura catches her first glimpse
of the man who will eventually become her husband, although in that moment she
is much more interested in his horses, the book's symbol of the nomadic, free-
spirited life to which she is attracted.

   Wilder never explicitly reveals any desire on the part of Laura to be a writer.
But in another example of the circularity between the life and work, we know that
she became one, and through that hindsight, the series transforms in the eyes of the
reader to a kind of Kunstlerroman. While *On the Shores of Silver Lake* picks up themes
from previous books like the tensions that pit adventure and freedom against civilization, home, and comfort, it also begins to define these tensions as part of Laura's
process of developing artistic vision. This theme will continue to unfold in other
books that take place in De Smet—*The Long Winter, Little Town on the Prairie,* and *These
Happy Golden Years.*

Sophie gets carsick easily and has complained about a stomachache ever since we
left Walnut Grove at 9:00 a.m. to head west on Highway 14 to De Smet. We arrive at 11:00, hot and grumpy, which is kind of a bummer since this town was the
setting of my favorite *Little House* books. This is the town where Wilder lived for
fifteen years, where she married Almanzo and gave birth to Rose, and where her
parents and Mary remained for the rest of their lives. This site should represent the
culmination of our trip, but all I want to do is find a place for Sophie to rest. I head
straight for our hotel and plead a sick child, but the desk clerk is indifferent. Our
room won't be ready until 3:00.

   Sophie says she might be hungry, so we go to the Oxbow Restaurant, established in 1976. I wonder if this restaurant had opened by the summer of 1976,

if this is one of the places where I ate one of my many grilled cheese sandwiches. In honor of that possibility, I order one, American on white bread. We sit below a shelf containing a Tennyson poetry collection, a Charlotte doll, and a china shepherdess, and I wonder how I ever subsisted on these tiny flat tasteless sandwiches.

It was in a café like this one thirty-one years ago, maybe even this one, where my aunt said to Jody, "You're like me. We read books we love over and over."

"So do I," I said.

"I don't know many people like that," Aunt Shirley told Jody, ignoring me. I'd felt excluded at school, with my friends suddenly obsessed with boys. But whatever uneasiness I felt about my aunt's illness, I thought of my aunt and cousin as members of my tribe who loved books as much as I did. And suddenly, I was being left out of this conversation, too.

Maybe my aunt sensed how uncomfortable I sometimes felt around her, how uncomfortable and guilty and scared it made me to watch her deteriorate. Her face had turned moony from the steroids, her movements slow from the disease. Her words sometimes were edged like the little serrations on a butter knife, seeming harmless at first but able to cut deep.

Now, years later, sitting in the Oxbow Restaurant, that bad feeling from my last visit to De Smet returns to me full force. I remember how all of the talkative enthusiasm of the first part of the trip had given way to tired silence, everyone dragging, seeming stern and distant. I felt drained from the heat, disillusioned, left out, my stomach churning. I was miserable, not able to belong to the same club as my cousin and my aunt, not able to belong anywhere, but temporarily unable to retreat to some space of my own, to read a book or think or write, to re-inhabit myself again. I identified strongly with Laura, wishing I could take refuge in my own version of an open prairie with untamed horses and fewer restrictions.

At the beginning of *The Long Winter*, Laura is still struggling with her attraction to wildness over civilization, still pulled toward a world that her gender precludes her from fully joining. Laura can't quite figure out how to belong anywhere, either. In the opening pages, she dreads moving to town; she's described as "as stout as a little French horse," an image that emphasizes her strength and identifies her with the natural world; and she and Pa have a discussion of free will, which is, Pa says, what separates humans from animals.[13] And yet sometimes free will doesn't mean much in the face of the brutality of nature, as when Laura and Carrie become lost in prairie grass, a scene that echoes an earlier one from *Silver Lake* and prefigures the family's helplessness when blizzards strike.

In that previous scene from *Silver Lake*, youngest sister Grace disappears, and there is a startling shift of point of view, the only break in the gentle third person rhythms of the entire series. All of a sudden, as Laura searches for her sister, the narrative voice turns to first person: "Oh, baby sister, I couldn't see you anywhere east or south on this hateful prairie."[14] In this cry of anguish, we hear Laura's fierce protectiveness of her sisters, her lament at what she's lost, her acknowledgment that sometimes the land she loves can betray her.

Grace is ultimately found, of course, and likewise, in *Long Winter* Laura and Carrie find their way, emerging from the prairie grass to discover Almanzo Wilder lying atop a stack of hay.[15] That Laura catches sight of him at the moment of safety subtly foreshadows Almanzo and Royal Wilder's heroic mission to save the town from starvation later in the book. Almanzo can lounge around lazily, tied to no one's schedule but his own, but he is also brave enough to venture out into harrowing conditions to bolster his community. He represents an appealing balance of the impulses that drive Laura, her longings for both freedom and safety. His brash courage and refusal of others' rules while still upholding the basic tenets of civilization begin to overshadow even Pa's adventurous spirit; Pa, after all, always has to consider the needs of his wife and daughters, whereas the unattached Almanzo is far more free to act as he chooses.

Still, although Pa may see himself as separated from animals by free will, like Laura he continues to be identified with nature through the book's imagery. He can't bring himself to shoot the jackrabbits that take refuge in his hay during a storm, and later he uses his fiddle to imitate the wind. Pa observes that the weather "seems to be holding back something that it might let loose any minute. If I were a wild animal, I'd hunt my hole and dig it plenty deep. If I were a wild goose, I'd spread my wings and get out of here."[16] This quote, of course, embodies the contradictory impulses that haunt both him and Laura: the desire to burrow down deep, the desire to flee.

But when the weather lets loose, all of this is moot. Everyone has to pull together to survive. Children become lost in snowstorms that leave them with bleeding eyelids; over and over, we hear about the nails in Laura's walls that are white with frost each morning, the house often buried in snow. The Ingallses struggle to stretch their small stores of food, they twist hay to burn, and they rely on imagination and art—reading, reciting, playing music—for psychic survival. And here is where Pa's powers begin to fade, the comfort he has always offered through song and nature vanishing in the terrible low point where he finally just can't play anymore. Nature is too treacherous; songs fail him. It is up to Almanzo and his brother to bring hope to the town again.

While *Little House in the Big Woods* offers the reader Pa's voice through the stories he tells, the point of view has stayed consistently Laura's through the rest of the series. But now, in *Long Winter*, whole sections are given over to Almanzo's point of view as he and Royal go out in the blizzard in search of food, as if Almanzo is starting to edge out Pa in Laura's imagination. As a child, I skimmed these parts. I wanted to stay with Laura. And as an adult, my first impression of these shifts is that they emphasize Laura's lack of freedom to move in the world, so that her perspective must disappear entirely if we're to leave behind the claustrophobic small space to which she is confined.

Sena Jeter Naslund interprets this shift in a much more positive light. In her Spalding lecture, she discussed the gradual movement throughout the books from Laura telling others' stories and imagining others' actions in limited ways to finally going all out in this book. In *Big Woods*, she has reproduced Pa's stories in his words; by *Prairie*, she has moved on to picturing what Ma is doing when she goes to the barn in a snowstorm, and Laura continues the process of breaking free of the boundaries of her own point of view when, in *Plum Creek*, she envisions the chores that Ma is performing out in the blizzard. Stories and songs throughout the books are another way of shifting out of her own immediate field of vision. And so, while the constraints on Laura as a girl intensify in the series' last four books, Sena sees the shift into Almanzo's point of view as a kind of ultimate power that Laura claims; she's the one writing the book, after all, the one allowed to rove anywhere in her imagination, exercising her omniscient ability to go where she chooses, including the minds and experiences of her characters. I love this interpretation, the subtle making of a writer that it documents and the triumph that it implies, the suggestion that the series is finally more about the way Laura's world opens up than the ways that it closes down. Still, the specter of the author Laura Ingalls Wilder haunts me, the woman who didn't believe in women's suffrage, which doesn't quite jibe for me with the young Laura who chomps at the bit and wishes to occupy a world where women aren't entirely welcome.

Laura never reconciles herself to De Smet, which she thinks of as "a sore" on the prairie.[17] I can see why, since the heat today is so blistering that it's hard to imagine cold or ice or snow in this town that ironically thrives because of the tourist industry brought by the very books that describe it in such negative terms. Sophie is flushed, though her stomach seems a bit more stable now. It's still too early to check into our hotel, so we drive to the museum, and, as usual, are directed to start our tour in the gift shop.

"Wow, it's hot," I say to the clerk. "How hot do you think it is?"

"Oh, I know," she answers without speculating about the temperature, though I really want to know. After years in northwestern Pennsylvania, I'm not used to heat like this.

We buy our tickets and browse through $75 sunbonnet-dress combinations and $35 Charlotte dolls. I hear a mother and daughter from North Carolina tell the guide that they are visiting Laura Ingalls Wilder sites to celebrate the daughter's thirtieth birthday.

"We were in Mansfield a few days ago," the mother says. "When a member of our tour group saw Pa's fiddle, she burst into tears."

"Yeah," the tour guide says. "It's not that unusual for visitors to cry."

"It's kind of a pilgrimage," the mother says. "But it was also 107 that day."

"Hmm," says our guide, a sixteen-year-old named Kiley, without commenting on today's heat. I wonder if employees have been instructed not to reveal the temperature. Maybe that's bad for business.

Kiley starts our tour, telling us that during the worst winter she can recall, in 1996 when she was six, she remembers lying in bed while her mother read *The Long Winter* aloud.

Within five minutes we've established that the three adults on this tour are all passionate readers who reread the series recently and dipped into some biographies as well. It's not many sixteen-year-olds who would have the poise and flexibility to assess the situation, adjust for the knowledge level and interests of her group, drop her tour guide spiel, and turn a tour into a conversation. Kiley manages this effortlessly as she leads us into the surveyors' house.

When the Ingallses move into this house in *Silver Lake*, Laura is astonished at how big it is, with a large front room, wood floors, glass windows, a bedroom, an attic, a pantry: "Laura thought there must be a great many surveyors to need so much space."[18] By our standards, the house is tiny. In the front room, Kiley points out displays of hay twists, wheat, and the kind of coffee grinder used to make bread flour during the long winter described in the powerful and harrowing book by the same name, structurally probably the tightest in the series. Though the Ingallses lived in the surveyors' house in 1879–1880, and the next book and the terrible winter it describes take place in 1882, it is the events of *The Long Winter* that dominate our imaginations as we walk through this house.

Early in *Town*, Laura says, "The prairie looks beautiful and gentle . . . but . . . seems like we have to fight it all the time." Though Ma responds with one of her platitudes, this one seems deeply felt: "This early life is a battle . . . the sooner you make up your mind to that, the better off you are, and the more thankful for your pleasures."[19] By the end of *The Long Winter*, Laura knows better than ever before the brutality of nature and is even more grateful for her pleasures; the gratitude that infuses all of the books becomes correspondingly intensified.

As we wander through the small rooms of the surveyors' house, I glance absently at the pantry, the lean-to, and the what-not shelf the real Pa made for the real Ma. One of the other women, the mother, says, "I'm really haunted by Mrs. Brewster in *These Happy Golden Years*. How old do you think she was—seventeen? Eighteen?"

"Young," Kiley agrees, and we look at her, struck by the idea that Mrs. Brewster was probably not much older than this slight girl in a sunbonnet and long cotton dress leading our tour. It's the second time on this trip that another visitor has brought up that knife-in-the-dark episode from *These Happy Golden Years*. It's one of those that sticks with you. When I was a child, the name "Mrs. Brewster" alone evoked an old hag, a woman in a black dress and pointy hat stirring her witches' brew. As an adult I realize that the sour, frightening woman in whose home Laura is forced to board while she teaches school was just a young, lonely, isolated teenager who'd left behind her family to follow her husband to the middle of nowhere.

We all pause, remembering the poor young woman who is viewed without mercy by the terrified Laura, who dismisses her as "a selfish mean woman."[20] I'm not entirely sure if the failure of compassion comes from the writer in her sixties or is just a function of the point of view of young Laura. The narrative voice presents Mrs. Brewster matter-of-factly, but gives us enough detail to regard her with far more understanding than Laura does. I missed this as a child, but now, as an adult, I see that Mrs. Brewster is the Madwoman in the Attic, the flip side of Laura, the woman without choices, the danger of what a person could become on the relentlessly unforgiving prairie.

Ann Romines writes about this same episode, recalling childhood perceptions of it that I find startlingly similar to my own, right down to the language she uses to describe it. She remembers Mrs. Brewster as "a creation of near-Gothic horror, nightmare fodder" and had long recalled "a chilling illustration . . . of Mrs. Brewster in the darkened bedroom, wielding her butcher knife." Eventually she realized that she was mixing up *These Happy Golden Years* with the edition of *Jane Eyre* she had read in early adolescence and picturing an engraving of Bertha Mason Rochester, "the prototypical Madwoman in the Attic, with wild hair and bestial features, leaning over the bed of another terrified young teacher, Jane Eyre. Bertha—trapped, desperate, and mad—is Jane Eyre's potential double, just as Mrs. Brewster is Laura's."[21] The edition of Wilder that I read as a child does have a Garth Williams illustration that, I realize, could also be straight out of Brontë. In it, a figure with scraggly dark hair and a flowing light gown approaches Mr. Brewster's bed with a large knife while Laura peers from a curtained partition that separates her own sleeping space from theirs.

The quick perking up of interest, the sudden shared connection of mutual Laura Ingalls Wilder fans never fails to amaze me, whether on a tour or in my daily life. When my new colleague Dani first arrived on campus, she told me that one of her favorite moments in the whole series is in *Little Town on the Prairie*, when Laura stands up to the new teacher, the cruel Eliza Jane Wilder, another young woman who in real life was in over her head. Carrie has been swaying while studying, causing her seat to rock, and, annoyed, Miss Wilder orders her to put away her books and "Just rock that seat!"[22] Reminiscing about this episode, Dani quotes her: "Just rock that seat!" But Carrie is too small to keep it moving, and Laura takes over, rocking that seat so loudly and vindictively that she and Carrie are sent home in disgrace.

Like Dani, I loved this part when I was young, and that quote brings it all back: "Just rock that seat!" I connected strongly to this book in general, probably because it focuses more on human conflict than the struggles against nature that often prevail. I especially liked Laura's battle with Eliza Jane, her villainous future sister-in-law, nicknamed "Lazy Lousy Lizy Jane" in a rhyme Laura assists in writing.[23] The portrayal of Eliza Jane Wilder is so ruthlessly negative that it surprised me to later learn that her real life counterpart was, if not a very good teacher, quite an interesting and progressive woman for her time, a single woman who accompanied her brothers to South Dakota and homesteaded her own land. In later life, she took in Rose during her high school years and gave her substantial help in completing her education. But more than fifty years after the young teacher sided against Laura, accused her falsely, and picked on Carrie, Wilder exacts her revenge, locking Eliza Jane for posterity in this irredeemably incompetent, cruel image, a portrayal in which Rose appears to have been complicit. As a child, I relished the story of strong-willed Laura's strength in the face of adversity and of her ultimate triumph; these chapters profoundly shaped my childhood belief that false accusations required no defense or retaliation, that the truth always comes out, and that a good person abides with dignity until that happens. It took me many years to conclude that sometimes the truth never comes out, or if it does, sometimes it comes out too late to do you any good.

Laura's victory, achieved through silence rather than speech, reinforced for me that a girl's best recourse was to keep quiet. And as Laura wages a war between duty and desire, she learns not to speak up, not to complain; a woman's voice, Ma reminds her, should be "ever gentle, low, and soft, an excellent thing in a woman"—a quote that I initially thought was Biblical, but later discovered was from *King Lear.*

Laura realizes that Ma hates sewing, but does it uncomplainingly because it's her duty. After an outburst against the pressures of having to study all the time in order to earn her teaching certificate at fifteen and provide her sister an education—a frustration that seems to me overdue given the responsibilities heaped upon the teenaged girl—Ma scolds her for "wooden swearing."[24] Laura doesn't swear, but her tone has suggested that she might possibly want to, and the mere possibility of this desire merits a reprimand. Even an all-too-human expression of exhaustion is too unladylike to be borne.

Ma advises Laura to tighten her corset and takes the girls to task for not wearing their corsets at night to keep their figures trim. By the time Laura cuts her bangs into a "lunatic fringe," we know that this is the closest she'll ever come to being truly unconventional.[25] The name of the hairstyle provides a subtle, jokey warning against anyone who strays too far. Who can hold it against Laura when, dreading teaching school, she gains new hope as she realizes that marriage could be a way out?

At the house built by Pa, where he, Ma, and Mary lived out the rest of their lives, our tour group expands to thirteen and we acquire a new guide, this time a middle-aged one.

"Wow, it's hot," I say. "What do you think the temperature is today?"

"Oh, I know," says the guide.

In the living room, she delivers a long speech about the Ingallses' life in De Smet. This room, we learn, was reconstructed from a photo Rose took with a box camera. The wallpaper was designed to match the snapshot, although the hues had to be estimated according to popular colors of the time.

Finally we're set free to wander around looking at family photos, Mary's pump organ, displays of beadwork and quilts, and Mary's Braille Bible. A young tour guide lets Sophie and me behind the rope to sit on Mary's squishy feather bed.

I remember the increasing feeling I had when I was thirteen that these were not people I would have liked. I remember the vague sense I had of them as narrow minded and mean-spirited and middle-aged and boring, real people who were nothing like the characters based on them. The irony of the tourist site is that we travel back to relive our experience of the book and yet the visit must inevitably spoil the illusion. But I don't remember what specific details spoiled my illusions in 1976. I don't even recall which displays that I'm viewing now were here all those years ago.

Like the one upstairs, a room reconstructed with things of Rose's, including a ponderous desk. I don't remember this room, but my memory prickles as I read a card next to the door, a paragraph that touts Rose's famous patriotism. A deliveryman from Latvia had confessed to Rose what a difficult time he was having making a living in America. Rose was so offended that she shouted at the man over and over as he retreated down the street, "Just go back to Russia!"

I feel nauseated. This is something to brag about, such an oppressive, uncompassionate manifestation of national loyalty? As my Chinese American daughter peers into the room, I find myself body-blocking the sign. Sophie has ambivalent feelings about being uprooted from the country of her birth and planted in another country that regularly declares its superiority to the rest of the world. She knows enough about the US's history of racial discrimination to be hesitant about embracing American ideals wholeheartedly. Would Rose have yelled at my complicated child, "Go back to China"?

When I was thirteen, I didn't know that I would grow up to parent a daughter from China. While I wasn't comfortable with Ma's attitude toward Indians, I certainly didn't recognize other more subtle but equally disturbing assumptions about race. Nor did I question what appeared to be Wilder's dismissal of a desperate eighteen-year-old pioneer wife. But this anecdote about Rose would have troubled me. And I wonder if this is the location, here in front of this door thirty years ago, where I made my final wrenching break with the *Little House* series. Was this the last straw, or was it a slow accumulation of various impressions that left me feeling so uneasy with the books?

The question of Rose Wilder Lane's role in the writing of the *Little House* books has continued to nag at me this whole trip. Wilder sites have, so far, skirted the issue, reminding me of how, when I was in my twenties, my mother and Aunt Gena expressed hostility about the very notion that Laura didn't write them alone. Maybe, even when I was thirteen, Aunt Shirley sensed that I was starting to break away from strongly held family opinions, that I would someday be fascinated by such ideas as the troubled, complex relationship between Laura and Rose that William Holtz describes in *Ghost in the Little House*. It enriched the series for me to imagine them as the products of the love and frustration of a mother and daughter, agendas and memories grudgingly merged, entering the past to make imperfect sense of each other.

Now, I get up my courage as I return downstairs. I approach the middle-aged tour guide and ask her, "What do you think about the scholarship suggesting that the books are a collaboration between Laura and Rose?"

"Laura was a professional writer," the tour guide says. "Rose certainly was her encourager and did some editing of Laura's work, but if you compare writing styles, the books read very differently from Rose's."

"But if you put Laura's manuscripts alongside the published work, they read pretty differently, too," I say. "It seems to me that a collaboration would have read differently from each of their individual work."

"Laura *was* a professional writer," the tour guide says. Her gaze darts away from me.

"Have you read any of the scholarship or compared the manuscripts?" I ask.

"I just know that Rose helped out. She didn't write the books," the woman says. She seems agitated. She excuses herself.

Nobody may ever know for sure what Rose's role was, but in larger if more abstract ways, the whole Wilder series is a metaphorical collaboration between Laura and her dead parents and sister. Whatever sibling rivalry lingers in the text, there is also a subtle tribute to Mary, who confesses in *These Happy Golden Years* that she wants to write a book someday—or maybe, she acknowledges, as with teaching, Laura can do it for her.[26] Perhaps Wilder's memory of that comment was one of the motivating forces that led her to write these books, particularly the first two, which are based as much on Mary's memories as her own.

Certainly the presence of Mary pervades every page far more than that of Wilder's younger sisters—after all, when I was a child we did call them the "Laura and Mary books"—and the daughter's hand is also evident even if the extent of her contribution is not. Rereading *The Long Winter*, I was struck by what a tight and suspenseful book it is, and it didn't surprise me to read in John E. Miller's *Becoming Laura* that this was the one that received the most reworking by Rose, who had once tried to write her own novel about the same legendary winter.[27] *Little Town on the Prairie* begins with a little prologue that bears Rose's stamp, one that establishes tension about the idea of young Laura going to work in town, among strangers, assisting a local seamstress, an idea that Ma and Laura's sisters find positively scandalous. This episode is also heavily fictionalized, since the real-life family had worked under much rougher circumstances not long before at the Master's Hotel. But it's an episode that lends a shape to the book, setting up a conflict about Laura's gradual emergence into the outside world.

I understand the protectiveness of the guide toward Wilder, as if to admit to a collaboration, would, in detracting from the myth of single authorship, diminish her achievement. It hasn't been that long since librarians of my childhood were horrified by series like Nancy Drew, given the ingrained assumption that ghostwriters or collaborative processes implied a violation of public trust or a compromise of artistic integrity. Now, of course, critics have reconsidered once widely accepted stances on collaboration and literary authority. The myth of single authorship is, it turns out, a relatively recent invention by "a bourgeois culture obsessed with individualism, individual rights and the myth of progress," writes Stanley Fish. "In earlier periods works of art were produced in workshops by teams; the master artisan may have signed them, but they were communal products."[28]

The idea of artistic genius that operates independently hangs on firmly in popular culture, allowing for a tradition that historically left the contributions of assistants, in particular wives, unacknowledged. In addition, children's literature has often been regarded less seriously than that written for adults, leading to a natural defensiveness among many who read and write children's books—a defensiveness that's predictably even more pronounced in the face of the stigmas surrounding series fiction that were reinforced by the genericism of productions of the Stratemeyer Syndicate. No wonder so many Laura Ingalls Wilder fans are protective of her image as the single author of these books, one whose reputation could be unfairly harmed by giving Rose Wilder Lane too much credit.

It's only 2:00 p.m. Our hotel room won't be ready for another hour. Sophie insists that she feels better, so we drive out to the Homestead, a complex of hands-on activities geared to children. This place, built on the site of the Ingalls family's claim shanty, wasn't here in 1976. I pay admission in the roomy log gift shop. "Sure is hot," I say. "Do you know how hot it is today?"

"Oh, it's not so bad in the shade," the clerk says.

I'm pretty sure that in the Midwest of my childhood, people relished exaggerating the temperatures, taking pride in our own hardiness. I'm regretful that protecting the tourist industry seems to be more important than bonding over hardship. Or maybe that's not it at all. I have a Pennsylvania license plate, so maybe they don't know I'm one of them. Maybe they're just showing the stoic faces that many midwesterners turn to outsiders.

Sophie and I hike down a treeless hill planted with prairie grasses, pausing to glance at a dugout replica before continuing to a cabin where a woman shows Sophie how to make a button string and weave a rag rug. She invites Sophie to lift a heavy iron and play a pump organ. Sophie gamely does both but sends me a look of pure despair.

She is more interested in running a cloth through an old-fashioned washing machine and a wringer, then hanging it out to dry. We decide to move on. "But you haven't done the Braille activity," the woman protests. I tell her that we'll come back.

At a barn with a stagecoach on display upstairs and a window with a view of miniature horses ranging around a nearby field, we wait for a wagon ride. Our driver is a young man, probably a high school student, who invites Sophie to take a turn at driving. She leads us in a zigzag, right off the path and on again, but we finally arrive, parched, at a one-room schoolhouse.

I sit in the back, sipping from the bottle of water I bought from the refrigerator in the entryway, as a guide directs the children to put on pioneer clothes, long dresses, bonnets, and aprons for the girls, knickers, vests, and caps for the boys. Sophie looks at me and sighs. She covets my adult freedom to just sit in the back of the room and not be expected to parade around in the heat in layers of clothing. The children march between the desks, then finally take seats for a mock school session.

Sophie resigns herself and then even kind of gets into it. The guide presents a Mother Goose riddle:

In marble walls as white as milk
Lined with a skin as soft as silk
Within a fountain crystal clear
A golden apple doth appear.
No doors there are to this stronghold,
Yet thieves break in and steal the gold.

Kids raise their hands, guessing the answer. "A fairy tale?" says one. "A coffin?" asks another.

Sophie raises her hand. "An egg," she says. I'm proud.

We bump and jostle back to the barn in the back of the wagon. By the time we disembark, Sophie's feeling sick again. We skip the Braille activity at the cabin and head back to town.

We pass signs along the way: "Abortion Stops a Beating Heart." "Pray to End Abortion." Next to our hotel, there's a field of white crosses in honor of aborted babies. There are no signs that say "Pray to end poverty" or "Pray to end ignorance" or "Pray to end lack of compassion." I'm getting pretty cranky. I park at the hotel and Sophie whips open the car door and runs to throw up in the bushes.

I check in and get my key to our second floor room before carrying Sophie from the car. She is flushed and limp in my arms. "Where's the elevator?" I ask the guy at the desk. He glares at me. "There are only twelve steps," he says, gesturing at the staircase that leads to the second floor.

I look up bleakly. I normally take stairs, but today I really, really want an elevator, even if, at forty pounds, Sophie's not that heavy. I hitch her up and slowly climb. I deposit her on a bed and head back downstairs for our bags, lugging them upstairs while the man stands and watches.

In the room, we crank on the air conditioner and Sophie drifts right off. After eating a sandwich I bring her from a Subway down the street, she says she feels a little better and claims she's up to attending the pageant, "These Happy Golden Years." So we head out into the heat once again.

The play sticks close to the books and the girl who plays Laura gets her right: sensible, practical, dutiful, spunky, and outspoken. And like the book *These Happy Golden Years*, the play ends, well, happily. We walk quietly through the dark to our car and drive back to the hotel. Despite the uplifting ending, though, I can't entirely shake my bad mood.

My original set of yellow *Little House* paperbacks stopped with *These Happy Golden Years*. But in more recent years the boxed set has been expanded to accommodate a slim little addition, Wilder's *The First Four Years*, a book whose dark mood echoes the one that has settled over me twice, thirty years apart, in De Smet. This book strikes me as proof that Lane must have had a hand in the others because Wilder wrote this one on her own. As a child, I didn't like it and read it only once, and as an adult, I understand why: it's shapeless, dire and Biblical in its repetitions, lacking the confident narrative structure and sharp narrative control of the other books, its point of view a kind of faltering omniscience as it recounts dismal facts about the hardships through which pioneer girl Laura transforms into a farmer's wife.

Reading along, I felt palpable relief when I reached the chapter "A Year of Grace." I assumed that "grace" referred to a reprieve from battles and sorrows. It just seemed to me that at some point things had to improve. But it turns out that the year of grace contains no grace at all. It is simply the period that Laura agrees to permit Almanzo to try farming for just a little longer, but to no avail. Their baby dies, their house burns, their crops fail, their debt increases, and Almanzo is permanently crippled after diphtheria and a stroke. The relentlessness of this book caused me to long for the shaping hand of Rose, politics and all.

In my twenties, I wrote an essay about the terrible disappointment I'd felt at thirteen in De Smet, that dark feeling of disillusionment that I also experience when I read *The First Four Years* and that seems to have settled over me now, so many years later. When I was thirteen, I couldn't figure out what to make of it. I decided that I'd been disconcerted by how boring and ordinary the Wilders were, after all, how without glamour, although in fact Laura Ingalls Wilder's official author photo taken when she was in her sixties shows a beautiful, gentle face. Maybe, I've always thought, I was disenchanted to discover that a simple way of life and the people who lived it were far more complex than I'd assumed. But now, as I get ready for bed in our De Smet hotel, it seems to me that there was more to my disillusionment than that.

I remember how, during the last days of the trip with my aunt and uncle and cousins, I was ready to go home. And then, throughout my junior high and high school years, as my classmates longed for nothing more than to someday get out of Kansas, to go to more exciting places, I just shrugged. Kansas was fine with me. If anyone asked where I wanted to live someday, I was stumped. The where never mattered to me nearly as much as the how. I knew only that I wanted to have lots of time to myself. I wanted to read and write and think and dream. I dreaded the reality that these might not be adequate life goals. I dreaded the knowledge that I might have to compress myself into expected roles, squish myself to be what others wanted. I longed, like Pa before the winter, to burrow down deep. But I knew that instead I might have to flee.

One second I'm lying in my hotel bed in De Smet, thinking about this as I drift off to sleep, and the next I'm sitting up, wide awake, electric with the realization that the last time I was here, my process of leaving home was just beginning. At thirteen, recognition was beginning to edge into my consciousness. I was starting to understand that I didn't want to live in a world that negated who I was or adapt to a life that went against my grain, and that the world of my childhood, shaped by the values of these warm homespun books, might be one of those places where I could not belong.

Despite my dread of the world outside, I was starting to realize that I was going to have to leave behind my childhood insulation. Laura's own choice seemed so easy, after living a life as a teacher that was completely unsuited to her, to escape by marrying at eighteen. Not that making a living was ever easy for her and Almanzo. But now I wonder how much Wilder's books and that trip when I was thirteen planted the seeds that led me to marry too young, almost as young as Laura, that filled me with terror about unfulfilled dreams as I watched my aunt's fade, that showed me that someday I was going to have to not just figure out how to make a living, but to walk away from my conservative, religious upbringing and build a life that didn't negate that, either.

The morning after the pageant, I wake antsy to get back on the road, out of De Smet. The man at the front desk, the one who scorned me yesterday when I asked for an elevator, mentioned to me several times that there were twenty-seven food items included in the hotel's free continental breakfast. We have been dreaming of fruit and bacon and eggs, but it turns out that the breakfast choices consist mostly of toast and cereal. We count the items to see if there are really twenty-seven, and indeed there are: two kinds of butter (regular and low fat), two flavors of syrup (maple and low-fat maple), one kind of cream cheese, three flavors of jelly, packets of honey, four kinds of bread, four kinds of cookies, and four brands of stale cereal. Waffles, coffee, water, and three kinds of juice round out the twenty-seven breakfast choices.

Somehow this all seems to me symbolic as I drive out of town. This was how circumscribed my choices felt at points in my childhood, what weighed on me so heavily when I was thirteen. Would I choose white bread or wheat, marriage and three children or marriage and four children, Sundays at a Baptist or Disciples of Christ church, a career as a teacher who wrote at night or one as a writer of the blurbs on the backs of books, a house in the country or one in the city? It never occurred to me back then that I could get married and then divorced or choose to adopt a baby as a single parent, that I could talk about books and writing for a living and not go to any church at all.

I was the product of books that seemed to promote nonconformity, creativity, and independence, but usually came out in favor of caretaking, family, community, and sacrifice. Thirty-one years ago, the tensions between these values were beginning to come to a head for me. I left De Smet feeling overwhelmed and scared, constrained and oppressed, afraid of the new knowledge that the world I'd grown up in was not the world where I was going to be able to stay. Now, all these years later, I instead feel giddy with happiness that I can return to the life I've made for myself, for the freedom I have as an adult that I never would have imagined at thirteen.

Passing through Mansfield, Missouri, on our way home is, I think, something of a formality, a necessary last stop after two weeks on the road, two weeks of log houses, sod houses, dugouts, old churches, schoolhouses, post offices, banks, jails, and depots, replica violins and china shepherdesses and Charlotte dolls, hand-dug wells and pump organs.

Retracing the path of Laura Ingalls Wilder has meant retracing my own journey, passing through places I once lived: Lincoln, Nebraska; Wichita, Kansas; Springfield, Missouri. When we leave Mansfield we will pass through Houston, Missouri, and see signs for Raymondsville, my mother's childhood home. I don't relate to the desire to keep on pressing west, but I realize that I have uprooted my life again and again in pursuit of a dream, looking for the life that felt right for me.

Rose Wilder Lane described her parents' motivation to move to Missouri as the "courage of despair."[29] I have experienced that courage of despair many times in my own life, that hopeful impulse to uproot myself to look for something better, in my case an MFA in one state, a PhD in another, three teaching jobs in three additional states. I can understand how barren Missouri, which my grandmother complained was nothing but rocks and sticks, could have represented a fresh start to the Wilders, a chance to start anew.

I've been to Mansfield several times, at least twice in my childhood and once in my twenties. The Laura Ingalls Wilder house and museum at Rocky Ridge Farm is the mother lode of memorabilia, smug in its riches compared to the poverty of where we've been. Rocky Ridge Farm is such a contrast to all those other sites that had to make do with replicas and period pieces that didn't actually belong to the Ingallses, but had been owned by the granddaughter of a minor character or resembled pieces of furniture or items of clothing mentioned in one of the books. Here, finally, is the real fiddle that belonged to Pa, the real bread plate that says, "Give us this day our daily bread," dishes, name cards, a table made from a cypress tree, a lamp fashioned from a cactus by Almanzo, who Sophie keeps calling "Orlando." Here are a needlepointed horse pillow made by Almanzo, Laura's dresses and a shawl she crocheted, handwritten manuscripts on yellowed tablet paper, and Mary's Braille slate and nine-patch quilt.

Sophie announces that she wants to live in the farmhouse built by Almanzo and Laura. We tour it with at least twenty other people, too many, sometimes, to fit into the rooms all at once. Our tour guide, whose feet hurt because she forgot to change out of her heels after Sunday School, tells us that we are one of three tours running that hour; 400,000 people a year come through this house described by one of the brochures as the home of "the greatly loved and internationally known authoress" whose daughter was also "a noted authoress in her own right."

As we wander through the rooms, I remember scattered images from my previous visits. Wilder's school tablet manuscripts, the wide-armed chairs where she sat to write, the narrow bed she slept in, the tour guide says, when she'd been up late working and didn't want to disturb Almanzo. Standing here, I am thirteen again, gazing past red velvet ropes at the living room, wishing I could see the books in Laura's library, the low shelves custom-built for her 4'11" height. Aunt Shirley comes up behind me. She silently ponders the living room and library. And then she says thoughtfully, "This makes writers seem pretty ordinary, doesn't it?"

I've always heard that you can't make a living as a writer. For years I've planned to be a teacher like my mom and write in my spare time, as a hobby. But then, last year, in seventh grade history class, my teacher started talking about Italy, where there are both mountains and beaches. A picture flashed through my mind: me sitting at a table, writing books, looking out the window at snow-capped mountains in the distance, listening to the crash of water on sand outside my door. And I thought: I don't have to be a teacher. I can be a writer and live in Italy.

I'm not really sure how I can fulfill this dream. But standing in Laura's house among all of her ordinary possessions, listening to my aunt's words, is like another revelation. Standing there among these remnants of an ordinary life in which writing and books mattered, I'm transformed. Thirty-one years later, remembering this, it's like a jolt of energy shoots through me, like that moment after an illness when I finally sit up in bed and open a book and start reading, or pick up a pen and paper and start writing, and suddenly I'm filled with unexpected joy, remembering: *This is my life. This is what I do.*

The Rock House, a gorgeous structure of native stone built by Lane as a retirement house for her parents, wasn't open during my earlier visits to Mansfield, but now it is. It has big windows and yellow and green rooms that overlook tall trees and rolling hills. Sophie wants to live here, too.

Lane was so particular, the guide says, that she made the contractors rebuild the chimney four times. This information is received with eye rolls and head shakes all around. I'm obviously not crazy about the image of Lane I've constructed through my own reading. So I don't know why I find it so irritating that instead of considering that she might have been a detail-oriented craftsperson or caring daughter who wanted the house to be just right for her parents, everyone immediately assumes that she was a domineering battle-axe. "Laura probably moved here to escape Rose," cracks one of the men in our group, and I find myself on the verge of defending Lane: without her particularity, neither the house nor the books would be so precise in their design. Grudgingly, I give her credit.

At the cemetery where the Wilders and Lane are buried, Sophie yells greetings at the earth above Laura's, Almanzo's, and Rose's graves. Rose's stone is as stern and dominant and militant as legend has her personality, a Thomas Paine quote carved on it: "An army of principles will penetrate where an army of soldiers cannot. Neither the channel nor the Rhine will arrest its progress; it will march on the horizon of the world and it will conquer."

I'm not really sure what this means, exactly, or why this quote was so important to Lane, who is credited with helping to inspire the modern libertarian movement. This gravestone seems as out of place in this cemetery as Lane was as a child growing up in Mansfield, where she was too smart and independent to fit in, a place she left young but came back to again and again because it's where her parents were.

And here they are still, sharing one marker labeled "Wilder," with only their dates and names, Almanzo James and Laura Ingalls, simple and somehow eloquent next to Rose's stone that is crowded with all the words that will fit.

We drive through Missouri and Ohio, passing billboards lamenting the "Aborted States of America" and instructing, "Whoever putteth away his wife and marrieth another commiteth adultery" and "America: A Land Built on Christian Values. Take God Out, We Will Fail." We pass quilt shops and churches, few of them named according to denomination but instead called things like "Wellspring," "Soul's Harbor," and "Faith Fellowship." In Ohio the Ten Commandments are divided between two billboards, five commandments each.

I feel the same vague sense of oppression I did every Sunday of my childhood. But the visit to Mansfield, that jolt of electrical memory, has left a lingering hum. I remember being a child, gently swinging the soft velvet rope that separated visitors from Laura's library, listening to my aunt's offhand comment about the ordinariness of writers. In that moment, excitement had pounded through me unexpectedly like an ocean surf, like the waves on the beach in my imaginary writing studio in Italy. And now, the memory alone returns me to that feeling again.

Thirty-one years ago, the Laura Ingalls Wilder trip showed me that someday I had to escape from a world where I would never fit.

What I'd forgotten is that it also showed me where I needed to go.

CHAPTER TEN

Prince Edward Island

Lucy Maud Montgomery's
Anne Books

BY THE TIME WE ARRIVE HOME from our Laura Ingalls Wilder tour/ Maud Hart Lovelace detour in the summer of 2007, Sophie can hardly stand to be in the back seat another moment. She whines and groans, sighs and bounces and shifts. She rolls her eyes at any reference to pioneers. She has had enough, or so I think.

We pull into our driveway and she says, "That was fun. Can we do it again?"

Soon I'm planning another trip, this time to Prince Edward Island, the territory of *Anne of Green Gables*. A few months before Sophie's ninth birthday, I start reading the book aloud to her.

After that, every night, she begs me to keep going, to read just another chapter about the red-haired orphan mistakenly sent to an aging and proper spinster and her soft-spoken brother. Having requested a boy to help out on their farm, they end up, instead, with a loquacious girl. I love the writing, the vivid and funny characterization and voice of Anne, her hot temper and hilariously overdramatic tendencies and vast fallibility. Sophie laughs uproariously at Anne's obsession with "bosom" friends. "Bosom!" Sophie keeps saying, collapsing.

I hear her on the phone with my friend Michele, whose daughter Kelsey has croup. "You need to boil some water and keep wood on the stove," Sophie says. "You need some soft flannel cloths, too. But what you really need is a bottle of ipecac to help her bring up the phlegm."

"So you mean that you want to steam up the room?" Michele asks.

"The book doesn't explain that part," Sophie says. She has watched the movie a few times, and she suddenly recalls a detail from it. "I think you need mustard plasters. It was the ipecac that saved Minnie May's life, though."

I'm impressed at how thoroughly Sophie has absorbed the episode in which the resourceful heroine of *Anne of Green Gables* provides medical care to Anne's bosom friend and "kindred spirit" Diana's baby sister.

Sophie gets a kick out of Anne's mishaps, like when she accidentally dyes her hair green, or when she breaks a slate over Gilbert Blythe's head after he calls her "Carrots," or when she inadvertently gets Diana drunk by serving her what she thinks is raspberry cordial but turns out to be currant wine. But it's Anne's voice that captivates us from the beginning, when she quite seriously asks Matthew, this gentle middle-aged bachelor whom she has just met, "Which would you rather be if you had the choice—divinely beautiful or dazzlingly clever or angelically good?" He is clearly startled by her query, but she is oblivious to his puzzlement and goes on pondering this question aloud, later concluding, "I'd rather be pretty than clever."[1] From that conversation on, he is beguiled by her, as are Sophie and I, as have been generations of readers. Soon after the book's publication, Mark Twain himself wrote to Montgomery that he found her protagonist to be "the dearest and most lovable child in fiction since the immortal Alice."

I've never before noticed how much the book is constructed through stories that the talkative Anne tells others about her experiences, so that it becomes a sort of third-person first person. Like so many of my childhood favorites and like many books of the era written in self-contained chapters so that they could be published as, or dismantled into, newspaper serials, it's slow and episodic, lacking the fast-paced chronological action of most of today's children's books. It's so funny and engaging that we hardly notice, though. Well, funny for the most part. Not the part where Matthew dies. I still get choked up by that.

I loved the first book in the series when I was a child, and into my teens I read the other available books, *Anne of Avonlea* and *Anne's House of Dreams*, books also passed on to me by my mom and aunts, though I don't remember them talking about Anne much.

After the Laura Ingalls Wilder trip when I was thirteen, I had turned into a restless, floundering reader. I wasn't that interested in the available choices. Not the contemporary problem novels from Scholastic order forms, stories about drugs and alcohol and poverty and sex and teen pregnancy; not the pleasant, conventional library novels from the 50s about characters who were alarmingly wholesome and obedient, white middle-class "good girls" who wore rounded collars and full skirts and faced conflicts like whether they would run into the boy they had a crush on at the malt shop.

Classics with teenage characters like the *Anne of Green Gables* sequels weren't wholly satisfying, either, but at least Anne felt like an old friend. In *Anne of Avonlea* and *Anne of the Island*, the title character, sixteen when the first sequel opens, is passionate about gaining an education as she dreams of being a writer. In the front matter of each novel was a list of later books in the *Anne* series, but to my disappointment, the others had fallen out of print and I didn't know how to obtain copies.

The biographies that had been staples of my childhood also ceased to engage me. Younger, I'd devoured most of the volumes from the Childhood of Famous Americans series, with silhouette drawings and duotone illustrations. Through these books, I first heard of Jim Thorpe: Indian Athlete (a reissued version has the new subtitle *Olympic Champion*); George Carver: Boy Scientist; Babe Didrikson: Girl Athlete; Sacagawea: Bird Girl (now *Young Pathfinder*); Amelia Earhart: Kansas Girl (entirely rewritten and changed to *Young Aviator*); or Helen Keller: Handicapped Girl (now subtitled, instead, *From Tragedy to Triumph*). Once promoted as biographies despite the fact that they had made-up dialogue, scenes, even whole episodes, reissued versions of these books now contain notes specifying that, while based on real events, the stories are fictionalized. To this day, I'm not sure how much I think I know about various noteworthy people is actually historically accurate.

Many of these biographies follow a standard formula, the most essential ingredient being the way the seeds of each subject's future profession were planted at remarkably young ages. Most of the books open when their subjects are between three and five years old. Maria Mitchell: Girl Astronomer is, at five, fascinated with the night sky, spends her childhood making scientific observations about the notches of leaves and the way water spreads on the floor, and carves math problems in sand at the beach. Young Amelia Earhart dreams of being a pioneer and builds a track from the shed roof so she can pretend that she's flying.

Not only were the subjects of these "biographies" clearly talented from birth, destined for greatness and meant to be whatever they eventually became, but they also seemed far more focused and certain, calmer and kinder than I was. The books told unambiguous stories about well-known people, avoiding any mention of turmoil, violent impulses, knotted-up stomachs, or cruel thoughts. Their stories were, as a result, simultaneously inspiring and discouraging.

When I was thirteen, home from the Laura Ingalls Wilder trip, I happened upon an adult biography of Helen Keller, Joseph Lash's *Helen and Teacher*. It startled me. The famous people who'd been sanitized in children's biographies came across as complicated and unpredictable, egocentric even while they were self-sacrificing, often choosing desire over duty. I didn't want to prefer this vision of humankind, but it seemed more true to me, more honest. As troubling as it was, it was also comforting to read something that reflected more accurately the world that I knew. It reassured me that I wasn't crazy, wasn't just paranoid or deluded about the real and perplexing ways that people thought and behaved. And so, gradually, the reasons that I read and wrote were beginning to shift. I no longer sought to simplify a disorderly world. I started reading instead to confirm that people were as complex and weird as I'd always suspected, and to try to figure out why.

But I continued to connect powerfully to Anne, her passion for books and stories, her fierce need to write. Now, the similarities that drew me to all of my favorite childhood heroines are obvious: not just that Betsy and Anne and Jo of *Little Women* often express the desire to be writers, but that we get to watch all of these girls, and Laura, come of age. But now I'm starting to note some significant differences as well. Like that, compared to the others, Anne doesn't really change much in the course of the first book, and while identity is central to the novel, it is really belonging that she seeks. She is always messing up and promising to change, but in the end, she doesn't really.

As with the early *Betsy* books—*Betsy-Tacy, Betsy-Tacy and Tib, Betsy and Tacy Go Over the Big Hill*, and *Betsy and Tacy go Downtown*, the *Anne* titles gradually expand their heroine's world—first she is just Anne of Green Gables, the name of the house where she grows up. Then she becomes Anne of Avonlea, the fictional town where Green Gables is located. In the third book, she is Anne of the Island—Prince Edward Island. After this, most of the *Anne* titles, the ones that were out of print during my childhood but that I later was able to read as a young adult—*Anne of Windy Poplars, Anne of Ingleside*—take on a similar naming strategy as the early *Little House* books. These titles imply no character transformation as Anne's world correspondingly widens, but instead resort to simply moving us around geographically. In Wilder's titles, Laura migrates from woods to prairie to creek to lake before the family settles in South Dakota and the book titles shift to reflecting events rather than geography. Later titles in both the Little House and Betsy series allude to interior lives and suggest external and internal struggles: *Betsy in Spite of Herself, Betsy and Joe, The Long Winter*. By comparison, the later Anne titles go flat. *Anne of Windy Poplars* and *Anne's House of Dreams* and *Rainbow Valley* identify where she is living, but these titles contain no hints of tension and as a result, somewhat like *These Happy Golden Years*, transmit a sense of complacency.

While Jo, Betsy, and Laura undergo processes of discovering who they are against social pressures and competing yearnings, Anne is from the beginning already who she is—her task is primarily to find acceptance by others who are always misunderstanding or underestimating her, as Elizabeth Epperly points out, and to learn to express herself in more sophisticated ways.[2]

But in the long run, identity is comparatively static for the heroine of *Anne of Green Gables*, while it fluctuates and develops for other literary heroines, a difference that becomes subtly apparent in an example as small as two characters' attitudes toward their own names. In Lovelace's *Betsy in Spite of Herself*, whose very title suggests the protagonist's identity struggle, Betsy decides to become "dramatic and mysterious"—and one of the first things she does toward that end is add an *e* to the end of her name.[3] Instead of "Betsy," she becomes "Betsye"—a conversion that, as a child, I assumed had an autobiographical basis because I was used to seeing the first name of her creator, Maud, written as "Maude." My frame of reference was the 70s TV show by the same name, but it turns out that in the nineteenth century, "Maude" was a far more popular spelling than "Maud." "Maud looks incomplete to the modern eye, despite her historical roots," says Abby Sandel, who writes a blog on names called Appellation Mountain.[4]

Betsy's journey of self-acceptance eventually brings her full circle, back to the original spelling of her name. But the "e" at the end of Anne's name is nonnegotiable, something we know from the get-go, since her name is spelled that way right on the cover of the book. Lucy Maud Montgomery (who not only shared the name "Maud" with Lovelace but who typically was called by that name by her friends and relatives) creates a heroine who is called "the girl" and "the child" throughout the opening of *Anne of Green Gables* because the point of view is Matthew's and he is so shy and so befuddled that he neglects to ask her name. In the third chapter, when Marilla does inquire, the child answers, "Will you please call me Cordelia?" Marilla is appalled. "CALL you Cordelia?" she replies. "Is that your name?" The child admits that it is not, but that she finds "Cordelia" to be "perfectly elegant" while Anne is "such an unromantic name." Anne finally concedes to being called by her name, though she also does a little bargaining: "But if you call me Anne please call me Anne spelled with an E," she says. "When you hear a name pronounced can't you always see it in your mind, just as if it was printed out? I can; and A-n-n looks dreadful, but A-n-n-e looks so much more distinguished. If you'll only call me Anne spelled with an E I shall try to reconcile myself to not being called Cordelia."[5]

This certainly implies that the spelling of her name on her birth certificate may have been "Ann," which connects her to many orphans from that time period (Irene Gammel traces these Anns back to James Whitcomb Riley's "Little Orphant Annie," from 1885, Mary Ann Maitland's "Charity Ann" from 1892, and J. L. Harbour's "Lucy Ann" from 1903).[6] However, at least from Chapter 3 of *Anne of Green Gables* on, Anne Shirley acquires the coveted "e" and distinguishes herself as a less ordinary kind of orphan, one with spunk and a sense of romance, an orphan perhaps a bit too upbeat to be believed. In real life, Juliet McMaster points out, being orphaned and then repeatedly exploited and rejected would most likely lead to a withdrawn and resentful child rather than one who like Anne is sunny and whimsical.[7]

Irene Gammel's *Looking for Anne of Green Gables* traces the years that Lucy Maud Montgomery wrote and published the first book in the series, examining both autobiographical sources and the ways that Montgomery drew from popular images of the era such as beauty icons, fashion plates, and advertisements. In it, Gammel calls attention to the way that hair color itself becomes a subtle determinant of hot-temperedAnne's personality. Anne does change outwardly, Gammel says, the evolution of her hair in itself a "fable of identity," as it turns from "'carroty' to 'auburn' to 'Titian red,' each with increasingly positive connotations."[8]

Rereading, I understand that it was from Anne and Betsy that I got the idea as a child to spell my name "Nancye" although my half-hearted attempt to gussy up my image was pretty short lived since I knew that I was at heart a plain old "Nancy." And it is from Laura and Anne that I derived strange fashion advice about appropriate colors to wear in my hair, although once again this was all theoretical since I rarely wore ribbons or any kind of hair accessories at all. Gammel sheds light on these peculiar color prescriptions of children's novels, attributing them to the 1878 work of an influential Victorian fashion columnist, Mary Eliza Haweis. Haweis decreed rules that may have been what forced blond Mary to wear blue and brown-haired Laura to wear red, and that, Gammel says, left Anne "forever debarred" from wearing a pink rose in her red hair: Haweis wrote that "Pink is suitable for most young faces, especially the fair, except when the hair inclines to red."[9]

Several critics describe the *Anne* books as feeling "modern," but it quickly becomes apparent that they don't mean the same thing as those who've deemed Maud Hart Lovelace's character Betsy as "modern." If Betsy could easily be a contemporary girl, her concerns about fashion and boys and identity not that different from those of today's teenagers, Anne, her longing for then-fashionable puffed sleeves notwithstanding, comes off as decidedly odd and old-fashioned in her whimsy and celebration of imagination and romanticization of female friendship.

Many readers are no doubt attracted to the glossed-over version of childhood and small town life represented in Montgomery's books. But despite that conventional surface of *Anne of Green Gables*, much of its humor comes from its underlying satire. Like Mark Twain, Gammel says, Montgomery was a "consummate social satirist" who gleefully skewers the self-importance and self-righteousness of small town rural communities.[10] This tends to be what critics are alluding to when they call Montgomery's book "modern"—her modernist playfulness that strikes me as more postmodern at times in its self-irony and metatextual elements. The books are thoroughly influenced by typical plot patterns of the day, as Epperly says: "dramatic reversals of fortune, suddenly discovered long-lost relatives, sentimental love scenes, and purple patches of description. But if the pieces are formulaic, they are also often very clever, suggesting the gifts behind the conformity, the artistic powers barely tapped by the marketable tale."[11] Gammel agrees, writing that Montgomery pokes fun at "Anne Shirley's wild mimicking of conventional literature and cliché, thereby poking fun at herself and her own mimicking of formula fiction. She created a text with a playfully modern irony underneath its quaint and old-fashioned vocabulary and nostalgic yearning."[12]

Sophie and I finish *Anne of Green Gables* right before I leave to teach at a Spalding MFA residency, but luckily I have on hand two copies of *Anne of Avonlea*. I devise this great plan in which we will both read while I'm gone, comparing notes each night. But she's busy, I'm busy, and we keep stalling. This book isn't quite as much fun as the first, as sixteen-year-old Anne defers her further education to stay home to help Marilla and teach at her old school.

Somehow, this novel feels to me a bit drab, despite the romantic-sounding name of Avonlea. The irony and humor of the first book seem to have vanished as Anne becomes the teacher at Avonlea School and helps Marilla to raise a set of orphaned twins. Suddenly Anne is startlingly sanctimonious—not just toward her pupils or the twins, but toward her friends as well. I feel a bit guilty about my negative reaction to this book, but Epperly, it turns out, is equally put off by it, irritated with the way Anne tries to fit in with everything and everybody and spends "much time preaching and teaching." Epperly further complains that "Anne does not let others be themselves. She actually commands them to be fanciful, is dismayed by their lack of poetry, and generally shows herself to be condescending." I'm a little relieved that Epperly is even more relentless than I am: "As an exploration of Anne's thinking and developing," she says, "the book is a qualified failure."[13]

Sophie never finishes it, but I come home and start *Anne of the Island*, my favorite of the two sequels available when I was a child, the one where Anne goes off to attend college. It was Nancy Pearl's favorite, too, she admits in *Book Crush*, because it was so romantic. I was also drawn to the portrayal of Anne's life at college, of the classes she took and her lively circle of friends. But I also liked the romance: in it, Anne receives no less than six marriage proposals and ultimately faces a dilemma between choosing the man who seems to be her ideal, Royal, and the one with whom she shares a deep friendship, Gilbert Blythe.

This sort of choice has long been a staple of young adult novels, so much so that readers are always taking sides; from the start, *Little Women's* fans were universally on Team Laurie and appalled when Jo married the hairy Professor Bhaer. Today, readers accustomed to choosing between Team Edward or Team Jacob (*Twilight*) or Team Gale or Team Peeta (*Hunger Games*) also have been known to discuss in online *Betsy-Tacy* forums whether they belong to Team Tony or Team Joe. Of all my favorite childhood heroines, only Laura, who takes a little bit of time warming up to Almanzo but once she does has no question that he is right for her, is exempt from this romance plot. The rest struggle. We the readers know what the "best" choice is, but still wait in suspense to see who Jo or Bella or Katniss or Betsy will choose.

As with many other single books that evolve into series, *Anne of the Island* was written as a result of reader demand, of fans who "pestered" Montgomery, asking her repeatedly what happened to Anne and Gilbert. The suspense accumulates until the very end of this book as to whether Anne will cast her lot with Royal, whose name itself suggests princes and fairy tales, or opt for a life with Gilbert Blythe, his last name alone suggesting carefree bliss. I remember the first time I read *Island*, breathing a sigh of relief when Anne makes the right choice, finally becoming engaged to the childhood rival who has emerged as her true soulmate. This may be the one way that Anne does change in the course of the books, learning, as Epperly says, "to distinguish between false and genuine romance," clearly a task of many girls' series heroines.[14]

I am happy to discover that Epperly also likes this book much better. "Gone is the moralizing narrator of the overtaxed *Anne of Avonlea*," she says. Anne has returned to her fun-loving, witty, well-read self, refusing to conform "to reader expectation, to cultural stereotype, or to accepted convention."[15]

Reading beyond the first three books in the series isn't so much a process of retracing my childhood as it is a return to my twenties, since it wasn't until then that the whole Anne set was reissued. I didn't read all of them until I was twenty-six. My divorce had been final for a few months, and I'd accepted a new college teaching job that required me to move to another state alone for the first time. In Springfield, Missouri, I knew almost no one, and before I cracked open the first Montgomery book, I was feeling lonely, unsettled, displaced, disconnected. But as I tore through the series on evenings and weekends, including those later installments that had been out of print when I was a child, I felt like I had found a community, even if it was just a fictional one, this gossipy and petty, warm and funny, often narrow-minded, occasionally open-hearted world of Avonlea.

Anne, a heroine reviewers inevitably refer to as *irrepressible, feisty, dreamy, spunky, spirited, vibrant,* and/or *charming,* kept me company, making me feel weirdly happy all the time. Soon, in real life, I'd bonded with a new colleague named Lisa who also loved the books, and my first hint of a social life in Springfield came when we got together for a marathon viewing of the first and second films directed by Kevin Sullivan.[16] The first sticks closely to the events of *Anne of Green Gables* while the second, which loosely combines *Anne of Avonlea* and *Anne of the Island*, remains true to the spirit and characterizations of Montgomery if not everything that happens in the books.

A couple of weeks before we leave for our trip, Sophie and I watch again those wonderful first two Sullivan movies, so beautifully cast and performed that the luminous actress who plays Anne, Megan Follows, remains in my head the image of Anne. I'm less impressed by the rather startling third installment of the series that I discover at a video store, Anne's espionage adventure in Europe during World War I. Gilbert has gone to war and because she hasn't heard from him for a while, she sets out to find him, her wifely devotion leading her to insistently and oh-so-realistically follow him into war zones. This is a bewildering deviation from the books, which never leave Prince Edward Island. But my disgust proves to be mild compared to what I find when I track down the 1934 black-and-white movie version of *Anne of Green Gables*.[17]

This movie, which I vaguely remember first watching with my mother, strikes me as cast very oddly by today's standards: the actress who plays Marilla, Helen Westley, who is appropriately solid and plain but not tall and thin, as Montgomery describes Marilla, predates Hollywood glamour. She doesn't appear to be wearing a bra, and her breasts are rather large; they droop to her waist. I can't take my eyes off of those sagging boobs. Talk about bosom friends.

Matthew, played by O. P. Heggie, has a grey look about him, which may be inevitable in a black-and-white movie. But he also gives off a sort of robotic accountant-mortician vibe, lacking the shy sweetness of Montgomery's characterization. The actress who plays Anne, who in either a publicity stunt or a fit of inspiration changed her original stage name, Dawn O'Day, to Anne Shirley, was sixteen at the time, and looks it, not like an eleven-year-old orphan. Or maybe I'm just critical because the Sullivan version is so well cast that it's impossible for anyone to live up to Megan Follows's portrayal in particular of the young Anne, much less Colleen Dewhurst's complex, no-nonsense but gradually softening Marilla and Richard Farnsworth's gentle Matthew.

The casting of the 1934 movie is only the tip of a problematic iceberg for a contemporary reader with feminist sensibilities. What really gets me is the way that Anne initially rejects Gilbert and then regrets it, trying desperately to regain his attention for the rest of the movie. This turns her a little bit pathetic, far more help-less than in the books, which throws into sharp relief the groundbreaking aspects of Montgomery's early *Anne* novels, such as her heroine's strong sense of self and refusal of many social expectations.

Unlike me, Montgomery seems to have liked this 1934 film, but then, her basis for comparison was a silent movie made in 1920 that is no longer available. Gammel reports Montgomery's reaction to this movie: "In one scene Anne appears at the door of her school, 'a shotgun in hand, standing off a crowd of infuriated villagers who were bent on mobbing her because she had whipped one of the pupils.'"[18] The title of the article in which Montgomery wrote this says it all: "Is This My Anne?"

After I finish rereading *Anne of the Island*, I get stuck. Maybe it's partly because I associate the rest of the books with my twenties, not with my childhood, that I find myself returning to them a bit grudgingly. That, and the heat. A few days before we leave for Prince Edward Island, it's ninety degrees. Our house, which has no air conditioning, holds heat like an oven as several days pass without the usual merciful nightly drop in temperature.

I'm plowing through *Anne of Windy Poplars*, which I'm finding pleasant if a little boring. Anne is now a school principal, a rather impressive position for a woman of her time, and the book is funny and folksy and mostly epistolary, Anne's letters to Gilbert during the three years she waits to marry him. Since her engagement has provided a happy ending to all of her own problems, she now turns her attention to procuring stepmothers for motherless children, reuniting lost loves, helping ogres get their comeuppance and reveal their humanity, freeing adult children from controlling elderly parents, and speeding along stalled courtships. Only once is Anne's meddling not ultimately appreciated; only once does she admit to making a mistake, but in this case, the couple, Terry and Hazel, are all the more happy for it.

I abandon the book to start packing, but the stifling heat makes it hard to move. Sophie and I are both slick with sweat in no time. So we lie on the downstairs couch bed with the fan blowing, watching reruns of the 90s series *Beverly Hills 90210*, which has the effect of making *Anne of Windy Poplars* look like a trail-blazing intellectual treatise. It's still impossibly hot when we get up at 6:00 the next morning to finish packing. I throw in the remaining books, the ones I still haven't read, planning to finish them on our trip.

Prince Edward Island, home of author Lucy Maud Montgomery for half of her life and the setting of most of her novels, is the destination for many annual "Anne-tastic" tours, as one website refers to them. Despite the heat, it seems appropriate that we're headed there in June, the month in which much of *Anne of Green Gables* is set—more than half the plot, Irene Gammel points out.[19] Two other fans are accompanying us to Canada: twenty-four-year-old Kellie, my former student who is now working on a library degree, an intrepid, constitutionally curious traveler who organized much of this trip and has offered to do the driving; and fifteen-year-old Mahita, whose father wrote me a notarized letter of permission to take his daughter out of the country but forgot her age and said that she was fourteen. And then, because her mother was away in India and both parents are required to sign, her father forged her mother's signature without pretending to change the handwriting.

We set out across New York, in and out of thunderstorms, crossing into Massachusetts. Veering away from Boston, we head up through New Hampshire and then Maine, passing lots of "Moose Crossing" signs, stopping to eat at Mike's Clam Shack, and then spending the night at a nearby motel. I'm a bit nervous about entering Canada with two minors who don't remotely resemble me, my Chinese American daughter as well as a teenager of Indian descent whose age on her passport doesn't match the age on her father's note, which has an obviously forged signature. If I were a border official, I would find this note extremely suspicious.

Luckily, the next morning when we reach New Brunswick, the border guard is nothing like me. He doesn't even ask to see the note. He cheerfully waves us through.

New Brunswick is beautiful. The sky is clear and blue and the fields and small towns remind me of the Midwestern US, clean and remote, the houses precise and geometric, compact boxes on spreading green lawns with few trees and no landscaping. We pass the occasional Tim Horton's, Dairy Queen, or McDonalds, but for the most part the only businesses we see sell tractors and semi-trucks. We struggle to convert prices as we buy gas by the liter instead of the gallon.

For lunch, we stop to use the "washroom" at a service station in Nackawic and to inquire where we can find the World's Largest Axe, for which we've seen a number of signs. "It's behind the marina," I think the woman says, and I get all excited about picnicking by water. It turns out that the axe is behind the arena, not the marina, but luckily, there is also water—the bluest lake I've ever seen, but then, all of the lakes, marshes, bays, and rivers we've passed in New Brunswick have been startlingly blue.

We stop to pay tribute to the World's Largest Axe, its 55-ton stainless steel head planted firmly in concrete, its 60-foot wooden handle slanting off into the sky. "This giant axe symbolizes the importance of the forest industry, past, present and future, to the town of Nackawic and the Province of New Brunswick," says the plaque beside it.

Back on the road, Kellie and I talk about the *Anne* books. Kellie listens politely when I go into professorial mode, observing the ways that Montgomery is preoccupied with issues of voice and language, marriage and female choice. I find amusing her endless fascination with doubling and twinning and actual twins, like the three sets of twins that young Anne was forced to care for as a foster child before the series begins, and then what seem to be exponentially multiplying sets of twins as the series progresses. There are elderly twins, young twins, and dead twins in portraits at a home that Anne visits. In *Anne of the Island*, a boarding house that Anne moves into is run by twins who embody the books' emphasis on balance and on women's options. Actually, the story goes, these two women *used* to be twins. Now one of them acts eighty, too old for her age, while the other, ridiculously, acts like she's thirty.[20]

Eventually, all talked out, Kellie and I put on the *Juno* soundtrack. All the way to PEI we keep replaying "Loose Lips" until all four of us can sing all the words without missing a beat, shouting the chorus: "We won't stop until somebody calls the cops and even then we'll start again and just pretend that nothing ever happened."[21]

If Laura Ingalls Wilder's books are about vision—mistakes of vision, loss of vision, developing vision as a writer—Montgomery's books are about voice—telling stories, talking too much, speaking with one's own voice, loss of voice, helping others to find their voices. Elizabeth Epperly comments on the development and suppression of Anne's voice, lamenting the way that she gives up "passionate articulation in favor of a conventional, maidenly dreaminess and reserve."[22] This gradual silencing of Anne has long bothered me, but as I continue to read, what will really alarm me is the way she goes from being a character with a distinctive voice to a silencer of others. In *Anne of Windy Poplars*, in yet another of many, many examples of twinning and doubling throughout the series, Anne encounters young twins who prove to be mean little hellions who pin down a little girl and paint her legs. Anne later decides that the girl deserves the abuse: "After all, Ivy Trent was a vain little monkey and had probably been very irritating."[23] This disturbing tendency to side with abusive behavior—and this fascination with twins—emerges more forcefully with the introduction of the young twins Dora and Davy who come to live with Anne and Marilla in *Anne of Avonlea*.

Dora, we repeatedly hear, is grim and proper, with perfect manners. She is "monotonous." When Anne leaves home, Dora "squeezes" out "two decorous little tears."[24] During a storm, we are told that it is doubtful that an earthquake could have disturbed her placidity.[25] So there we have it—the perfect model of girlhood, embodying every womanly characteristic that girls are encouraged to strive for, a representative of the feminine virtue that Montgomery frequently endorses—and Montgomery is merciless toward her. Over and over, Marilla and Anne feel perfectly righteous in announcing that they prefer mischievous (and sometimes downright mean) Davy, who not only hurts his sister but cries when he misses out on the pleasure of seeing her get hurt. And Anne and Marilla don't just admit that they prefer Davy. They frequently mention that they "like" him better. The narrator can't ever mention that Davy is "harum scarum" without adding that Marilla "liked the harum scarum best of all."

Not that Anne isn't always trying to tame him. For a while, Montgomery is so enamored of Davy, even Anne fades into the background, aggrieved when he uses a bad word, lecturing him on how it's wrong for little boys to use slang, correcting him when he admires a "bully splash," since in this time period, "bully" is apparently a highly vulgar if enthusiastically complimentary adjective.[26] Anne rarely takes the active route of outright scolding him, but instead generally adopts a passive approach to improving him by revealing that his behavior hurts her. Anne directs intense energy to domesticating Davy, but poor Dora, already tame, functions only as a prop, a foil for the more interesting boy character, whose speech Anne must help to shape into acceptable form.

The theme of voices and speech creeps into the narrative in both obvious and more subtle ways as Davy characterizes an echo as a sound that "sasses back" or when Montgomery writes about "voiceful memory."[27] But in the midst of all of this emphasis on voice, Anne talks less and less while others talk more and more. I think back to books I read in graduate school, like Carol Gilligan and Lyn Mikel Brown's *Meeting at the Crossroads* and Mary Pipher's *Reviving Ophelia*; Anne could be a case study in one of these books, which deal with how girls become silenced and tentative as they transition into adolescence, losing their senses of self. Gilligan's, Brown's, and Pipher's work resonated strongly with my own experience of going from talkative, confident child to silent, unsure teenager, but it didn't occur to me how much even fictional girls replicate this pattern, turning into role models who subtly compel readers to also conform.

While they adhere to some societal expectations, characters like Anne and Jo resist the pressure to marry more insistently than later heroines like Laura and Betsy. And like Maud Hart Lovelace in her *Betsy* series, Montgomery presents multiple options for women. Marilla has never married and isn't considered the lesser for it, and Miss Lavender, up until her departure, is a spunky role model. But Anne's friends desire the "happy ending" that she's not yet willing to admit that she wants. Diana, who becomes engaged, acknowledges that there's a "romance about a thin old maid"—but concludes that she must marry because she's bound to end up fat.[28]

Davy himself is beginning to process these issues, announcing that when he's married he will "put his foot down and say, 'Mrs. Davy, you've just got to do what will please me cause I'm a man.'"[29] Davy's "wisdom" is frequently cited, as when he announces that a woman would be better off living with a widower with eight children than a sister-in-law.[30] Such comments are unquestioned in a climate where homey casual misogyny is taken for granted, allowing Anne to speak unironically of "henpecked husbands,"[31] and all of her friends to humorously deem their friend Phil's "beaux" her "victims." The preoccupations with voice and marriage, and the pitfalls of maintaining a voice after marriage, intersect on many occasions: in one of many such instances, a woman is described as having a "face like a hatchet" with a tongue that is "sharper still." When one character dies, another says of her, "nobody . . . ever loved poor Atossa . . . not even her husband. The doctor said he died of dyspepsia, but I shall always maintain that he died of Atossa's tongue."[32]

Such examples serve to reinforce the danger of women's words and opinions, as do comments like when Anne tells Phil, "Jonas likes you better for your big brown eyes and your crooked smile than for all the brains you carry under your curls." Perhaps such comments are all the more jarring amid the many progressive attitudes these characters express, particularly for 1915, when this book first appeared. Aunt Jamesina, whose daughter has a master's degree, speaks out in favor of higher education for women. And, after all, Anne and her friends are, unlike many women of the time, going to college, and Phil remains a character who can't be silenced even when she becomes less frivolous and flirtatious after falling in love. "Oh, why must a minister's wife be supposed to utter only prunes and prisms?" she laments when corrected for using slang (the phrase "dig in")—and then defends slang, which she says is only "metaphorical language." She then wisely concludes that she'll be perceived as stuck up among the parishioners that her future husband serves if she doesn't share their language.[33]

While women's voices are the subject of much discussion, while finding, altering, or suppressing their voices are issues confronting Montgomery's heroine and her friends, Anne is also finding a voice as a writer. She receives some good advice from neighbor Mr. Harrison, who tells her that she's "too young to write a worthwhile story." He tells her to wait ten years, then to write "of people and places" she knows, let her characters talk in "everyday English," and give her villains "a chance." Gilbert is the one who offers this advice in the Sullivan production. This is excellent advice even if it does mark, in both the movie and the book, a troubling shift into presenting men as the primary bearers of wisdom. Eventually, these suggestions transform Anne's approach to writing, a positive development. Anne is apparently unaffected by the climate around her of ambivalence toward storytelling, which acquires frivolous undertones when Aunt Jamesina says, "My daughter used to write stories before she went to the foreign field, but now she has turned her attention to higher things." Though Anne doesn't take this comment especially seriously, it does capture one of her central tensions: how to be a writer but still remain properly womanly, how to cling to "the highest ideals" and never write from "a low or unworthy motive."[34]

Language is a double-edged sword. It can be a conduit to inspiring and entertaining others, but it can also be a tool of self-deception, a way to conceal truths. This comes across humorously when Dora insists that a tomcat should be referred to as a "gentleman cat" while Davy maintains it should be a "Thomas pussy." Montgomery makes fun of the prudery that leads to such euphemistic language even while her characters are perpetually reprimanded for their slang. And Anne delivers one of her more mature insights when she says, "We are never half so interesting when we have learned that language is given us to enable us to conceal our thoughts."[35]

Not too long after, Anne, brooding about Gilbert's absence from Avonlea, thinks, "Oh, Avonlea was going to be so lonely—with Diana gone." Of course we know by then that it's Gil she misses most, even if she can't admit it to herself; here, Montgomery enters into Anne's conspiracy as she filters this reflection through her heroine, yet uses the dash to wink at us as well. Anne's great self-deception is that she loves Royal, not Gilbert, and she manages to entertain it right up to the last few pages. "I do know my own mind," she says at one point. "The trouble is, my mind changes and I have to get acquainted with it all over again."[36]

Phil cautions Anne about letting her imagination run away with her. "You've tricked something out with your imagination that you think love, and you expect the real thing to look like that," Phil says. We know how right she is long before Anne recognizes the flat, somewhat sappy Royal as the wrong choice for her, a recognition that is a long time coming because from the beginning, she has been so seduced by his flashy uses of language. Upon their first meeting, he laments the time he spent in Europe with his ailing mother, saying, "I am reconciled to the loss of years that the locust has eaten." My immediate response to this is "uh-oh" even as Anne swoons over how romantic he is. Even sensible Aunt Jamesina is "carried away by [Royal's] unfailing and deferential courtesy, and the pleasing tones of his delightful voice," which delivers many "poetical compliments" to Anne.[37] Pleasing voice? He sounds whiny to me.

Since love is one of the book's unspeakable emotions, Anne is naturally attracted to someone who appears to articulate what is inarticulable—even while she si-
lences Gilbert for doing the same thing in far more sincere fashion. There is an odd
interlude toward the end of *Island* when Anne substitute teaches and helps spur on
the twenty-year courtship of the woman she boards with—a courtship stalled, it
turns out, due to promises and secrets that have never, in all of these years, been
allowed into the open. What a contrast when Royal offers a proposal to Anne "as
beautifully worded as if he had copied it, as one of Ruby Gillis's lovers had done,
out of a Deportment of Courtships and Marriage."[38] His proposal is sincere and
flawless—and leaves her cold. Once again, Anne's task is to find middle ground between silent passion and over-the-top expressions of fleeting emotions.

The Confederation Bridge, the eight-mile span of concrete that crosses the Nor-
thumberland Strait, connecting New Brunswick to Prince Edward Island, feels like
being in the middle of nowhere, no land in any direction, only the bridge and
the water below. It's late by the time we arrive on the island and find our small
white-sided cottage in Cavendish. We wait for the morning to drive to New London to exchange money and get gas. "See you again," calls the guy at the service
station.

Unlike, say, Putnam, Connecticut, where no one seems to have heard of Gertrude Chandler Warner or the *Boxcar Children* books or have any idea why there's
a boxcar-turned-museum planted smack downtown, unlike some Laura Ingalls
Wilder sites where people are vaguely familiar with the TV show but haven't read
the books, this place takes visible pride in its connections to *Anne of Green Gables* and
makes literary references right and left. Some cars bear license plates with a picture
of Anne's face, a green-gabled house in the background, and the slogan, "Home of
'Anne of Green Gables.'" We pass a cabin complex called "Kindred Spirits" and
another called "Bosom Buddies." We pass the Lake of Shining Waters Amusement
Park. There's a Bright River Café, Marilla's Pizza, Green Gables Keepsakes, an
Anne of Green Gables Golf Course, the Anne Shirley Motel and Cabins, the Anne
Shirley Bed and Breakfast, Ingleside Lodge, the Green Gables Bungalow Court, and
Matthew's Market.

There is, in addition, a dizzying array of Anne-related sites and activities:
Montgomery's childhood home; a combination post office/museum to commem-
orate that Montgomery once worked at a post office; Green Gables Village; and
Avonlea Village, all in Cavendish. There is a museum at Montgomery's birthplace
in New London and in a house where Montgomery boarded while teaching for a
year in nearby Bideford. We skip the latter along with several others that are open

to the public: the house where Montgomery lived when she taught in two near-by towns as well as homes of her paternal grandfather and maternal aunt. We also miss the house where Montgomery got married, which is now owned by her great-grandson. There, he organizes weddings patterned after Montgomery's own.

In addition to all of these tributes, Prince Edward Island is a place so proud of a writer that one of Montgomery's poems is the island's official anthem and Anne has appeared on a postage stamp. Film scholar Theodore F. Scheckels reports that to many Canadians, Anne ranks right up there with the moose, the beaver, the Mountie, and the Habs, a Canadian hockey team.[39] And since at least 1923, this area has been referred to in print as "Anne of Green Gables country," attracting tourists who loved the books and, later, the Kevin Sullivan movies. "Some young islanders grow up believing that Anne really existed and are disappointed when they first learn that Anne, like Santa Claus, is fictional," writes Epperly.[40] Montgomery, herself an enthusiastic visitor of literary sites near Boston the first time she traveled there and later on her honeymoon in Scotland and England, was cynical about her own fans and their intrusions: "Every freak that has written to me about [*Anne of Green Gables*] claims to be a kindred spirit," she once complained.[41]

After an early lunch, we start the round of Montgomery attractions. First we visit the land in Cavendish where her childhood home used to be. There, she was raised by her grandparents and wrote the first two books of the *Anne* series. This is now a Canadian National Historic site operated by descendants of Montgomery, a relatively unembellished site that is the one considered most authentic by scholars.[42] We enter through a low-budget rustic-looking cabin inside a picket fence, where tickets are for sale and a few items are on display, like Montgomery's typewriter, her desk with pigeon-hole slots, and a first edition of *Anne of Green Gables*. The post office that Montgomery's grandparents ran out of their house is the reason that, according to legend, she was brave enough to send her work to publishers: when it was rejected, she could be the first to intercept it, thus not exposing herself to the gossip of local busybodies. Here in this cabin we also see the old post office scales and a cancellation stamp with the words "Cavendish, PEI."

Down a path, there's a wooden cover where Montgomery's grandparents' well used to be and, nearby, a big hole in the ground: the old basement and foundation of their house, which was excavated in the 1980s. Quotes from Montgomery's journal are posted on interpretive signs every few feet. I would like to take a leisurely stroll past a large garden with little green rows of sprouts, down paths bordered by a split rail fence, contemplating the quotes, but it's way too cold—much colder and damper than we were expecting. This doesn't stop Sophie and Mahita from climbing all the trees, the many birches and spruces and poplars and apple trees on the property, echoing the pastoral setting common to popular girls' fiction of Montgomery's time.

Since we are freezing, in the time-honored tradition of all tourists who come unprepared for the weather, we go in search of a shop to buy sweatshirts. We stop at the Friendly Fisherman Restaurant, which has a sign advertising a gift shop with a complete line of Anne products. After pausing to take pictures of each other hugging a nine-foot wooden statue of a bearded fisherman in a yellow slicker, we browse the aisles of the gift shop, trying on straw Anne hats with red braids and purchasing warmer clothing.

Following a brief stop at the local post office, which doubles as a Montgomery museum, we head on to a place called "Green Gables." This is a complex that includes the home once owned by Montgomery's cousin on which Green Gables was based. Displays about Montgomery's life and a film occupy the first building. The film, which is in English, French, and Japanese, talks about all of the people who come to Cavendish "in search of the idyllic setting" of the books.

Everything, it turns out, has been translated into Japanese, much to my surprise: audio recordings, signs, advertisements. This is my first inkling of the Japanese fascination with the *Anne* books, a subject I will read about later in greater detail. Mike Snow explains that Anne appeals to the Japanese because of their "love of nature and beautiful scenery, devotion to innocence, ready identification with underdogs, appetite for those who are frank and spontaneous (in contrast to the repressive nature of Japanese society) and simple nostalgia."[43]

According to Yuka Kajihara, a Japanese reader named Hanako Muraoka was given a copy of *Anne of Green Gables* in 1939 and was "so charmed" that she translated the book into her native language. Her translation, *Akage no An* (which translates to "Red-haired Anne") was a hit when it appeared in 1952 during a time when General Douglas MacArthur himself advocated introducing to Japan American juvenile books like Laura Ingalls Wilder's and Montgomery's in order to give hope to young people in a nation devastated by World War II.[44]

The book has remained popular in Japan, writes Kajihara, at first because of the many orphans created by war, more recently because of Japan's movement toward more insulated families with two working parents, which "has caused many Japanese youth to feel abandoned by parents and relatives." Anne, Kajihara says, "gives readers comfort and courage." The obsession with Anne has spawned pastry shops, cafés, home furnishing boutiques, inns, and prefabricated homes. These are referred to as "houses of Red Haired Anne" and made to look just like Green Gables, except for bathroom sliding doors and extra space for storing shoes. A college of social work and nursing, the School of Green Gables, has as its central philosophy to educate students to be "positive and bright like Anne." Magazines focused on "Learning Anne-ish Lifestyles" include articles on "cooking, quilting, having tea, picnicking, and developing an imaginative appreciation of nature." A theme park called "Canadian World" operated in Hokkaido for many years, including a replica of Green Gables, Canadian staff who demonstrated log-house construction and quilting, and a red-haired girl imported from PEI who dressed up as Anne and responded to tourists' questions about Canada.[45]

Irene Gammel writes that Japanese-English language textbooks for junior high students have also used excerpts from *Anne of Green Gables* such as the chapters "Mrs. Rachel Lynde Is Properly Horrified" and "Anne's Apology." In the first, Anne meets neighbor Mrs. Lynde, who calls her "skinny" and "homely" with "hair as red as carrots." Anne flies into a rage and then, in the subsequent chapter, is forced to seek Mrs. Lynde's forgiveness, though her apology is a funny, unexpected one. Gammel explains that for Japanese readers, "the formal, ritualistic politeness, the cult of humbleness, and repression of anger associated with the ideals of traditional Japanese femininity reverberate in the novel. Anne's outburst may well help alleviate readers frustrated with repression and silence."[46] In this light, it is doubly sad to me that Anne, who early on is such a role model of spunk and outspokenness, gradually evolves in later books into quite the opposite.

At the Green Gables complex, we pass through the museum and gift shop, then through a barn-like structure, where we pause to pretend to milk a big fake cow. And then, there it is, the house on which Green Gables was based, the home of Montgomery's cousins. This is where things get really weird. Because of consumer demand and a public desire "to experience Montgomery's fictional world rather than the historical reality of Cavendish," the farmhouse was transformed to more closely mimic its fictional counterpart.[47] Displays include "Marilla's" shawl with the once-missing amethyst broach and "Anne's" brown silk dress with puffy sleeves.

Even though the criticism has avoided the temptation to mix up the lives of Lucy Maud Montgomery and her creation, tourist sites like this one have given in to it wholeheartedly. But of course by now I'm used to confusion between the fictional and the real, which makes a certain amount of logical sense in Laura Ingalls Wilder country but struck me as weirder in Mankato at "Betsy's house" and "Tacy's house," sites named after people who never actually existed. Hannibal, Missouri, which we passed through on our way to Kansas one year, is full of ice cream parlors and souvenir shops named after Twain characters as well as buildings labeled "Tom's House," "Becky's Cave," and "Huck's house," but, as Mary Morris points out, nothing named after Jim.[48] Even though I'm getting used to this widespread if selective habit of mixing the fictional and the real, somehow I'm still not sure what to make of a display of a shawl and a dress presented as if these people really existed.

In a small shop, we stop for "raspberry cordial," raspberry-flavored crème soda. Mahita staggers around like a drunken Diana in order to more fully re-create the *Anne of Green Gables* experience. Still shivering in the cold, we stroll down a path labeled "Lover's Lane," a wooded trail with dandelions and forget-me-nots growing alongside. Montgomery really did refer to this place by that name, and it became the model for "Lover's Lane" in the book. I don't remember any bugs on the fictional version of this trail, but clouds of nonfictional ones swarm annoyingly in front of our faces. One dies down the front of my shirt. Mahita runs off to "frolic" (her word) in a beautiful green meadow like Anne, but her illusion is quickly disrupted by little flags stuck in the ground and men in golf carts rising over the hill.

We take a walk through the Haunted Wood, another wooded path among trees, wildflowers growing alongside, indistinguishable from Lover's Lane. We sing "Loose Lips," the song from *Juno* that we all memorized in the car during the long passage through Maine. "Send me an IM, I'll be your friend," we all chorus together, which seems somehow highly appropriate and completely inappropriate at the same time, a song about friendship in this place associated with the friendship of Anne and Diana, a song referencing modern technology in this place associated with an old-fashioned novel, a song from a contemporary movie about teen pregnancy in this place dedicated to childhood innocence.

Finally we're just so cold and wet that we abandon Anne and take refuge in a *Ripley's Believe It Or Not* museum. There we admire trucks made of matchsticks, a candy box and portraits made from lint, a sculpture of Abe Lincoln constructed from human hair, and a huge ship carved from jade. And it turns out that we haven't altogether escaped Anne after all: we find a portrait of her painted on a grain of rice. Not to mention that I've just started reading *Anne's House of Dreams*, and this Ripley's museum seems straight from the collection of the character Captain Jim, who has traveled around the world gathering treasures. His house is full of "curios, hideous, quaint, and beautiful," each with "some striking story attached to it."[49]

On our way to dinner, we're delayed by the Tour de Prince Edward Island, which just happens to be passing through Cavendish. We wait to cross the street, not realizing for a few minutes that the cemetery edge where we're standing has a huge arched sign proclaiming it "The Resting Place of L. M. Montgomery," as if another hundred people aren't also buried there. We dutifully venture in to locate Montgomery's gravestone. Two pine trees stand guard on either side, a flower garden spreads out in front, and a fence and chain provide added measures to keep tourists at bay. The Reverend Ewen MacDonald, Montgomery's husband, is listed first, followed by "Lucy Maud Montgomery MacDonald." There is no mention of *Anne of Green Gables.* Montgomery is only identified as "Wife of Ewan McDonald." I'm not sure which is the correct spelling of his name.

Once the last straggling cyclist has passed and we can finally cross the street, we have dinner and take a walk on the beach, where a woman yells at Sophie and Mahita for climbing a dune. "Respect the Island!" she yells, jarring us out of any notion that this place that has become such a vivid part of our imaginations can be in any way ours.

The next morning we visit Montgomery's birthplace in New London, a house where her parents lived for a few years. It has the same narrow white siding as our cottage along with the requisite green shutters and trim. The brochure identifies this place as home to the "authoress of the famous ANNE books" and assures us that "As you walk through the rooms of the birthplace, you will thrill to the realization that it was in this house that Lucy Maud first saw the light of day."

We wander back and forth across the seamless transition between museum and gift shop. Montgomery's wedding dress and slippers, made before there were right and left shoes, are on display, and cases hold replicas of pages from her scrapbook as well as various manuscripts, publications, and correspondence. Upstairs, the rooms are furnished by donated pieces to look the way they might have during Montgomery's time. A plaque tells us that one small room is where Montgomery was born. "And this," Kellie cracks, gesturing at the other bedroom, "is where Lucy Maud Montgomery was conceived."

We proceed to Avonlea Village and yet another gift shop. The number of available Anne-related items rival the Laura Ingalls Wilder ones I saw last summer: the *Anne of Green Gables* birthday book, coloring book, cookbook, diary, journal, and press-out model house; stationery, plates, giftwrap, mousepads, postcards, woodcuts, jigsaw puzzles, lollipops, watercolors, clocks, wall hangings, birdhouses, and plaques; t-shirts, sweatshirts, and hats, though, disappointingly, none like the ones once sold at Canadian World in Japan that said "Anne of Green Gapole."[50] Anne's image is everywhere, along with images of white houses with green trim. "The ideal consumer," write Jeanette Lynes, "will find little amiss in seeing a CD-ROM or a computer mouse pad in an old-fashioned country store, or a ninety-dollar doll based on a literary character who was a penniless orphan."[51]

Overwhelmed by the sheer amount of merchandise, Sophie and I buy a little Anne doll to go in the dollhouse my dad made me when I was seven. With help from friends, Sophie and I restored it a few years ago, and it strikes us now that like the majority of tourist buildings here, it also has white siding and green trim. Our Anne doll will spend the next few years migrating around the dollhouse, dozing in bed, reclining on the couch, dangling by her feet from the balcony, or standing on her head in the toilet.

The rest of the Avonlea Village complex is closed. The season doesn't officially start until next week. But we're allowed to walk around, gazing at buildings painted in bright colors, like a fictional idyllic village. There's a schoolhouse, an old church, a restaurant, a raspberry cordial bottling company, a chocolate shop, a museum of photographs taken by Montgomery, yet another re-creation of Green Gables, and "Matthew's carriage ride," which during tourist season includes a hat with red braids on the seat so that sweaty visitors can take turns impersonating Anne being picked up at the train station.

There is also a theater, gardens, and picnic grounds with a duck house, perhaps to suggest the duck house whose roof Anne falls through in *Anne of the Island*, though this one has an intact roof and several live ducks plumped out on the lawn. The whole place smells of fresh paint as men roll pastel colors onto the buildings. It's like a small-scale Disney World, designed to appeal to our nostalgia and our belief in childhood innocence and simplicity.

We take a bike ride that afternoon, stopping for ice cream. Someone yells at us for walking our bikes along the boardwalk, reminding us again: we're just tourists, and apparently unintentionally obnoxious ones. Rather than feeling closer to a favorite character, this trip is actually making us feel more distant.

While we sit on the steps in front of a cow gift shop, Mahita says, "Wow, this is the first time we've been here that we haven't been inundated with images of Anne." It's true. It's like a silence after a deluge of noise, a strange lull after two days of being surrounded by Anne dolls and mousepads and embroidery kits and license plates.

Then Kellie points out that Anne's Chocolates is right next door, and that behind us, in a window, is a bag of Anne of Green Gables potato chips. Later, on the beach, we construct our own absurd-looking Anne in the sand with gray rocks for her eyes and red rocks for her mouth and braids. I think of our organic Anne as something between a caricature of Anne as commodity and a tribute to Anne the character. She is our own ambitious attempt at folk art, like the pantyhose Ingalls family back in Burr Oak, Iowa.

Beyond us and our Anne-in-the-sand, the ocean is blue and green and yellow and red as it washes in over the red dirt. "The west was a glory of mingled hues, and the pond reflected them in still softer shadings," Montgomery writes in *Anne of Green Gables*.[52] *Anne's House of Dreams*, which I am still reading, seems to describe our own walk along the "fine surf . . . dashing on sand and rock in a splendid white turmoil—the only restless thing in the great, pervading stillness and peace." Soon after, Anne says of the ocean, "Tonight it seemed so free—so untamed—. Something broke loose in me, too, out of sympathy."[53]

In *Anne's House of Dreams*, Captain Jim marvels at the ocean's proximity: "Nice and far from the marketplace, ain't it?" he asks. "No buying and selling and getting gain. You don't have to pay anything—all that sea and sky free. . . ."[54] In Anne of Green Gables country, we are never far from the marketplace—especially not the next day, when we head to Charlottetown. For several hours, we wander, dodging the Tour de PEI, which we have apparently followed. All the streets are closed as clusters of bikers in their skin-tight gear hunch forward in single-minded focus, whizzing by, service vehicles following rapidly behind. When the way is temporarily clear, we open gates and race across streets as fast as we can before anyone runs us over.

We walk along the harbor, stopping to browse in shops selling jewelry and crafts and t-shirts dyed with local mud, sporting the words "No White Dogs." We puzzle over the outlawing of white dogs here and gradually realize that "No White Dogs" is actually a popular saying alluding to the red dirt that inevitably leaves white dogs tinted a rust color, reminiscent of Anne's braids. We visit a park of sand sculptures being prepared for tourist season. Artists hack out the minute details of a sand umbrella, scoop water from a bucket to wet the sand and shape a man's nostrils, put the finishing touches on a small village that contains a sand lighthouse and a sand church complete with sand steeple. On the street we run into a costumed Anne, greeting people to advertise tonight's play, "Anne of Green Gables: The Musical," the main reason that we're here.

This turns out not to be a homey, local outdoor pageant like at Laura Ingalls Wilder sites. It's a professional production in a large theater with comfortable seats. The musical brings to mind others with female heroines, particularly those played on the screen by Julie Andrews. As Avonlea women organizing a charity drive sing "Great Workers for the Cause," I can't help but think of "Sister Suffragettes" from *Mary Poppins*. The song "Did You Hear?" in which the small community demonstrates its prejudices against outsiders reminds me of "How Do You Solve a Problem Like Maria" from *The Sound of Music*. "She's a vision / She's a hussy / She's a terror / She's a tartar," the townswomen sing. It's like a more mean-spirited version of the nun's exasperated lyrics about Maria, "She's a riddle! She's a child! She's a headache! She's an angel! She's a girl!"[55]

Last summer at the Laura Ingalls Wilder pageants, I often suspected that the actors were channeling Michael Landon and Melissa Gilbert rather than Pa and Laura Ingalls, and here I have a similar feeling. The actress who plays Marilla is even made up to look like Colleen Dewhurst, and the young woman who plays Anne holds her head the same way that Megan Follows does. It's like I'm watching interpretations of interpretations.

Of course it's impossible to capture in a two-hour play all of the book's plots and subplots, themes and nuances, but I'm a little disappointed that the production focuses on Anne's relationship with Gilbert, never mentioning their academic rivalry and barely alluding to her wish to be a writer. The script also puts significant emphasis on Anne's struggle to "fit in," leaving out most of the "scrapes" that show her trying to rein in her vivid imagination without giving it up altogether. In the play, Anne doesn't jump on a bed that turns out to contain a sleeping Aunt Josephine. She doesn't pretend to be the dying Lily Maid floating down a river, forced to cling to a bridge when her boat sinks. She doesn't psych herself out about the haunted wood, convincing herself that it really is haunted.

The play also omits many episodes that show Anne being initiated into domesticity. She doesn't find a rat in the pudding, accidentally get Diana drunk on what she thinks is raspberry cordial, or put liniment in the cake. The play does contain references to Anne's struggles with cultural expectations toward girls, to her dying her hair, trying to bleach her freckles, and longing for puffed sleeves. But mostly the musical rushes to show how Anne is embraced and loved by the community. This Anne is less self-dramatizing, more wild and rebellious. I'm having trouble recognizing her.

The next day, in another break from Anne, we go to see the bottle houses in Edgmont, driving along the periphery of PEI. It's windy and in some places the water is part red, part blue, while in others the colors mix, some more influenced by the soil, some reflecting the sky, others caught in the middle of a battle between soil and sky. The water is violet here and there but mostly brackish with hints of purple like a bruise, sometimes blue or green, stitched with white caps along the waves, frothy in the wind.

The whimsy of the bottle houses is something that the young Anne, at least, would appreciate. There's a giant bottle at the entryway to this little complex of flower and rock gardens, a pond and a fountain and small buildings constructed from more than 25,000 old bottles of different shapes, sizes, and colors combined with cement to form walls. There's a six-gabled house, a round tavern, and a chapel, with pews and an altar and a pump organ made of bottles, designed so that light streams in like light through stained glass, colors playing on the floor.

It's too cold for me to walk on the beach that afternoon, so while everyone else goes off, I return to reading *Anne's House of Dreams*, which I learn from Epperly was written soon after *Anne of the Island*, long before the boring *Anne of Windy Poplars*. This novel, perhaps the best of the sequels, is full of fog and humidity and wind and storms, and in it, newlywed Anne is allowed to grow and deepen.

In this novel, Anne departs from her usual friendship with "wholesome, normal, merry girls like herself" and befriends Leslie Moore, "a tragic appealing figure of thwarted womanhood." In an ostensibly sensitive, intimate scene, Anne tells Leslie, "the life you have to live has warped you a little, perhaps."[56] Even though to my twenty-first century eyes, this seems a bit patronizing toward a woman who has endured loss after loss, *Anne's House of Dreams* is nevertheless very much a book about women joining forces to weather grief, a novel described by Epperly as a "tightly woven, wise story" about "self-discovery and integration."[57]

Anne's House of Dreams reminds me strongly of *Jane Eyre*, which heralded my breakthrough into reading adult classics when I was fifteen. It turns out that Charlotte Brontë's novel was also formative for Montgomery. Like Jane Eyre, Anne is an orphan with a plain name who must create her own sense of family. Throughout Montgomery's series, the emphasis on opposites and doubling and on striking middle grounds between relying on intuition and rationality, on sorting out the differences between fantasy and reality, on struggling between duty and desire, passion and discipline, and voice and silence, echoes Brontë's themes.

As the allusions become especially obvious in this novel, Anne can no longer be Jane's parallel because, now married, Anne can't experience comparable conflicts to her single young nineteenth-century counterpart. So Leslie becomes the heroine of the story, not so much Jane as Bertha, Rochester's mad wife who is kept hidden away in the attic. Like Bertha, Leslie is caught in a distressing and impossible moral bind. Once a beautiful girl full of promise, she was forced at sixteen to marry an abusive, alcoholic man in order to save her mother's property—much like Bertha. But unlike her, Leslie isn't locked in an attic by a husband who pretends that she doesn't exist. Instead, her husband mercifully disappeared at sea, and now Leslie is free to get on with her life, right?

Nope. Captain Jim, the "hero" of this novel, runs across a brain-damaged man who has lost his memory and is now in a boarding house. This man has the same eye color as Dick, and so Captain Jim concludes that he is Leslie's lost husband.

And since it's a wife's duty to take care of her husband (and apparently any man who has eyes the color of her husband's), Captain Jim does the "right thing" and dumps this man on Leslie. While many readers find Captain Jim charming, I often find him tiresome, his voice the most dominant one in the book, drowning out Anne's presence with his long-winded stories. And his meddling in Leslie's life, his determination to make her do her "duty," especially irritates me.

The community is, on the surface, very sympathetic to Leslie's plight, one that parallels Jane Eyre's struggles against duty and desire when, in the time-honored tradition of heroines who must choose between love interests, she has to decide whether to cast her lot with the passionate but deceptive Rochester or her cold but righteous cousin St. John. Even Brontë thinks that duty can be taken too far, though, and can't bring herself to overly prolong the possibility that Jane will end up with St. John. Montgomery refuses to take such a firm position on the side of desire and to release Leslie from the community's absurd insistence that she perform her "duty." Even as the neighbors try to assist Leslie, they acknowledge that she is trapped for the rest of her life, enduring a "living death," and has "no prospect except waiting on Dick Moore all her life."[58] When a handsome writer arrives on the scene and falls in love with Leslie, it is understood that this romance can never be.

Leslie's writer-beau is the one who eventually takes on the task of penning Captain Jim's story, something Gilbert has suggested that Anne do to her protests: "You know what my forte is. The fanciful, the fairy-like, the pretty. To write Captain Jim's book as it should be written one should be a master of vigorous yet subtle style, a keen psychologist, a born humorist and a born tragedian. A rare combination of gifts is needed." I'm peeved at Gil for seeming to accept this logic, and find him downright sadistic for advocating an operation that would restore "Dick" to his former self. Nevertheless, he and Captain Jim eventually become the unwitting instruments who free Leslie. While Anne favors withholding the truth to protect her friend, it is Gilbert and Captain Jim who ultimately respect Leslie enough to inform her that the operation exists and to leave the decision up to her. And Gilbert is sensitive enough to comment that "Duty in the abstract is one thing; duty in the concrete is quite another, especially when the doer is confronted by a woman's stricken eyes."[59]

Since Anne and Gilbert serve as the rational centers of the book, Montgomery uses Captain Jim and Cornelia to explore male and female extremes. These two characters constitute another set of doubles in the book, counterpoints for each other. Cornelia hates both men and Methodists. She believes that "us women ought to stand by each other" and presents Leslie as a victim of weak and bad men, though she also blames her mother's selfishness. Surprisingly to me at least, Cornelia considers that the vote for women would be a burden, another way to force them to clean up men's messes. Anne and Gilbert particularly enjoy Cornelia's visits because they like to make fun of her speeches afterward. But ultimately Cornelia is good hearted and extremely protective of Leslie, and she surprises everyone by marrying a once-hairy prophet-like guy, Marshall—once he gets a haircut and a shave and she would no longer have to be seen with a "perambulating haystack."[60]

Captain Jim also has a good heart and boundless admiration for Anne. For being one of those "rare people" who "never speak but that they say something," he is quite loquacious and sometimes a little precious. He has remained faithful fifty years to his drowned sweetheart and holds as many stereotypes of the opposite sex as Cornelia—women can't write, women are illogical—but Anne and Gilbert never have a good laugh over him.[61] However, Epperly comments that "Captain Jim's dismissal of women's writing seems funny in the story, since Montgomery is writing his story."[62]

Eventually, Leslie discovers the truth—that, in another example of doubling/twinning, the man everyone thought was Dick is actually his cousin George. Gilbert and Captain Jim, the two characters most oppressively insistent in their kindly manner that Leslie do her duty, become the ones lauded for setting her free. The book ends happily: Leslie has a future and Anne remains, as Gilbert addressed her early on, "my Queen Anne—queen of my heart and life and home." But by then Anne has suffered the death of a newborn. Eventually, in a cutesy passage, she is delivered another child by the stork and, ignoring the advice of male childcare experts, speaks to him in baby talk.[63] In later books she will continue to rebel against similar advice, like stern admonitions against kissing sons. In *Anne of Ingleside*, Montgomery writes in response to this advice, "She only felt pity for the writer of it. Poor, poor man! For of course [the writer] was a man. No woman would ever write anything so silly and wicked."[64]

I love the Brontë echoes and the subversive elements of this novel, but I'm a little grateful that I didn't first read it until my twenties, with all of its emphasis on women's duty. As a child or teenager, I doubt that I would have recognized how Montgomery often undercuts her own messages. After all, at fifteen when I first read *Jane Eyre*, I rooted pretty hard for Jane to end up with Rochester. A couple of years later, when I first read *Wuthering Heights*, I enthusiastically admired the doomed love of Cathy and Heathcliff. My students find my former teenage concept of romance to be insane. They find Rochester a jerk, a manipulator, a "player." They find Heathcliff disturbed and dangerous and abusive.

After paying $40 to get onto the Confederation Bridge and head home, we drive and drive and drive and finally reach the US border, where the American official isn't quite as easygoing as the Canadian one from a few days ago.

"Do you have any oranges, tangerines, or clementines?" she asks, and Sophie giggles because of the redundancy of the question. The woman frowns at her and asks her how she knows the adults in the front seat. A wicked little gleam flashes through Sophie's eyes, the kind that suggests that she's pondering whether to claim that I kidnapped her, but then she says, "That's my mom." The woman then questions Mahita, who identifies herself as a friend. The woman asks if she's brought a note from her parents. I pretend to be casual while I produce the forged, inaccurate note. Seconds tick by as we wait silently. The woman asks for our passports. She looks at each. She examines the note. She appears to be comparing a passport to the note. We all hold our breaths, not daring to fidget or shuffle or blink.

"Have a good trip," she says, passing back our papers.

I confess that I only make it through one more Anne book, *Anne of Ingleside*, another of the books that Montgomery wrote some years after the others to fill in gaps in Anne's life. In this book, Anne has stopped writing; she instead is "writing living epistles" in the form of raising children.[65] Sometimes the book is about Anne, with mildly funny, gossipy stories and a subplot in which she's afraid that her relationship with Gilbert is in trouble. Much of the time the book is about the children, full of cutesy stories about their adventures and mishaps. The book starts to feel schizophrenic as it moves from marital anxiety to adorable stories from the children's perspectives. It's hard to tell if this is a book for adults or children. And of course Anne has twins (girls) and a son, Walter, who believes in fairies, and at this point, I feel no remorse in giving up on the series.

I think back to the first friend I made in Springfield, Missouri, Lisa, a bond forged by our mutual love of Anne. I wonder what has become of Lisa. I wonder how she feels about Anne today. I google her, thinking maybe I will send her a note, find out if she's ever reread the books, introduced them to her children. I am saddened to discover that she died of breast cancer a year ago.

During her two-year fight against the disease, Lisa was part of a support network. They called themselves "Kindred Spirits."

CHAPTER ELEVEN

Concord, Massachusetts

Louisa May Alcott's *Little Women*

"I CAN'T EVEN COUNT HOW MANY TIMES I've read *Little Women*," Aunt Shirley had said one day during our Laura Ingalls Wilder tour. We'd been sitting at a Formica table in a diner in De Smet, SD. A fan whirred in the window while I ate my usual grilled cheese sandwich and rippled potato chip lunch out of a red basket.

"Me neither," Jody said, sipping her unsweetened ice tea, smugly, I thought. Jody was special. She had been named Jo after Jo March, which made me extremely jealous. Not only that, but she was once diagnosed with scarlet fever, such a cool, literary disease, the one that had led to the stroke that blinded Mary Ingalls and triggered the rheumatic fever that resulted in congestive heart failure in the case of Lizzie Alcott, the model for *Little Women*'s Beth.[1] Of course, by the late twentieth century, Jody could just feel all literary, take some antibiotics, and be done with it.

I could never live up to Jody, and at thirteen, though I identified with Jo and her writing aspirations, I could count how many times I'd read *Little Women*: once. Though my mother and aunts were always alluding to it, I'd been slow to pick it up, finding the title off putting. It seemed to reflect an adult rather than child's sensibility, appearing to embody notions about femininity that felt old-fashioned, outdated, weirdly patronizing and sanctimonious. Like writer Anne Trubek, I thought it sounded like "a prissy book for girly girls."[2] It didn't help that the girls in the book were, with the exception of twelve-year-old Amy, teenagers, too old for me as a pre-teen to find especially interesting.

Maybe it was wise that, that day in South Dakota, I kept quiet about my mixed feelings toward *Little Women*. As Aunt Shirley and Jody talked about it, I became exceptionally absorbed in peeling off the part of my bread that, placed too close to the pickle, was now stained green.

"Have you even read it?" Aunt Shirley turned her attention to me.

"Yes," I answered in the most indignant tone I could muster.

"You didn't like it, though." Aunt Shirley dismissed me.

"I did, too," I protested, but she and Jody shook their heads as if they had seen right through me. Their disapproval of my incomplete passion for the book allowed them to bond more deeply with each other, affirming their membership in a club that became even more illustrious by virtue of my exclusion.

A few years before, Aunt Shirley had started doll collections for us. She had always loved dolls. Antique ones stared from every surface in her living room: cracked porcelain, molded plastic, scraggly rag, withered cornhusk. In a glass case she kept two smiling china head dolls that stared out of wide, lashless eyes, giving me the creeps, especially when I thought about how these were the closest things to a baby girl my aunt would ever have. "Have you seen the Madame Alexander *Little Women* dolls?" she asked Jody, then said to me, "You never liked dolls. You never played with them."

I had played with dolls, just not all that maternally. I'd never cradled them and pretended to be a mother. Mostly, I'd cast them in dramas I made up. So maybe that explained why my aunt and cousin ignored me when I protested, "I did, too," going on with their conversation as if I hadn't spoken.

I resolved to reread *Little Women* as soon as I got home. And I must have, though I can't remember; when I was older, I did list the book as among my childhood favorites, and I've always remembered Jo fondly. But I never felt properly committed to Alcott's characters, not enough to read beyond *Little Women*. As many times as I picked up *Little Men*, I just couldn't bring myself to be interested in the fates of a bunch of children, mostly boys, whom Jo takes under her wing. First, I was too young to be interested in Alcott's teenage March sisters; by the time I began to identify with them, I was too old to really engage with the children of the sequels.

Christmas 1976 rolled around, and with it came the promised *Little Women* dolls from Aunt Shirley. For Jody, Jo, the heroine, the writer, special-ordered because there had been none in stock. For me, Amy, the brat, blond with a white dress and yellow polka dotted overskirt. I smothered Amy with tissue paper, my smile stiff. I hated her and I hated Jody, who exclaimed smugly over her Jo doll in her red underskirt and white eyelet peplum. I read just as much as Jody and I was the one who wanted to be a writer, and I'd absorbed enough of those Childhood of Famous Americans books to know that talent should be visible from a tender age. So I took the Amy doll as a sign of my aunt's lack of faith in me: somehow she had failed to notice, failed to register, my incipient writer self. The next year we both got Marmee, the next year, Meg. Aunt Shirley never gave me a Jo doll.

One morning when I was twenty-four, I sat up in bed and said, in a tone of profound disbelief, "Amy?" My aunt had been dead for seven years, but I was as hurt as if she'd given me the Amy doll the day before. Jody said, "It was because I had brown hair, like Jo, and the same name. You were younger and blond, like Amy."

But even at twenty-four, my memory of being identified with Amy seemed like the most hurtful of insults, even if Aunt Shirley wasn't as put off by poor Amy as I was. Nevertheless, when, at twenty-six, I received my MFA in creative writing, Aunt Gena and Jody presented me with a blue Madame Alexander box.

"A wrong is being righted," Jody said.

I shuffled through the tissue paper, lifting out the Jo doll with the brown hair and the red and white outfit, touched at finally receiving the gift I'd been hoping for, absurdly, throughout my teenage years, the affirmation that I was more like Jo than like Amy.

Today, if Jo were to come to life and enroll at our local high school, she would be quickly deemed a "loser" by my own daughter. Sophie is impervious to the romantic image of the prototypical writer heroine whose adolescent production is largely melodramas and fairy tales that she scribbles in her attic garret while eating piles of crisp apples. Jo has "odd, blunt ways" and expects to be "the old maid of the family" because she is not "one of the agreeable sort."[3] When Jo cuts off her hair to sell it in order to help her family, her mother, sisters, and even the neighbor boy Laurie constantly lament the loss of it, saying mournfully and repeatedly, "Your one beauty!" Their dismay is so acute, one begins to wonder how hideous Jo really is. But that didn't matter to me as a young teenager. It was Jo's passion for writing and misfit ways that I focused on. Described in a PBS documentary about Alcott by various readers using adjectives that include "impetuous, rambunctious, ambitious, moody, passionate," Jo was the one who was not only determined to be a writer, but who was always fighting against limitations on girls and women.[4]

Then there's Amy. In the book's early chapters, the "conceited" Amy performs the inexcusable act of burning Jo's manuscript—the only copy—to get revenge when her sister refuses to take her on an outing. I was horrified by this. Jo eventually forgives her sister, but I never did, and never warmed up to Amy, who would have been the popular one at Sophie's school as she gets older and boys start noticing her in a way they never noticed Jo. Even though Amy also becomes an artist, I still resolutely disliked her.

Aunt Shirley's death from lupus was far less beautiful and graceful, quiet and dignified than *Little Women*'s Beth's fictional death. "There is a lovelier country . . . where we shall go, by and by, when we are good enough," Meg says early in *Little Women*. Beth replies, "It seems so long to wait, so hard to do. I want to fly away at once, as those swallows fly, and go in at that splendid gate."[5]

Many contemporary readers have found shy, retiring Beth to be, according to Harriet Reisen, "alternately pathetic and infuriating."[6] Not me. As a child and young teenager, I saw her as a saint to be emulated, the perfect representative of passive girlhood, without ambition or opinion, even if she is, as Janice Alberghene and Beverly Lyon Clark put it, "so fully self-effacing that she dies."[7] I figured that I just wasn't virtuous enough to rise to her standard. Growing up, I imagined, I'd become more like Beth and learn to embrace with a joyful heart whatever came along, even death.

But my aunt was in her forties and she was nothing like Beth. She was enraged by her own declining health and imminent demise. Fury inhabited her eyes more and more as the years passed. I never once heard her speak yearningly about entering "that splendid gate." If she ever looked forward to lying on a cloud while playing a harp and singing praises day and night, she didn't tell me about it. She was in pain. She was leaving behind a family. She was angry.

It turns out that the death of Alcott's sister Lizzie, the model for Beth, was more similar to my aunt's than to Beth's; Susan Cheever writes that Lizzie "lashed out at her family with an anger she had never before expressed."[8] As an adult, I'm surprised to be surprised by this, and by Marmee's confession early in *Little Women* that she has been angry every day of her life.[9] I somehow failed to pick up on this when I was young, even though my own teenage years played out against a backdrop of confusion and anger at the death that hung over us all.

I didn't know how to respond to my aunt's barbed comments or my mother's irritation and anguish at her sister's increasing paranoia, or the family disruptions, like when my aunt and uncle abruptly packed up and left a holiday gathering. I didn't know what to make of the accusations and arguments I overheard on the phone or in whispers on the stairs outside of Jody's bedroom, where we sat frozen. While Marmee's comment about her own anger is an allusion to her daily struggles, not the intensified emotions of coping with terminal illness, I'm surprised that I once skimmed over this rather than finding in it a validation of my own turbulence.

But then, the point of Marmee's speech is that anger should be suppressed. In fact, this is a running theme throughout *Little Women*. Take when Jo's fury with Amy for burning her manuscript results in Amy nearly drowning. Judith Fetterley points out that in the book "female anger is so unacceptable that there are no degrees to it; all anger leads to 'murder.'" In fact, she notes, any female's negative emotion or act of even the most minimal selfishness has dire consequences, as when Beth ends

up catching the scarlet fever that leads to her death because Jo is too busy writing to help the desperately impoverished Hummel family and Beth goes instead.[10]

In comparison to the happy striving of the March girls to be virtuous, I felt
that something was wrong with my family, everyone angry and on edge in the face
of death instead of appropriately sad, mournful, and selfless. After our Laura Ingalls Wilder trip, as my aunt grew sicker, I tried to avoid her, tried to avoid her
resentment and delusional thinking. At fifteen, I was shaken when she called me
and pleasantly asked me if my mother had been talking about her and what she'd
been saying. Later, I overheard my mother on the phone with my Aunt Gena. Mom
was outraged that Aunt Shirley had interrogated me. "Is Nancy upset about it?"
Aunt Gena must have asked, but I only heard my mother's side of the conversation:
"Oh, no. She's not very perceptive," she said, as if she really believed that I hadn't
noticed the closed doors and whispers, tense glances and strained conversations,
half-uttered sentences that halted when we kids entered the room. Sometimes I
overheard my mother agonizing to others on the phone: why had my aunt changed
so much? Was it the disease's attack on her central nervous system, was it the cor-
ticosteroids, or did those things simply lower inhibitions and allow my aunt to do
and say mean things she'd wished to all along?

"You girls don't really remember your Aunt Shirley," my mom said to me and
Jody many times when we were adults. "You were pretty young when she died."

But I'd been seventeen, Jody nineteen, old enough to remember plenty and
grieve her loss. While Aunt Gena may have given Jody permission and space to
mourn, my mother always made it clear to me that Aunt Shirley's death was not
my grief. She made it clear that it would have been presumptuous for me to claim
any sense of loss or sadness, and even, later, any memories of my aunt. I struggled
for many years to process her death and reconcile all of the tension in my family
with such literary examples as the peaceful sorrow at the loss of the ever-angelic
and patient Beth.

My own daughter's experience with *Little Women* is far less fraught; she was introduced to it by the 1949 film with June Allyson.[11] Once when Sophie was about
five, she emerged from the den and dashed past me, where I was marking student
papers in the living room. "I'm watching *Little Women!*" she called. "I have to change
my clothes!" Soon she came back downstairs wearing a long skirt from her costume
box. "Christopher Columbus!" she exclaimed regularly, Jo's favorite slang phrase.

Now she's fourteen, and we're getting ready to go to Concord, and I read parts
of the book aloud on the porch on a long summer evening. I find that Alcott's vocabulary makes me kind of chipper, the repetitions of words like *task, duty, eager,*

cheerful, cozy, heartily—what Ann Douglas calls a "blank-check Victorian vocabulary" that reappears with "sprightly monotony."[12] It takes me back to the summer I re-read Laura Ingalls Wilder, who was born the year before Alcott's book was published. Though her books were written much later, Wilder's recurring words like *happy, cozy, pretty, snug,* and *sweet* echo the tone and sometimes overlap the content of Alcott's.

Sophie laughs often at Alcott's sly comedy. For instance, after nurturing Beth forgets to feed her bird, who dies, Amy suggests that he might be revived in the oven. "He's been starved, and he shan't be baked now he's dead!" Beth responds indignantly before retiring to her room "overcome with emotion and lobster."[13] Even though Sophie finds this amusing, she has little patience with the lessons imparted at the end of each chapter, like that concern with fashion and one's appearance is deeply degrading and that all play and no work makes life boring and chaotic. I find that I don't really buy these lessons anymore, either. I'm a little shocked that I ever did.

"Mom, no offense, but how can they be so worshipful toward their mother?" Sophie asks me. "I mean, they're my age, and I love you and all, but I really hate you, too." I just roll my eyes, remembering the feeling, at fourteen, of desperately wanting to hang on to the security of home and desperately wanting to separate from it, all in the same moment. While all of my favorite heroines miss their families, the ease of the process of separation appears to correlate with the publication dates of the books: in the 1860s, Jo is reluctant to leave home or to embrace change; in the early 1900s, Anne's desire for more education finally takes her away from Avonlea; in the 1930s, we find a late nineteenth-century Laura chomping at the bit to start her own life with Almanzo; and by the early 1950s, an early twentieth-century Betsy is brave enough to set off overseas rather than sabotaging her longing to travel the way Jo does. And yet, of all of these heroines' creators, Louisa May Alcott, the only one who remained unmarried, seems to be the one who experienced the most tension herself about her independence, eager both to travel and to be on her own in the vibrant world of Boston, often returning to live with her parents, always intent on providing financial support for her family.

Sophie nudges me and I go on reading aloud. But as I hit one of Marmee's particularly long moralizing speeches, Sophie dozes off.

Although I can't pinpoint the exact ages that I read *Little Women*, it's as if Jody and I absorbed the book by osmosis from the time we were little. And yet, it's also a book that carries so much cultural weight, a book so well-known and so much more highly regarded by some academics than it was when I was young, a book that has been written about and analyzed and discussed and loved by so many, I found myself putting off rereading it for years. Unlike with Laura and Betsy and Anne, I never entertained any illusion that I owned Jo. Just as I had a vague sense that my mother owned grief, that it was a feeling I didn't have a right to, I saw *Little Women* as a book that belonged to my mother and aunts. And it turned out that many people, friends and famous writers alike, felt a sense of possession as well. How could I compete?

Harriet Reisen lists famous fans, including J. K. Rowling, Gloria Steinem, Cynthia Ozick, Gertrude Stein, Simone de Beauvoir, Ursula Le Guin, Bobbie Ann Mason, and Geraldine Brooks, whose own novel *March* envisions the lives of the March parents.[14] In 1989, when American governors were asked to name their favorite childhood books, two of the three women governors chose *Little Women*.[15] While none of the forty-seven male governors mentioned Alcott's book in their responses, *Little Women* does have its male fans. George Cukor made the first movie version in 1933 because he had such an emotional affinity with Jo.[16] Even somewhat dimwitted *Friends* character Joey, who loves *The Shining* but finds it so frightening that he keeps it in the freezer, becomes attached to Alcott's book. Beth's impending death upsets him so much that Rachel offers to put *Little Women* in the freezer, too.

Alcott's books were so popular in her time that, according to Harriet Reisen, readers eagerly awaited their release "with a fervor not seen again until the Harry Potter series of J. K. Rowling."[17] Long before *Little Women* was taken especially seriously by the academy, Alcott's work thrived in popular culture, inspiring movies and TV adaptations, musicals, operas, and anime. It's been translated into more than fifty languages and spawned the usual catalogues of merchandise—t-shirts, magnets, puzzles, notecards, dolls, diaries. "For a century," writes Ann Douglas, "American middle-class girls read all of Louisa May Alcott's books for children simply as a part of being young, and of growing up."[18]

My mother was a preschooler when the George Cukor film of *Little Women* came out in 1933, the year after *Little House in the Big Woods* was first published; she probably borrowed Alcott's book from a neighbor or the library a few years later, or maybe her mother already had a copy. Whenever my mom discovered the books and the film, they would undoubtedly have resonated with her own impoverished childhood. Although Alcott's book stresses many other themes, Cukor's film, like Wilder's work, puts the emphasis on "the financial struggles of the Marches and presents them as a kind of idealized American family who are brought together by hard times, perhaps a message an audience pulling together behind Roosevelt's

NRA would be especially ready to hear," Susan R. Gannon writes.[19] Also as in Wilder's books, the conflict between duty and aspiration looms large.

"Mothers who loved the book pass it on to daughters who may translate the March girls' problems a little differently, but identify with them no less strongly," Gannon writes.[20] I don't know if my mother and aunts, invested in more traditional ideas of gender roles, connected to the book's representation of what it means to become a woman, Jo's rebellion, or its view of art that somehow proves inspiring and more memorable than Jo and Amy's eventual abandonment of it. Alcott's work can be read on so many levels, mixing matriarchal and patriarchal traditions, both reinforcing and challenging gender roles, and both encouraging and constraining artistic impulses, that it's hard to decode in retrospect all of the dimensions of my family members' attachment to it.

Though she had enough of an independent streak to delay marrying until she was thirty and to cultivate careers as a teacher and a businesswoman, my mother was committed to making me into a lady and somewhat horrified when I embraced feminism. "But you gave me *Little Women*," I wanted to protest, a book in which, as Judith Fetterley puts it, "the figure who most resists the pressure to become a little woman is the most attractive and the figure who most succumbs to it dies."[21]

Jo, the resistant character, is always being scolded for her unladylike ways. She refers to herself as a "business man" (and then corrects it to "business girl") and is reprimanded by Meg for attempting to "make a guy of yourself" and for her "romping ways" when she runs. Jo's opposition to Meg's marriage and her famous announcement that she wishes she could marry Meg herself "and keep her safe in the family" speaks more to her desire to keep her family intact than any incestuous lesbian leanings, and her frustration with being a girl seems to have more to do with restriction than a real desire to be male. She tells Laurie, "If I were a boy, we'd run away together, and have a capital time; but as I'm a miserable girl, I must be proper and stop at home." Eventually she is praised by her father for no longer being his "son Jo." He says, "I see a young lady who pins her collar straight, laces her boots neatly, and neither whistles, talks slang, nor lies on the rug as she used to do." Jo, the most critical of all heroines of female indoctrination, is also, paradoxically, the only literary heroine ever to be cured of slang.[22]

Who wouldn't want to be a man in a society where women aren't allowed to run, travel, or lie on the rug, who have to carefully guard their speech, a society where women are regarded as children while men are assumed to be paragons of wisdom? "Your father . . . never loses patience—never doubts or complains—but always hopes, and works and waits so cheerfully. . . . I asked him to help me so, and he never forgot it, but saved me from many a sharp word by that little gesture and kind look," Marmee tells Jo, communicating a paradigm for marriage that precludes equality between partners.[23] "Little women can only love up, not across or down," Fetterley says. "They must marry their fathers, not their brothers or sons." Thus Meg marries John Brooke, their relationship like one of an impetuous child and patient parent, Laurie marries Amy, "who is a fitting child for him," and Jo ends up with the older and wiser Professor Bhaer.[24]

Alcott herself, who said she had a man's soul and a love of pretty girls, was notably more consistent than her best-known heroine when it came to avoiding traditional gender roles, never marrying and famously declaring, "I'd rather paddle my own canoe." Even more famous is Alcott's response to the pressure to marry Jo off to Laurie, protesting about the girls who wrote to ask "who the little women marry, as if that was the only aim and end of a woman's life. I won't marry Jo to Laurie to please anyone."

Early on, Jo describes her ambitions: she wants "to do something splendid . . . something heroic or wonderful that won't be forgotten after I'm dead . . . I think I shall write books, and get rich and famous." She sees no contradiction between this and Marmee's wish to see her daughters "well and wisely married, and to lead useful, pleasant lives. . . . To be loved and chosen by a good man is the best and sweetest thing which can happen to a woman."[25]

By the end of Little Women's sequel, Good Wives, which is now routinely published in the same volume as the original text and labeled "Part Two," Jo succumbs to Marmee's vision, marries, and seems to give up her writing. But Alcott did no such thing, creating a tradition of women writers like her successor Lucy Maud Montgomery who retain their ambition and independence much more forcefully than their own heroines do. In Little Women's final chapter, Jo comments on the youthful ambition beyond which she has now supposedly matured: "The life I wanted then seems selfish, lonely, and cold to me now. I haven't given up the hope that I may write a good book yet, but I can wait, and I'm sure it will be all the better for such experiences and illustrations as these."[26] At this, Jo gestures at her family, a scene that recalls for me the one in Anne of Ingleside in which Anne says that she has not altogether given up writing, then, referring to her children, says, "But I'm writing living epistles now."[27]

Maybe readers should have seen this coming. After all, throughout the book, Jo's best writing is not, as Elizabeth Lennox Keyser points out, the result of passion or ambition, but of her love for her family. And though Amy largely gives up her painting as well, Keyser sees her as the more subversive one and possibly the better artist, since she is less fearful of being assertive, taking risks, and appearing selfish or foolish. "As the pampered baby of the family, she does not feel the need to earn its love or fear its disapproval," says Keyser. "Therefore, from the beginning of the book, she is the least willing to engage in self-sacrifice."[28]

At any rate, whatever the source of the book's appeal to my mother and aunts, and likely their mother before them, it was, according to Elaine Showalter, a radical departure from girls' fare of its time. And while it's become standard to criticize Alcott for compromising her imaginative vision in favor of commercial success by marrying off Jo, albeit to Professor Bhaer rather than Laurie, while I too have fallen prey to this very tendency, Showalter defends Alcott. Showalter insists that such criticisms demand a twentieth-century ending of separation and autonomy which comes from a romantic model of genius, one that women have simply never been able to live up to. "Because it is derived from male experience and mythology, genius requires a woman artist either to sacrifice the feminine side of her personality, or to labor continually under the sense of infinite artistic inferiority," Showalter writes, arguing that Jo "exchanges the model of male 'genius' for a more realistic feminine model that is based on training, experimentation, professionalism and self-fulfillment" and that Jo's "writing will be stronger for years as wife, mother, and teacher."[29]

Little Women's popularity with women and girls notwithstanding, it was historically fashionable to belittle it; a 1938 Odell Shepard review of an Alcott biography is typical, claiming that one reason for Alcott's popularity is that "the American public is itself immature in thought and mood."[30] This was still the prevalent attitude when I entered college in 1981. As an English major and psychology minor, I plowed through reading lists that were dominated by Hemingway, Fitzgerald, Faulkner, and Freud and almost completely devoid of any women writers or thinkers. My relationship with *Little Women* became even more uneasy as I read writers and studied from professors who were largely dismissive of work like Alcott's. In his story "Bernice Bobs Her Hair," one of F. Scott Fitzgerald's characters says of *Little Women,* "What modern girl could live like those inane females?" Writer Lavinia Russ reports being told by Ernest Hemingway, "you're so full of young sweetness and light you ought to be carrying *Little Women.*"[31]

Sometimes I goaded my mom and Aunt Gena, gleefully reporting to them my discovery that Alcott had disdained her most popular book, dismissing it as sentimental and moralistic, calling it her "worst scrape," amazed by the success of a work that eventually made her feel trapped, as Ann Douglas puts it.[32] I was obnoxious in my sense of having been absolved of my lifelong crime of ambivalence toward the book, my perpetual mixed feelings, my stunted emotional ability to cultivate unadulterated passion toward what the other women in my family had loved.

But by the time the critical tide turned, seemingly abruptly, I welcomed it. One minute, *Little Women* was absent from the canon, ignored by the academy, Alcott's name rarely considered as important as those of her detractors like Hemingway and Fitzgerald or her older contemporaries like Henry David Thoreau, Ralph Waldo Emerson, or Nathaniel Hawthorne, even if she was the only woman writer included in the Authors card game of my childhood. The next minute, or so it seemed to me, Alcott's work had been reassessed. Suddenly, it was being considered as a legitimate topic in academic journals devoted to women's and American literature rather than remaining segregated to the children's literature "ghetto." Eventually, it was excerpted in the *Norton Anthology of Women's Literature.* "Where else . . . could we have read about an all-female group who discussed Work, Art, and all the Great Questions—or found girls who wanted to be women and not vice versa?" asks Gloria Steinem.[33]

It's a book that influenced so many of the books I loved in childhood, and continues to filter into young adult literature such as a recent novel that is both a satire and tribute, Lauren Baratz-Logsted's 2011 *Little Women and Me.* In it, a contemporary girl falls into the book and becomes the "fifth March sister" who anachronistically nails each of the characters with her brief descriptions: Meg is the "prig"; Jo is the "rebel," the one who "really rocked," the "alpha girl," the one you'd never catch "wearing skinny jeans or eating salad just to impress a boy." Beth, who Emily compares to Oprah, is the "least cool . . . but she was so sweet and kind."[34] The book achieves its humor largely through such jarringly slangy, anachronistic references to the past and through its commentary that echoes the reactions of even the most affectionate contemporary reader. When Laurie admits to watching the March family through the window and Jo offers to leave the curtains open, narrator Emily says, "Oh, good one, Jo . . . way to enable the stalker."[35] And Emily's twenty-first-century insistence on initiating a competition with Jo over Laurie highlights just how revolutionary Alcott's book was in its focus on solidarity between women and on women's communities. Originally titled *The Pathetic Family* (which meant "worthy of sympathy" rather than "inadequate"),[36] *Little Women*'s title comes from a letter from the March girls' absent father. But his influence pretty much stops there. This is a female-centered world in which even the family's surname, March, is a transformation of Alcott's mother's, May.[37]

The summer day in 2012 when Sophie and I finally set off for Concord, it's been more than thirty years since Aunt Shirley's death, my mother and Aunt Gena have also been gone for several years now, and Sophie is a few months older than I was on my childhood Laura Ingalls Wilder trip. It's a clear blue day, five years after

Sophie and I drove through Laura Ingalls Wilder Land, and as we head across up-state New York, an orange flag tears loose from an "oversize" load and flies under my tires. Above us, little birds seem suspended in the air, shivering. In a highly mobile, increasingly digital age where we are always speeding along roads and skipping along over the surfaces of Facebook and Twitter, a time when publishers keep failing and bookstores keep closing, my sense of urgency and longing about totally immersing myself in the experience of a book has become even more intense. Though experience has often proven me wrong, I still imagine that seeing the places where authors lived and where books are set will somehow deepen my connection.

In downtown Concord, there are no flapping teeth above a building with a sign saying "Docta Angus Wilk's Extractions," a creepy image from the 1939 movie. On our way to Orchard House, where Alcott wrote *Little Women*, we instead pass a store called "Thoreauly Antiques," my first clue that in Concord (pronounced "Conquered"), Thoreau is pronounced with the accent on the first syllable, so it sounds like "Thorough."

I have misread the hours for the Alcott home, and so we arrive at a tiny lot at the bottom of a hill before it opens. Sophie thinks that getting out of the car so early will make us look too nerdily eager, but it's a nice day, so I leave her to read in the front seat while I walk up to the three-hundred-year-old house with narrow brown siding.

Sitting on a bench, I admire the garden that has been designed after a description of the one in *Little Women* and that, according to a marker, is planted and tended by volunteers. I try to identify Meg's roses, heliotropes, and myrtle; Jo's sunflowers; Beth's sweet peas and mignonette, larkspur, pinks, pansies, and southernwood, "with chickweed for the birds and catnip for the pussies"; and Amy's bower with "honeysuckles and morning-glories hanging their colored horns and bells in graceful wreaths all over it, tall white lilies, delicate ferns, and as many brilliant, picturesque plants as would consent to blossom there."[38]

It's pleasant out here, surrounded by trees, maybe even the one that inspired the description of the March sisters riding a tree limb when they can't have a horse.[39] Up above in a picnic area, a group of girls are practicing a play. As 10:00 nears, employees start emerging from the house, setting up a table and guest book outside.

I wish Sophie weren't being so stubborn. Now that she's fourteen, I am the most embarrassing person who ever walked the Earth, so it's not just that she wants to wait in the car—she wants me to wait in the car, too, reticent and unobserved, rather than stroll freely out in the world, too eager, too excited, too needy, too unprotected from the critical eyes of others. I remember feeling like this as an adolescent, wanting to just be able to remain unobserved and feeling ashamed at the mere existence of my own mother, so irritatingly insistent on taking up space and being seen and heard. But now I think, wow, even in this day and age when readers are largely impatient with passive Beth, girls still go through a phase of being so self-conscious that the solution is self-erasure? At least I hope that it's just a phase.

Grudgingly, Sophie joins me when the staff finally open the doors. I buy our tickets, and then we browse in the gift shop for thirty minutes, pondering collectibles, an audio and video rack, notecards and dolls, reproductions of nineteenth-century toys, mugs and posters and tote bags. As usual, I spend most of my time looking through the books, mysteries by Anna Maclean in which Louisa has become a sleuth, many biographies and commentaries related to Alcott's work and family, and children's books and thrillers by the prolific Alcott herself. There's a new edition of her first published book, *Flower Fables*, a small volume that was originally privately printed. Skipping over this book but turning through others, I become so absorbed I'm the last person to enter a small room where the tour starts with the viewing of a video. Though I was the first in line to buy tickets this morning, there is nowhere for us to sit.

The video is narrated by Susan Sarandon, who played a very forward-thinking twentieth-century Marmee in Gillian Armstrong's 1994 movie version of the book.[40] From the video, we learn about the influence of the great men of Louisa's father's circle, including Emerson, Hawthorne, and Thoreau, who once told young Louisa that a cobweb in the grass was a fairy's handkerchief. Sophie and I seem to be the only ones in the room who find this cloying. Or at least we're the only ones who laugh.

I think back to all of the references to fairies and the personifications of flowers in girls' literature, in the *Anne* series, in the *Jennifer* series, those images that once made me feel that my imagination was inadequate. Now I wonder if all of that sappiness traces back in a direct lineage to Thoreau, who thought he was doing the Alcott girls a favor by referring to the woods as "fairy land," unaware that he was planting a seed that would shape the imaginations of generations of girls, making me feel hostile toward him 150 years later. Alcott saw this whimsy as a way to get her own foot in the door; after *Flower Fables* first appeared, she said, "I hope to pass in time from fairies and fables to men and realities."[41] But first she wrote two subsequent, equally fanciful manuscripts that never found publishers, titled *Christmas Elves* and *Beach Bubbles*.

After the film, we continue the tour of the house where Alcott wrote *Little Women* in 1868, starting in the parlor where "Meg" (Alcott's sister Anna) got married. That's when it becomes especially evident that the emphasis of the tour is more historical than literary. It walks a careful line between conflating Alcott's life with *Little Women*, a book many visitors may not have read, and emphasizing the Alcott family's legacy not just in literature, but in "art, education, philosophy, and social justice," as the Orchard House website says.[42]

According to Anne Trubek, the original organizers of the museum created it as a "shrine to domesticity," and that emphasis remains; the Orchard House's website rhapsodizes that more than 50,000 visitors a year "discover what it means to be 'home.'" But, Trubek comments, the Alcotts were "anything but the idealized American family enshrined by founders of the Orchard House museum." It is likely that many visitors would see the real Alcott family, who supported abolitionist John Brown, progressive education, and women's rights, as a "bunch of weirdo radicals."[43]

The docent—as museum tour guides seem to be more commonly called in the eastern US—steers clear of controversy as she informs us that Louisa was not the only outstanding family member. The whole family had impressive gifts. Louisa's older sister Anna was an actress. Her younger sister Lizzie loved music. Her youngest sister, May, was a "talented" artist, mother Abigail was a reformer, and father Bronson was a transcendental philosopher, radical educator, and child psychology pioneer. "So see," the docent says, "It wasn't just Louisa who was talented!" Heaven forbid, I think, that the author of a book about putting others first would be allowed prominence on a tour of the home where she set that book. The tour carefully avoids any references to the feminist, passionate Louisa caught between the expectations of her father, the needs of her family, and the commercial demands of the publishing industry. The tourist industry seems to exert similar pressures, requiring careful balance, presenting the most generic possible images of beloved writers.

We walk under low ceilings across slanty floors with wide painted boards, making me feel like I'm in a funhouse. Eighty percent of the furnishings were owned by the Alcotts, but a few items are clearly reproductions. Like the "mood pillow" in the parlor, a sausage-shaped orange pillow.

"When the pillow is upright, that means you are welcome to join Jo in her room, but when the pillow is down, it means *Don't come in, I'm in a writing vortex*," the docent explains. Luckily for us, the current position of the pillow favors the social Alcott over the reclusive creative one, as the docent points out: "So, as you can see, the pillow is upright, so we are all welcome to join her upstairs."

I'm overcome by an overpowering urge to knock the pillow flat. Sophie is also eyeing it thoughtfully. She whispers, "Let's push the pillow over."

We stand pondering it for a moment while the rest of the group files toward the stairs. The docent remains rooted in place, watching us, clearly intending to keep a firm eye on each member of the group and then take up the rear as she herds us upstairs. Maybe every tour group has a rebel or two. Perhaps there have been troubling pillow tipping incidents in the past.

We sigh and head up the stairs.

"Can I slide down the banister?" Sophie whispers.

"Are you trying to get us kicked out?" I ask.

Upstairs, we crowd into Louisa's room with its sleigh bed and tiny built-in writing desk, called a "shelf desk," like a half-moon mounted to the wall between two windows, fake manuscript pages on top. I think of my big, messy desk at home and wonder at the small space on which Alcott wrote long books as well as many articles and stories for magazines like *Godey's Lady's Book* and *The Youth's Companion*. This tiny desk is the place where so much originated that would connect to and shape my favorite childhood books and my own values and imagination. *Little Women*'s influence on me and the other writers I loved was prodigious, whether directly mentioned as when Lovelace's Betsy borrows the book from a neighbor, or indirectly shaping episodes, values, and character portrayals in many books for girls. But Alcott also impacted generations of readers in perhaps more roundabout ways through the stories she published in these prominent nineteenth-century magazines, and a whole line of writers followed her example. *Godey's Lady's Book* appears throughout the *Little House* books, Ma Ingalls sharing back issues when other ladies come to visit, some of the issues undoubtedly containing stories by Alcott. Lucy Maud Montgomery's grandmother subscribed to *Godey's Lady's Book* and it was in this magazine that Montgomery found one of the source texts for *Anne*, the story "Charity Ann"; it is likely that Montgomery encountered Alcott's stories there also. Then there was the *Youth's Companion*, where Montgomery also had early publications, and which also made it to the frontier and influenced young Laura Ingalls; Laura saves a pile of *Youth's Companions* to open on Christmas Day in *The Long Winter*, giving her and her family something to look forward to in the midst of bleakness.

It's not just Alcott's desk that's small. The bed also seems tiny compared even to a twin bed of today, even though Alcott was relatively tall, 5'9" or 5'10". The docent points out a painting by youngest sister, May, of an owl on the fireplace. As we continue the tour, she points out more examples of May's artwork, especially in her long narrow room, which has sketches of mythological figures on the woodwork, and doors and bracketed shelves to hold flowers, and horses running along one wall, pulling a chariot surrounded by a rambunctious crowd. The docent always identifies May as a "talented artist," never allowing the word "artist" to slip out unmodified by the word "talented."

I've seen the four illustrations that May created for the first edition of her sister's book. They are amateurish, the girls peculiarly unattractive, with pointy noses and chins. Oddly, Jo only appears once, in a frontispiece group portrait of the girls gathered around Marmee, the focal point of the picture. Beth, supposedly thirteen, appears to be a toddler. Jo dreamily gazes out over her sisters' heads. Susan R. Gannon attributes the awkwardness of these figures to May's attempt to give her sister's characters "the conventionalized features and bodies of fashion illustrators, but her lame efforts produce figures with infantile heads and bodies that cannot convincingly stand, sit, or gesture." The individual illustrations show Amy skating, Beth welcoming Father home, and Meg admiring herself in the mirror—the latter so odd that editors of Alcott's letters described it as "freakish."[44]

Underneath the story of these illustrations seems to brew a tale of intense sibling rivalry. In *Little Women*, May's counterpart Amy eventually concludes that there's a difference between talent and genius and that she's merely talented. It wouldn't be surprising if aspiring artist May were stung by that portrayal. Maybe it was a small act of revenge for May to deny Louisa's counterpart Jo a starring role in an illustration. Although May's illustrations were quickly dumped from future editions of *Little Women* by its publisher, over time her art improved and matured and was exhibited in Paris salons, and she once protested that Louisa did not "monopolize all the Alcott talent."[45]

Throughout the house we see evidence of May's education as an artist as she copied famous paintings, like her versions of Joseph Turner seascapes on the walls of the master bedroom, where we also view a handmade flying geese quilt on the bed. In the adjoining nursery, a *Pilgrim's Progress* game hangs on the wall, an unacknowledged allusion to the way Alcott borrows from John Bunyan's book in the structure of part one of *Little Women* as she follows a year in the lives of the March sisters.

Back downstairs, we shift our focus to Bronson Alcott. His spacious study is packed with books, and his hat and mantel clock are also on display. Little niches contain busts of Plato and Sophocles. This room with its library table and desk seems luxurious compared to Louisa's with its tiny writing desk, but for much of history, Bronson's work was generally considered more influential than that of any of his daughters. In fact, before 1982, dissertations centered on Bronson's work outnumbered those on Louisa's by more than 2 to 1. She gained on him and then surpassed him in the five-year period afterward, and by 1987, she took a twenty-to-one lead.[46] As we stand in Bronson's study, we learn about his educational innovations and other pioneering activities. The original vegan, Bronson once renounced wool so as not to insult the sheep and insisted that his family eat only "aspiring vegetables," those that grew toward the sun, avoiding root crops that pointed toward hell.

As we move out of the study into the kitchen and dining room, once again the contrast is stark between the intellectual world of Bronson's study and the domestic world that the women occupied, with sister Lizzie Alcott's melodeon and mother Abby Alcott's green and white china set, and, displayed on the countertops, a breadboard, tin spice chest, and wooden bowls. It's like a visual representation of one of the central conflicts in *Little Women*, Jo's sense of being split between the freedoms of the male world and the restrictions of the female one, much as Alcott and her heroine also value women's community and culture.

After lunch, we head to the Wayside, just down the highway. This house was called Hillside back when the Alcott girls lived here for four years as children and has had many famous residents, including Nathaniel Hawthorne and Harriet Lathrop, who wrote the *Five Little Peppers* series of children's books under the name Margaret Sidney. I remember finding the first of the twelve books in this series, *Five Little Peppers and How They Grew*, among the used books in a Goodwill store when I was young. In an early variation on the four-children family configuration, the Peppers were, like the Marches, poor in money but rich in love, a matriarchal clan who, instead of calling their mother "Marmee," refer to her as "Mamsie." I wish I could ask my mother and aunts whether they read these books or saw the series of *Five Little Peppers* movies that appeared starting in 1939, when my mom was ten.[47]

The Wayside is now a National Historic Park site, not because of its history of housing famous writers but because Minutemen lived there during the Revolutionary War. We buy tickets in the barn where the Alcott sisters gave their theatricals and which, as my eyes adjust to the transition between the sunny outside and the dark interior, I initially think is full of people. Gradually I see that they are just statues—of Louisa May and Bronson Alcott, Nathaniel Hawthorne, and Harriet Lathrop. Bronson Alcott reads, a pile of books and his hat on the bench beside him. Louisa May Alcott poses dramatically in her cape and broad-brimmed hat as if staring nobly across a wind-swept plain. Hawthorne remains busy at work at his writing table. Harriet Lathrop rocks in a chair, wearing a shawl and lace blouse, hair in a bun. In her lap is a sign that says "Please do not touch figures," thwarting my plan to perch on her lap because I am so dying to rest, and there is, in typical nineteenth-century historical house tour style, no place to sit.

According to the park ranger who leads the tour, twelve published authors have lived in this house. It feels more like an apartment building or boarding house, since each of the most notable of these authors wrote in totally different areas, and since the house was repeatedly renovated. We enter through what once was the Alcott family's bathroom, which has a colorful floor like a star quilt block pattern. Unlike most people of their time, the Alcotts bathed daily. But subsequent owners turned this room into a kitchen, and the two couples with us exclaim over how low the counters were, how grueling it would be to bend over them for long periods.

"The Hawthornes and Lathrops had servants," the guide reassures them, and the couples say, "Oh, well," seeming relieved. "That's right, in the movie they had servants," says one of the women. Though she mentions the movie several times, and it becomes evident that she means *Little Women*, I never quite figure out which version she's talking about, although when it comes to servants, for us the most memorable scene is in the 1949 version when Aunt March shrieks up the stairs to her maid, "So-phie!"

Sophie and I have watched all of the movies, although I tend to get distracted by things like the fact that all of the actresses are the wrong ages for their characters. For instance, in 1933, Katharine Hepburn was twenty-six when she played fifteen-year-old Jo; in 1949, June Allyson was thirty-two, though somehow she dissolves into the role of Jo more thoroughly for me than the refined and already monumentally famous Hepburn did. In 1933, Joan Bennett, who plays twelve-year-old Amy, was twenty-four years old and pregnant; Elizabeth Taylor played her sixteen years later at seventeen and in a blond wig.

In the 1994 version, all of the actors are about the right age, but the first time I saw it, I was too busy being mortified to appreciate this. In it, Alcott's humor is usurped by earnestness, giving the movie a saccharine feeling that seemed exponentially magnified because I was watching it with my mother, who never got emotional about movies. I was also relieved that there were no sex scenes that I would be forced to watch in the company of my mom. So it wasn't until later viewings that I noticed how much Susan Sarandon's Marmee focuses on social justice rather than self-abnegation and humility, as Susan Gannon points out. The surprisingly feminist Marmee encourages Jo to go make her way in the world: "Go find your liberty!" she exclaims. Anne Hollander concludes that the movie's approach to social issues was meant to suggest that the March family is "ahead of their time and would have been more at home among us."[48]

Maybe this is the movie version that the woman on our tour keeps referring to. I never quite figure it out as we walk through the rooms where each writer worked. On one end of the house was Louisa's teenage bedroom, with its own door to the outside. Hawthorne added upstairs rooms, including the tower that became his study, which he called the "Sky Parlor." We go up a very narrow staircase to view his revolving bookshelves and curtained bookcase and the landscape paintings on the upper parts of three walls, murals painted after his death. On the standing desk where Hawthorne wrote, there's one of those fake manuscripts common to writers' houses. Back downstairs in a living room in the middle of the house was where Harriet Lathrop produced her *Five Little Peppers* books at another impossibly small table. The tour guide tells us that Lathrop chose the name Pepper because she didn't know anyone with that last name. "Dr. Pepper," says one of the men, and we laugh, but the tour guide just smiles politely, like she has heard this a lot.

Long before this childhood home of Alcott's was occupied by Hawthorne, long before Alcott's work influenced Lathrop's, the Alcott family's lives were intimately intertwined with those of their contemporaries, Concord the hub for the writers who constituted Bronson's circle and set the stage for Louisa May's writing. All of those transcendentalists hung out together or lived overlapping lives, suspicious of the corrupting power of institutions like organized religion and political parties, promoting the kind of independence and self-reliance that Laura Ingalls Wilder's books would someday carry to extremes.

Ralph Waldo Emerson was at the center of all of the literary activity in Concord, living back when a philosopher could be accorded rock star status. He was heavily in demand as a lecturer, delivering up to eighty per year. Henry David Thoreau lived with the Emersons and worked as a handyman before he headed out to the woods to live deliberately and suck the marrow out of life. Margaret Fuller spent time here when she agreed to edit Emerson's transcendentalist journal, the *Dial*. Nathaniel Hawthorne lived and wrote in two homes nearby at various stages of his career. Bronson Alcott and his family popped in and out of the Emerson house, from which the girls borrowed books. Emerson also loaned etchings to "talented artist" May, and she copied one onto her bedroom wall in Orchard House.

The Emerson house isn't far from the Wayside, but it turns out to be no bucolic stroll. The whole pastoral and peaceful image of Concord has kept me from fully comprehending, until I'm actually doing it, the unpleasantness of walking alongside a highway in 90 degrees while traffic whips by. Emerson himself refused to live in his wife's hometown of Plymouth, Massachusetts, because, as he wrote to her, "Plymouth is streets. I live in the wide champaign." Nowadays, one would be hard put to find the wide champaign. Concord is streets.

At the Emerson house, women in long skirts open the door and give me Kleenex to mop my brow. They laugh merrily at the idea that Concord might create shady paths between historic sites, sparing tourists the walk alongside a highway reeking of fumes, cars pummeling past.

By now, historic house tours have begun to blur together, all of the portraits on walls, the subject of each elucidated and enumerated, and the artfully placed objects on shelves, mantels, and tables: plaster busts, bisque candlesticks, oil lamps, pincushions, clocks. What will stand out in my memory of the Emerson house is the pew-like bench upholstered in red velvet among other replica furniture in Emerson's study, where we're allowed to sit, a rare and unexpected treat. Copious numbers of sadistic chairs populate the rooms of historic houses, many arranged in half-circles facing the docent, but we are always warned not to sit on them. Emerson's couch will prove even more memorable, since across the street, at the Concord Museum, is a duplicate or rather, reversal, of what we've just seen, a replica study containing Emerson's actual couch, which we can view through glass. And then I turn a corner and there, as part of an Annie Leibowitz exhibit called "Pilgrimage," there's a photograph of Emerson's inescapable couch.

After the Emerson house and the Concord Museum, we do a whirlwind tour of the area, making quick trips to Sleepy Hollow Cemetery and Walden Pond and then Salem and the House of Seven Gables, which inspired the Nathaniel Hawthorne novel by the same title, and which one tourist confuses with the *Anne of Green Gables* house, making me feel as if I've come full circle. At Author's Ridge in Sleepy Hollow Cemetery, pencils, pens, notes, a hotel-sized container of jam, a Euro, and a yuan lay scattered around the unassuming little stone marked "L.M.A." Right above hers, Emerson's grave has drawn a small crowd, strolling, picnicking on a low stone wall, and taking pictures of the grave littered by pencils and notes, now covered by dirt. Walden Pond is not an especially serene spot to contemplate nature and simplicity but an ordinary swimming beach littered with scantily clad visitors on a sweltering day. In the Walden Pond parking lot, an oddly chaotic location, stands a very small replica cabin, with a very small replica writing desk and a statue of Thoreau staring with what appears to be complete astonishment at the existence of his own left hand.

That night, I wish I had a DVD player so that I could view the PBS documentary I bought at Orchard House, "Louisa May Alcott: The Woman Behind Little Women." It won't be till later, at home again, that I will be able to watch the program, which mixes commentary and re-enactments. After putting a period on her last sentence of *Little Women* and sending off her manuscript, the actress who plays Alcott falls exhausted but exhilarated onto her bed. My attention starts to wander, then is abruptly yanked back. I have to rewind, thinking that I heard wrong. I didn't.

Alcott, a current theory goes, had lupus.

Lupus, like my Aunt Shirley, who owned all of Alcott's books and read and reread them, who must have read biographies as well, must have had some knowledge of Alcott's health issues even though the lupus theory didn't appear until around 2003, long after Aunt Shirley's death. It was in 2003 that two doctors, Norbert Hirschhorn and Ian A. Greaves, published a paper about Alcott in *Perspectives in Biology and Medicine*. They had studied the signs and symptoms in her journal entries and examined an 1870 portrait in which they observed what appears to be a classic butterfly rash across her nose and cheeks, also one of the early symptoms that Aunt Shirley experienced.[49]

Kay Redfield Jamison has observed that Alcott's patterns are consistent with bipolar disorder.[50] But the patterns of creativity described—wild energy, periods of depression and rest, pain and fatigue, months in bed—sound to me less like a mood disorder and more eerily like the cycles of flare-ups and remissions I remember from my aunt and from memoirs about lupus I read later, trying to understand what it had been like for her. I wonder if, reading Alcott, my Aunt Shirley ever felt a twinge of familiarity, ever recognized her own life in the details of Alcott's experience.

I used to half believe that my aunt was haunting me. It started, when I was twenty-one, with the memory of her voice that sometimes played inside my head, calling me "Nancy Grace"—"Nancy Grace, watch out!"; "Nancy Grace, be careful," that sort of thing. She was the only person who had ever called me Nancy Grace. Once I had a phone number that had previously belonged to a family named Grace, so people were always calling, saying, "Miss Grace?" My lights flickered strangely and one morning I woke up from a dream in which a voice said, "Nancy Grace, I want what you have." "What?" I asked. "Your life," it said. And then it added, "Christine Rossini." I sat up in bed and said, "You mean Christina Rossetti?" Then I went back to sleep.

Later that day I tracked down an English literature anthology to look up Christina Rossetti, a poet I'd heard of but never read. The first poem reprinted there was called "Echo" and it began:

Come to me in the silence of the night
Come in the speaking silence of a dream. . . .
Yet come to me in dreams that I may live
My very life again though cold in death. . . .[51]

I remember how chills lifted the hairs on the back of my neck, how I slammed the book, winter shadows pressing in, making the room feel colder. She wants my life, I thought. But I wasn't really afraid. And, a few years later, when I decided I was going to adopt a child, to raise a little girl, my aunt's lifelong dream, I stopped feeling haunted. When my cousin Jody also adopted a baby girl, I imagined that Aunt Shirley's ghost was even more pleased, slowly fading away. And yet her influence remains in the books that I read in childhood and have reread these last few years, her voice joined by the chorus of my mother's and Aunt Gena's, still returning to me through these books and the speaking silence of dreams.

Epilogue

Amherst, Massachusetts, and Emily Dickinson

CONCORD, MASSACHUSETTS, AND LOUISA MAY ALCOTT were, I thought, the end of my journey through my favorite childhood books. But as long as I was nearby, I couldn't resist visiting Amherst, the home of Emily Dickinson, a poet no one in my family had ever read except me, and not until I was a junior in high school.

While Louisa May Alcott, born in 1832, spent much of her life in Concord, down the road in Amherst, Emily Dickinson had been born in 1830; both died when they were fifty-five. The two couldn't have been more different: Dickinson remained obscure her whole life while Alcott was once invited to stand on a stage and turn slowly around so that the audience could simply view her, a beloved author. Alcott, who produced bestselling children's books and big sweeping thrillers that she revised minimally, and Dickinson, who wrote mostly unknown tiny carefully constructed poems that detonate like little bombs, probably never met, though Dickinson's brother and sister-in-law, Austin and Susan, lived next door to her and hosted many literary figures at their home, including Emerson and Harriet Beecher Stowe.

That day in Massachusetts, it's been years since I've picked up my copy of *The Collected Poems of Emily Dickinson*. The last time I really thought about her was a few months ago when Sophie announced while we waited for our food at a Mexican restaurant, "Today we learned about how Emily Dickinson murdered her husband. And wrote about it."

"Emily Dickinson didn't have a husband," I said, startled. "I don't think she murdered anyone, either. She definitely didn't write about it."

"Oh, I meant her lover," Sophie corrected herself. "Mrs. T. was telling us all about how when Emily Dickinson was a kid, and her pets died, she kept their bodies."

"She kept her dead pets?" I said. In high school, I'd written my junior research paper on Dickinson's attitude toward religion (ambivalent, I concluded) and in graduate school, I'd taken a Dickinson seminar, and I didn't remember any of this.

"And then she killed her lover and sprinkled lime around to keep people from smelling his corpse and then she slept with it," Sophie said.

At which point the thick fog of confusion cleared. "That's not Emily Dickinson," I said. "It's a short story by William Faulkner. 'A Rose for Emily.' Are you sure she said it was Emily Dickinson?"

Now it was Sophie's turn to look confused. "We had these reading questions about Emily Dickinson, and then she started telling us all this stuff about her," she said.

"Maybe you should ask her tomorrow to make sure," I suggested. Sophie's a good student, but she's capable of spacing out and missing vital transitions, which I hoped was what had happened.

A few days later, I saw Kelsey, Sophie's classmate, a generally more attentive student. "I heard you learned about Emily Dickinson the other day," I said.

"Yeah!" Kelsey answered. "We learned all about how she killed her lover!"

In Amherst, we have popovers for dinner with my friend Anna ("Popovers," Sophie says. "They have them for breakfast in *Little Women*." A detail I'd forgotten.) Anna, it turns out, lives across the street from the cemetery where Emily Dickinson is buried. Anna attends Dickinson study groups, and I keep hoping she'll become a docent at the Emily Dickinson museum.

Walking around Amherst with Anna, my memory keeps prickling, sort of like when the blood supply has been cut off to my foot and I shake it and it tingles, awakening. It's been a while since I've really thought about Dickinson's place in my own teenage reading journey, the part she played in my transition into adulthood. I don't remember paying much attention to the mythology that cast Dickinson as a wacko. I don't remember buying into popular images of her as a "fragile woman-child, a wraithlike spinster, a proto-goth weirdo."[1] But I can't remember exactly what it was that I was drawn to when I started reading her obsessively at the age of seventeen.

Of course when I was younger, I'd run across many much-anthologized poems, like "A narrow Fellow in the Grass" and "I'm Nobody!" but at some point in high school, Dickinson had stepped forward and carved out a place in my imagination. Maybe it started with that research paper on Dickinson and religion. I don't remember.[2]

And yet, details flood back to me in Amherst. I'm seventeen, no longer reading children's books about girls who want to be writers. Instead, though not yet a comfortable reader of poetry, my lifelong interest in biography leads me to push through the two-volume Richard Sewell treatment of Dickinson. I've started writing cryptic poems and letters with lots of dashes. I have altogether broken away (I think) from the reading guidance of my mother and aunts. I read authors they've never heard of and books they'd never be interested in, by Chaim Potok, Theodore Dreiser, Jane Austen, Thomas Hardy, Emily Dickinson.

Every day, I wear a cardigan and my gold locket carved with flowers and vines, a gift from my boyfriend. I feel drably romantic. I'm planning to marry my boyfriend. We even have a wedding date picked out in 1985, after we finish college. We're going to move to New York City where he'll attend an Episcopal seminary and I'll work for a magazine before I quit to stay home (my idea, not his) with our four children, who will all have Biblical names (his idea, not mine). I remember this with amazement: a self who was still embedded in such a conventional idea of my life, and yet so drawn to an unconventional poet and her work.

Anna leads us to Dickinson's grave, through a cemetery that feels as gothic as the winding staircase and precarious ladder up to the bell tower of the nearby Episcopal church that Anna attends, with its claustrophobic stone-walled room. Anna took us up there last night, where light filtered through small, square stained-glass windows and glinted off complicated mechanisms. Below and a few blocks away, in this cemetery, long weeds grow around wafer-thin gravestones, the words worn off, the stones leaning every which way. An apartment building stands alongside it, its balconies overlooking the graves.

We find Emily Dickinson's, so close behind the iron fence that surrounds the family plot that it's a little hard to read: "Born Dec. 10, 1830 / Called Back May 15, 1886." The grave is surrounded by notes from other visitors weighed down by rocks, along with pencils, coins, and a plastic daisy. We want to leave something, too, but all Anna can find in her pocket are three Altoids. I make sure there are a sufficient number of dashes as Sophie writes out a note with a miniature golf pencil on a scrap of paper:

Dear Emily,
For you—
Some altoids—breathe
Peacefully—
And mintily—
July 31, 2012 Sophie, Nancy, and Anna

Sophie draws a little bee on it, which seems to me extremely appropriate and maybe even kind of psychic given Dickinson's love of nature. "Bee! I'm expecting you!" I think, words from poems I haven't read in years popping into my head. As we stroll through the cemetery, Sophie and I giggle extremely inappropriately over the gravestone of a woman who appears to have been named "Thankfully Dick" and the angel-wing-shaped tombstone that resembles boobs.[3]

The next morning, we start the tour of the Emily Dickinson house in the back parlor, where our guide Marianne, a junior at Bryn Mawr, sticks closely to historical fact but also quotes liberally from poetry and letters. Portraits of Dickinson's mother and father hang on one wall and the rare existing images of her hang on the other. There is the daguerreotype of her at sixteen, hair parted in the middle, two flat wings on the sides of her head, ribbon tied around her neck; the family later doctored this picture to make her look "more feminine," giving her curly hair and adding a fichu and ruff, fussy-looking fashions that I hope are never revived. There is also a painting of her and her brother and sister as children, grouped around a book. Their heads all seem too big for their bodies, floating above white collars, Emily and Lavinia's made of lace, Austin's a spread collar still typical of men's dress shirts.

"They look like bobbleheads," Sophie whispers.

We move on to the front parlor with its marble fireplace, then on up the stairs to view Dickinson's white dress in a glass case in the upstairs hall. Dickinson's bedroom is even sparser than Alcott's. There's a sleigh bed and washstand and Franklin stove and mahogany chest, where Lavinia found 1,775 poems after Emily's death. Dickinson's tiny little writing desk sits between two large windows, one of which looks out onto Main Street. The train station was next door ("I like to see it lap the Miles—And lick the Valleys up—" I think), so anyone who came to Amherst walked past this house.[4]

There seems to be a popular notion that Dickinson never left her bedroom. ("She would have lived longer if she would have went outside," as one viewer of a YouTube video put it in the comments section.) This notion can only be maintained by anyone who's never read a Dickinson biography, poem, or letter, which demonstrate that she was an avid gardener and roamed the family property with her Newfoundland, Carlo, named after Mr. Rochester's dog in *Jane Eyre*. Her writing reveals rich natural surroundings and a highly developed sense of humor, not the sad closed-off life of the stereotype. Certainly while some of her poems contain dark elements, her body of work taken as a whole has never struck me as depressing or angry so much as playful, funny, ironic, passionate, engaged: "To be alive—is Power—."[5]

A member of our tour group asks if Dickinson ever read Walt Whitman, and Marianne says no, but that she wrote, "I hear he is disgraceful."

"Wasn't she kidding?" Anna asks. Dickinson was always kidding, tongue in cheek, making fun, resisting anyone else's definition of her.

Lavinia's bedroom has been dedicated to Dickinson's poetry, with boards on the walls displaying her poem "A Chilly Peace infests the Grass" and a reproduction of it in Dickinson's handwriting. We sit on benches and discuss her form and word choices. I wish all of the writers' houses would do this. It's like a little review that reminds me of what drew me to her work, not just how Dickinson herself seemed to provide an alternative to a conventional life, but the way her letters and poems seemed so wicked, subversive, quirky, self-contained.[6]

Back when I was in high school, Dickinson was still regarded as "a quaint and helpless creature, disappointed in love, who gave up on life," as Lyndall Gordon describes the conventional conception of her.[7] Much of what was then available were the heavily edited versions of the Dickinson poems, their dashes removed, their slant rhymes standardized, their rhythms turned into what Christopher Benfey calls smooth, lulling melodies.[8] At one time, she was seen as a sentimental poet, represented by lines like:

If I can stop one heart from breaking
I shall not live in vain
If I can ease one life the aching
or cool one pain
Or help one fainting robin
Unto his nest again
I shall not live in vain.[9]

Even Adrienne Rich sees this as a puzzling departure from Dickinson's usual work rather than as a satire of sanctimonious, treacly verse, with its over-the-top final image. I doubt that when I first read this I understood how the ridiculous picture of the fainting robin marks this poem as a tongue-in-cheek send-up of her day's popular verse. But even at seventeen and eighteen, I don't remember being drawn to the sweet, bland image of Dickinson represented by a face-value reading of this poem, but to what Benfey calls her "explosive phrasing, abrupt shifts of tone, shocking images, offbeat rhymes," the "pressure [she puts] on the individual word."

After my boyfriend and I broke up, I found solace in imitating Dickinson, writing in a disjointed fashion that seemed to echo my own chaos of mind. In the process, I became distracted by the joy of finding language to make the invisible visible, to try to give form to the nebulous the way Dickinson's poems did, poems like "After great pain, a formal feeling comes—," which comforted me by its eerily familiar description of the cycle of grief.[10]

Eventually, I left Dickinson behind to proceed through various other obsessions, like one with Sylvia Plath, a prerequisite for aspiring young female writers. At some point, graduate degrees made me more leery of Dickinson's work; I was struck full force by how complicated and difficult it was, even if, when I was working on my MFA school, the joke circulated that you could sing any of her poems to the "Yellow Rose of Texas." Of course, one of my professors pointed out, since Dickinson used the standard alternating tetrameter and trimeter hymn stanza, you could sing Dickinson to a number of tunes. While teaching at a Christian college, I led groups of students who knew their hymns thoroughly in choruses of "Because I could not stop for Death—" to the tune of "Amazing Grace" and "I heard a Fly buzz—when I died—" to the tune of "What a Friend We Have in Jesus" to demonstrate Dickinson's form and her irreverence.[11]

More than fifteen years after my initial teenage fascination with the poet, while studying for a PhD, I enrolled in a Dickinson seminar. I was happy to discover that the common image of her had lost currency, the portrait of her as virgin recluse/ crazy spinster who retreated from society after being jilted in love. The burning question of the day was, instead, who was Master, the intended recipient of three unsent love letters? Was it Samuel Bowles or Otis Lord, men to whom she wrote many letters? Who was Dickinson talking about when she wrote, "Wild nights— Wild nights! / Were I with thee / Wild nights should be / Our luxury!"?[12]

Several of my classmates felt affirmed by the notion that Dickinson's famous reclusiveness could be explained if she were a lesbian, engaged in a lifelong affair with her sister-in-law Sue Dickinson—an affair that had to be hidden according to the dictates of social mores. And it's true that Emily's letters to Sue are quite ardent even if there is no other evidence for an affair. When my classmates argued that "Safe in Their Alabaster Chambers" was about Emily and Sue taking refuge from the world in their own timeless love, "untouched by morning and untouched by noon," my friend Deb and I stared wide eyed at each other: it sounded to us like the poem was describing corpses in caskets ("rafter of satin") that were sealed up in vaults ("roof of stone"). It sounded like the poem was making fun of conventional religious beliefs ("Sleep the meek members of the resurrection. . . . oh what sagacity perished here!").[13]

Of course, with that poem, my whole high school junior research paper was rendered ridiculous as well. It didn't sound to me like Dickinson was quite as ambivalent toward religion as I'd suggested. It sounded to me like she didn't think much of it, at least not the heavy-handed doctrines of the organized kind. Hmm, she seems to be saying in this poem. Look where their piousness got them.

Deb often occupied herself that semester with wickedly satirizing unssupported interpretations, putting forth especially memorable theories on the "pregnan-cy poems" of Emily Dickinson. "My period had come for Prayer—" Deb would quote, or, "Wherefore so late—I murmured— . . . My Period begin."[14]

Critics since have written about pregnancy, miscarriage, and birth imagery in Dickinson, so Deb's joking interpretations weren't as far out of left field as we thought. Dickinson's work defies too-literal analysis, and interpretation is further complicated by the fact that like most writers, she doesn't limit herself to her own direct life experience.

Dickinson's poetry can be so difficult, so cryptic, her life itself such a cipher, that she's the perfect candidate for readers to project whatever they want onto her, whatever will make her most like us. "Tell all the truth but tell it slant—" she wrote. "Success in Circuit lies." And so, the question endures: What truths was Dickinson's poetry telling about her life? And how do you explain her seclusion?[15]

I totally understand the impulse to diagnose dead writers, especially mysteri-ous ones like Dickinson. Back in the early 90s, lots of people I knew, including me, were hooked on the Myers-Briggs personality inventory, which lead to Myers-Briggsing everyone else to death. Some Myers-Briggs fanatics specialized in typ-ing famous dead people, concluding that Dickinson was an INFP, which is close enough to my own personality type, an INFJ with strong P tendencies, to consti-tute proof that Emily Dickinson and I would have hit it off.

So I can relate to the way, in attempting to account for her reclusiveness, read-ers have projected their own situations and disorders onto her, claimed for her diagnoses that were fashionable at the time, or found real if ambiguous evidence suggesting possible explanations: doomed love; depression; agoraphobia. They've argued that she suffered from schizophrenia or Asperger's (based on odd phrasings and wild dashes); anorexia ("I had been hungry, all the Years"); sadomasochism ("Amputate my freckled Bosom! / Make me bearded like a man!"); Bipolar Disor-der ("Inebriate of air—am I— / And Debauchee of Dew / Reeling—thro' end-less summer days— / From inns of molten Blue—"); Seasonal Affective Disorder ("There's a certain Slant of light / Winter Afternoons— / That oppresses, like the Heft / Of Cathedral Tunes—"); childhood incest ("In Winter in my Room / I came upon a Worm / Pink lank and warm" or "So keep your secret—Father! / I would not—if I could—"); Lupus ("Pain—has an Element of Blank—"); and epilepsy ("He fumbles at your Soul / As Players at the Keys— / Before they drop full Music on— / He stuns you by Degrees—").[16]

When I read the recent biography *Lives like Loaded Guns*, author Lyndall Gordon had me completely convinced that Dickinson had epilepsy. Some of Dickinson's odd habits, from wearing white dresses to passing rapidly through her father's parties, then disappearing, make sense if she was trying to prevent or disguise illness, especially in light of the way epilepsy was regarded at the time. Considered a form of mental illness, it would have been potential grounds for lifelong institutionalization. In this light, withdrawing from society, keeping scrupulously clean, and living a quiet, low-stress life become not eccentricity but sensible acts of self-protection. Furthermore, Dickinson's many descriptions of the creative process could certainly double as depictions of seizures.

But some of the truths that Dickinson tells slant may always remain a mystery. Norbert Hirschhorn, the same physician-writer who posthumously diagnosed Louisa May Alcott with lupus, doesn't buy the Emily Dickinson epilepsy theory, and his well-reasoned argument throws me back into doubt.[17] That's the way it is with Dickinson. It's hard to know exactly what to think.

But the fact that remains is that she was a woman, admittedly privileged, who nevertheless had to go against many expectations to make a space for her writing, something that, in retrospect, she did fearlessly, unapologetic. In contemporary times, conceptions of Dickinson have shifted radically. She is no longer regarded as the pitful wacko poet of my daugher's teacher's lesson. In her essay on Dickinson, Adrienne Rich notes that "The terms she had been handed by society . . . could spell insanity to a woman genius." But Dickinson didn't allow that, says Rich:

> I have a notion genius knows itself; that Dickinson chose her seclusion, knowing she was exceptional and knowing what she needed. It was, moreover, no hermetic retreat, but a seclusion which included a wide range of people, of reading, and correspondence. . . . She carefully selected her society and controlled the disposal of her time.[18]

Now, such ideas are echoed again and again throughout the criticism. "Like many artists, Dickinson needed a great deal of time alone for reading, contemplation, and writing—a requirement that has rarely been questioned when enjoyed by male writers," write Ellen Louise Hart and Martha Nell Smith.[19] "Others may see Emily's reclusiveness as a symptom of a problem—but I always see it as a solution to one," says Rose Lichter-Marck:

> It was the 19th century, and Emily Dickinson, a woman, wanted to be a writer. So she retreated from the obligations that would have absorbed her time and energy: marriage, motherhood, keeping up appearances, the social expectations that came with her family's privileged status. . . . Writing po-

etry made another kind of liberation possible. It gave her the opportunity to inhabit multiple, shifting selves beyond the limited identity her class and culture offered her.[20]

Dickinson's critics no longer see her as a helpless victim of fate, even if she did suffer from agoraphobia or epilepsy or depression. "Rather than choose victimhood," concludes Amy Pence, "she chose art."[21] "The Brain has Corridors—surpassing / Material Place—," I think.[22] And: "The Soul selects her own Society— / Then—shuts the Door—."[23] Dickinson was a woman who found immense freedom within a situation that appeared circumscribed, someone who lived a full and productive life rather than one engaged in a futile fight against restrictions, one who used her writing not merely to cope but to transcend her circumstances.

Entering the Evergreens, the home of Sue and Austin Dickinson, Anna says, is like being walloped by the past. We step into the front hall of the house that has remained unchanged for one hundred years and been compared to an archeological site.[24] As my eyes gradually adjust to the dark front hall, I notice the peeling paint and wallpaper. We file into the parlor with its mishmash of original furniture, its worn yellowish chairs and carpeting peeling up from floor. In the dining room, narrow floorboards are set in intricate patterns. In the kitchen with its wide floorboards, cooking implements from the time period are displayed on countertops alongside plastic strawberries and asparagus. Upstairs, we look through windows into a maid's room. "Look, a maid stripper pole!" Sophie says of its one pillar. We pass a nursery with a cradle, a rocking horse, and a tricycle that has a huge front wheel. The tour wraps up in Austin and Sue's room, where once again there are benches where we can sit.

I feel inspired, as if I've finally found what I was looking for on my tours of authors' houses, a feeling of connection not just to the writer who once lived here, but to her words, and through them to my earlier self that first connected with those words. Emily Dickinson initiated me, finally and fully, from all the thwarted possibilities of the heroines of children's literature into adult life and permission to find my own way.

Outside, we pass a silhouette sculpture of Dickinson and a later well-known resident of Amherst, poet Robert Frost, sitting on rocks facing each other, engaged in dialogue. Books lie open beside them, one containing a poem by Dickinson about a lost jewel that she couldn't hold on to—a metaphor for a poem? —and one by Frost that is more familiar to me: "Two roads diverged in a wood, and I— / I took the one less traveled by, / And that has made all the difference."[25] Another poem I first encountered in high school, another poem that mapped for me my journey ahead, that offered courage to find my own way.

As we drive out of Amherst, we pass an enormous pile of old tires, hundreds and hundreds stacked in a field.

"So ugly it's beautiful," I say.

"So pathetic it's cool," replies Sophie, who has her own distinct taste and may never love the same books I did, who breaks away from me a little more each day, ready to find her own way, too.

I am at the end of a journey that has taken me from Wisconsin to Kansas, Minnesota to Iowa to Missouri, to Prince Edward Island and Massachusetts, through books by Laura Ingalls Wilder and Maud Hart Lovelace, Lucy Maud Montgomery and Louisa May Alcott and a whole slew of other childhood favorites, through my own childhood reading journey as I moved into more mature understandings of literature and my own life. Along the way, I've been lured by more writers' houses—I want to go to Brontë country someday, and why didn't I go see Edith Wharton's house in Massachusetts while I was there?

I've also been sidetracked a couple of times by *The Wizard of Oz*, a work that is particularly ubiquitous. Whenever I mention that I'm from Kansas, it's like a requirement for people to respond, "I don't believe you're in Kansas anymore." I've never read Frank Baum's books, but I saw the movie a million times while growing up in a state that issued license plates that said "Land of Ahs." Today I live in Bradford, PA, long rumored to have once briefly been home to author Frank Baum, whose father made his fortune in the oilfields in the late 1800s. Popular notions of my home state were shaped in many people's minds by images from the film: farms and wind and homespun people, yellow brick roads and winged monkeys and munchkins.

Dorothy is an imaginative heroine I didn't especially relate to, and it is true that I'm not in Kansas anymore, the place where, when all is said and done, Dorothy longs to return. At the end of the movie she says that "if I ever go looking for my heart's desire again, I won't look any further than my own backyard; because if it isn't there, I never really lost it to begin with." This was the message I grew up with, that there was no place like home, that there was nothing I should desire beyond my own backyard.

My journeys the last few years have included a few nods to Dorothy, like a quick spin through *The Wizard of Oz* museum in a small building storefront in Wamego, Kansas, which displays first editions and translations and spinoffs and toys and dolls and life-sized tableaus of each character. The first shows Dorothy in her braids and her blue-and-white checked dress, a basket over one arm, Toto draped over the other, standing by a white picket fence. There are flowers behind her, and rolling hills hoed into rows, and fluffy clouds in the distance, a sunny and idyllic Kansas scene. Sophie turns a cartwheel in the haunted forest and sits on the throne of the Wizard, looking wise, before we go next door to have lunch at Toto's Tacoz, which are, as described, "Toto-ly Oz-some."

Another day, we pass through Chittenango, New York, Baum's birthplace, but "Everything About Oz," also a storefront-turned-museum, closed a few years ago. I may never know how it presents my home state in contrast to the Wamego museum. All we can do is view the yellow brick path through the downtown sidewalks and then drive on.

Growing up, I fully expected to stay put my whole life, to achieve permanence and value stability above all else. Instead I married at twenty, then divorced at twenty-five and never remarried, I adopted a child and raised her alone, I moved and struggled and negotiated until I could read and write for hours every week, none of this quite the life I or my mother or aunts imagined for me but one that suits me. All of my favorite children's book heroines had imaginations and dreams and talents, and all of them expected to do work that mattered to them, ideas that outweighed in my memory the more traditional aspects of their stories as they married, kept house, and had children or prepared to. Those favorite books laid the groundwork for me, at fifteen, to discover Charlotte Brontë and then at sixteen, to discover Emily Dickinson and then, to continue finding writers, especially women, who broke my world open. It turned out that books were my home even more than Kansas was, and that to find what I was looking for, I would have to stray far beyond my own backyard.

As we drive away from Amherst, a Mary Chapin Carpenter CD plays. "I dwell in possibility," she sings,[26] startling me with Emily Dickinson's own words, and the rest of the poem continues to unwind in my memory:

I dwell in Possibility—
A fairer House than Prose—
More numerous of Windows—
Superior—for Doors—[27]

Dickinson was describing poetry and the way it enables the speaker to view a world, at least metaphorically, far beyond her own backyard, allowing her to spread "wide my narrow Hands / To gather Paradise—." But in this moment it seems apt as it resonates against all the literature I read growing up, all of the windows it opened and the doors it allowed me to step through.

Notes

PROLOGUE

1. Personal correspondence with Sara King, Fall 2004.
2. Virginia Woolf, *Mrs. Dalloway*, 157.
3. Ibid.

CHAPTER ONE

1. *Little House on the Prairie*, starring Michael Landon and Melissa Gilbert, was an Ed Friendly/NBC Production and ran from 1974 to 1983.
2. Laura Ingalls Wilder, *Little Town on the Prairie*, 223.
3. Wilder, *These Happy Golden Years*, 270.
4. Dar Williams, "Traveling Again," from *The Honesty Room*, Razor & Tie, 2008, CD; Kristen Hall, "Following My Compass," from *Be Careful What You Wish For*, High Street Records, 1994, CD; Kirsty MacColl, "No Victims," from *Kite*, Virgin Records, 1989, CD; Bonnie Raitt, "The Road's My Middle Name," *Nick of Time*, Capitol Records, 1989, CD; Patsy Cline, "I'm Moving Along" by Johnny Starr, Capitol Records, 1959.
5. Maud Hart Lovelace, *Carney's House Party*, 12–13.
6. Donald Zochert, *Laura: The Life of Laura Ingalls Wilder*, 11.
7. David Laskin, *The Children's Blizzard*, 272.

CHAPTER TWO

1. Elizabeth Caudill, *Did You Carry the Flag Today, Charley?* 51.
2. Lucy Maud Montgomery, *Anne of the Island*, 106.
3. Ibid., 133.
4. Virginia Sorensen, *Plain Girl*, 33.
5. Louisa May Alcott, *Little Women*, 113.
6. Sorensen, 54.
7. Ibid.
8. At the same time, Sena Jeter Naslund pointed out to me Pa's comment in *The Long Winter*: "What do you say we all get together and kind of ration it out, on a basis of how much our families need to last through till spring?" This resonates, if unconsciously, with the Marx dictum "From each according to his ability; to each according to his need."
9. Ursula Nordstrom, *The Secret Language*, "like everyone else," 74; "In the months and years ahead," 74; "things others cannot understand," 120.
10. Lois Lenski, *Strawberry Girl*, "Jefferson Davis Slater," 11; "physical feature," x.

11. Ellen Herman, "The Family Nobody Wanted, 1954," Adoption History Project, accessed 27 January 2013, http://pages.oregon.edu/adoption/topics/familynobodywanted.htm.

12. Irene Gammel, *Looking for Anne of Green Gables: The Story of L. M. Montgomery and Her Literary Classic*, 213.

13. Montgomery, *Anne of Green Gables*, 29.

14. Gammel, 213.

15. Noel Streatfeild, *Dancing Shoes*, "She's adopted," 7; "in a manner of speaking," 93.

16. *Cheaper by the Dozen*, directed by Shawn Levy (2003: United States, 20th Century Fox).

17. Lenora Mattingly Weber, *Make a Wish for Me*, 21.

18. Weber, *Meet the Malones*, 39–40.

19. Ibid., 41.

20. Weber, *The More the Merrier*, Chapter 12.

21. Weber, *Beany Has a Secret Life*, 172.

22. Weber, *Make a Wish for Me*, 162.

23. Weber, *Happy Birthday, Dear Beany*, 174.

24. Eunice Young Smith, *The Jennifer Gift*, 33.

25. Montgomery, *Anne of Windy Poplars*, "happier," 89; "dullest room sparkled . . . troubles," 92, 107.

26. Flying Dreams, accessed 8 July 2014, http://flyingdreams.home.mindspring.com/donna.htm.

Chapter Three

1. Lizzie Skurnick, *Shelf Discovery*, 227–28.

2. Ann Romines, *Constructing the Little House*, 23.

3. Skurnick, 38.

4. Romines, "traditional male initiation," 24; "achievement," 51; lyric mode, 51, quilt, 180.

5. Ibid., 53.

6. Beverly Cleary, *Ramona the Pest*, 18.

7. Anita Clair Fellman, *Little House, Long Shadow*, 205.

8. Gabrielle Mitchell-Marell, "Little House Under Renovation," *Publishers Weekly*, 4 December 2006, accessed 12 February 2013, http://www.publishersweekly.com/pw/print/20061204/3266-little-house-under-renovation.html.

9. Fellman, 208.

10. Ibid., 200–201.

11. Christine Heppermann, "Little House on the Bottom Line."

12. Fellman, 1.

13. Wendy McClure, *The Wilder Life: My Adventures in the Lost World of Little House on the Prairie*, 8.

14. John E. Miller, *Becoming Laura Ingalls Wilder: The Woman Behind the Legend*, 168.

Chapter Four

1. Lucy Maud Montgomery, *Anne of Avonlea*, 157.

2. Ibid., 111.

3. George P. Landow, "The Dead Woman Talks Back: Christina Rossetti's Ironic Intonation of the Dead Fair Maiden," Victorian Web: Literature, History, and Culture in the Age of Victoria, accessed 21 August 2013, http://www.victorianweb.org/authors/crosetti/gp11.html.

4. Montgomery, *Anne of Green Gables*, 124.

5. Montgomery, *Anne of Avonlea*, 169.

6. Ibid., 92.

7. Ibid., boys averse to expressions of affection, 205; "porridge," 128.

8. Ibid., 244.

9. Montgomery, *Anne of the Island*, "the year is a book," 151; "denuded of romance," 234.

10. Montgomery, *Anne's House of Dreams*, 15.

11. Louisa May Alcott, *Little Women*, "exclamation points," 178; "paradise," 45; "Laurie loved them," 64.

12. Maud Hart Lovelace, *Betsy and Tacy Go Downtown*, 113.

13. Lovelace, *Betsy and the Great World*, 279.

14. Lovelace, *Heaven to Betsy*, 48.

15. Anna Quindlen, foreword to Maud Hart Lovelace's *Betsy and the Great World/Betsy's Wedding*, x–xi.

16. Betty Brock, *No Flying in the House*, "butterfly's wing," 98; "without getting a scratch," 103; "wind to the stars," 144.

17. Ibid., 121.

18. Ibid., 154–55.

19. E. B. White, *The Trumpet of the Swan*, "egg of supreme beauty," 18; "like a swan," 26; "high purpose," 47; "peaceful and enchanted," 162.

20. Quoted in Anita Clair Fellman, *Little House, Long Shadow*, 124.

21. Carolyn Keene, *The Clue of the Broken Locket*, 66.

22. George Selden, *The Cricket in Times Square*, 107.

23. Louise Fitzhugh, *Harriet the Spy*, 276.

24. Ibid., drive nails through her head, 207; terrified of everyone, 146.

25. Ibid., 174.

Chapter Five

1. Anita Clair Fellman, *Little House, Long Shadow*, 205.

2. Little House on the Prairie, Independence, Kansas, accessed July 2009, http://www.littlehouseonprairie.com. Content has since been changed/updated.

3. Fran Kaye, "Little Squatter on the Osage Diminished Reserve."

4. Laura Ingalls Wilder, *These Happy Golden Years*, 3.

5. Dennis McAuliffe Jr., "Books to Avoid," Oyate, accessed 24 September 2010, http://www.oyate.org/index.php?option+com_content&view+article. The "Books to Avoid" feature has since been discontinued and removed from this site.

6. Quoted in Fellman, 228.

7. McAuliffe, "Books to Avoid."

8. Kimberly Meyer, "Little Log Houses for You and Me."

9. Wilder, *Little House on the Prairie*, 134.

10. Ann Romines, *Constructing the Little House*, 66.

11. Wilder, *Little House on the Prairie*, 47.

12. Romines, 74.

13. *The Wizard of Oz*. Directed by Victor Fleming, King Vidor, Mervyn LeRoy. Metro-Goldwyn-Mayer, 1939.

14. Fellman, 75.

15. Ibid., 79.

16. McAuliffe, "Books to Avoid."

17. Wilder, *Little House on the Prairie*, 236–37.

18. Quoted in Fellman, 229.

19. Wilder, *Little House on the Prairie*, 237.

20. Ibid., 136.

21. Romines, 66.

22. Ibid., 65.

23. Ibid., 78.

24. Wilder, *Little House on the Prairie*, 324.

25. Ibid., 335.

CHAPTER SIX

1. Maud Hart Lovelace, *Betsy-Tacy*, *Betsy-Tacy and Tib*, and *Betsy and Tacy Go Over the Big Hill*.

2. Julie A. Schrader, *Maud Hart Lovelace's Deep Valley: A Guidebook of Mankato Places in the Betsy-Tacy Series*, ii.

3. Lovelace, *Betsy-Tacy and Tib*, 2–3.

4. Alexandra Lange, "Original Gossip Girls," *New York Magazine*, 1 November 2009, http://nymag.com/arts/books/features/61737/.

5. Sadie Stein, "Stars in the Sky: A Tribute to Betsy-Tacy," 1 August 2013. http://jezebel.com/5378305/stars-in-the-sky-a-tribute-to-betsy+tacy.

6. Peggy Orenstein, *Cinderella Ate My Daughter*, 111.

7. Sharla Scannell Whalen, *The Betsy-Tacy Companion: A Biography of Maud Hart Lovelace*, x–xi.

8. Ibid., "an interesting past," 96; Mike Parker, 147.

9. Amboy Area Community Theatre, "The Curtain Goes Up on 'Deep Valley Vignettes—Betsy-Tacy on Stage," accessed 27 September 2010, http://amboymn.govoffice2.com.Amboy.

10. Bettijane Levine, "Commitments: The Never-Ending Story: Why is it that some adults never seem to outgrow the Betsy-Tacy books? Perhaps it's because they recall a simpler era when imagination reigned supreme," *Los Angeles Times*, 9 October 1995, http://articles.latimes.com/1995-10-09/news/ls-55095_1_betsy-tacy-books.

11. Lovelace, *Betsy-Tacy and Tib*, 1.

12. Ibid., 19.

13. Whalen, 72.

14. Lovelace, *Betsy and Tacy Go Over the Big Hill*, 8.

15. Lovelace, *Heaven to Betsy*, 11.

16. Whalen, 72.

17. Lovelace, *Heaven to Betsy*, 187.

18. Lovelace, *Betsy Was a Junior*, "barbarians," 178; "sorority-fraternity business," 217; "bad reputation," 188; "fondness for the crowd," 188-89; "different kinds of people," 242.

19. Lovelace, *Betsy and Joe*, 574.

20. Lovelace, *Betsy and the Great World*, "deepest interests were social," 23; "unthinkable," 329.

21. Lovelace, *Betsy's Wedding*, 628.

22. Quindlen, foreword to Maud Hart Lovelace's *Betsy and the Great World/Betsy's Wedding*, viii.

23. Lovelace, *Betsy-Tacy and Tib*, 49.

24. Lovelace, *Heaven to Betsy*, 167–68.

25. Lovelace, *Betsy in Spite of Herself*, 350.

26. Lovelace, *Betsy and Joe*, 413.

27. Ibid., 412.

28. Lovelace, *Betsy and the Great World*, 85.

29. Whalen, 421.

30. Lovelace, *Betsy's Wedding*, "castles in the air," 387; "Rules for Married Life," 425; "not just as a girl," 600.

31. Lovelace, *Betsy and Tacy Go Downtown*, 72.

32. Lovelace, *Heaven to Betsy*, 67.

33. Lovelace, *Betsy in Spite of Herself*, 379.

34. Ibid., 443.

35. Lovelace, *Heaven to Betsy*, "little Poetess," 184; "good for writers to suffer," 283; "having improved her art," 283; "purpose and promise," 324.

36. Lovelace, *Betsy in Spite of Herself*, 646.

37. Lovelace, *Heaven to Betsy*, 79.

38. Lovelace, *Betsy in Spite of Herself*, "deepest thing," 652; "anything but harmless," 653.

39. Lovelace, *Betsy Was a Junior*, 69.

40. Lovelace, *Betsy Was a Junior*, "affectionate strolls on the campus," 152; "lullabies," 207.

41. Lovelace, *Betsy and Joe*, 580–81.

42. Lovelace, *Betsy and the Great World*, 9.

43. Lovelace, *Heaven to Betsy*, 275.

44. Lovelace, *Betsy and Tacy Go Over the Big Hill*, "gaiety and kindness," 125–26; "gibberish," 130; "lovely place," 140.

45. Ibid., 75.

46. Lovelace, *Betsy in Spite of Herself*, 464.

47. Lovelace, *Betsy and the Great World*, "coming to stare," 114–15; "less than perfect," 252.

48. Lovelace, *Betsy-Tacy*, 10.

49. Betsy-Tacy Society, "Betsy's House History and Restoration," accessed 27 September 2010, http://www.betsy-tacysociety.org/houses/betsy.

50. Levine, "Commitments: The Never-Ending Story."

51. Book Club Girl, "Betsy-Tacy Convention—Day Two!" accessed 19 July 2009, http://www.bookclubgirl.com/book_club_girl/2009/07/betsytacy-convention-day-two.html

52. Amboy Area Community Theatre, "The Curtain Goes Up on Deep Valley Vignettes —Betsy-Tacy on Stage."

53. Meg Cabot, foreword to Maud Hart Lovelace's *Betsy Was a Junior/Betsy and Joe*, v.

54. Sarah M., "More About Betsy, Tacy, Tib and Maud Hart Lovelace," A Library Is the Hospital of the Mind, 29 October 2009, http://libraryhospital.blogspot.com/.

55. Amy Lauters, "Partnering with Betsy-Tacy Society," Beyond Little House, accessed 23 April 2010, beyondlittlehouse.com/2010/04/.../partnering-with-the-betsy-tacy-society.

56. Cabot, "What Little Girls Are Made Of," *Wall Street Journal*, 3 October 3 2009, http://online.wsj.com/article/SB10001424052748704471504574447514006375536. html.

57. Nell Musoff, "They're Wild for Ingalls Wilder at LauraPalooza," Mankato Free Press, 15 July 2010, http://mankatofreepress.com/local/x829293805/They-re-wild-for-Ingalls-Wilder-at-LauraPalooza.

Chapter Seven

1. Virginia McCone, "Sod Houses at Sanborn," http://www.sodhouse.org/.

2. Personal correspondence with Dania Rajendra, 24 September 2011.

3. Laura Ingalls Wilder Museum website, Walnut Grove, MN, http://www .walnutgrove.org/.

4. Glen Meakum, "The Politics of Laura Ingalls Wilder: Dr. Paul Kengor Interviews Dr. John J. Fry," Center for Vision and Values, accessed 2 August 2013, http://glenmeakem .com/2009/09/23/the-politics-of-laura-ingalls-wilder/.

5. Donald Zochert, *Laura: The Life of Laura Ingalls Wilder*, 166.

6. The *Mental Floss* commentary was accessed on 24 September 2010 at http:// mentalfloss.com and no longer appears to be available. Mike McComb's "WTF Little House on the Prairie" is at http://wtf-littlehouse.blogspot.com/.

7. Wilder, *On the Banks of Plum Creek*, 17.

8. Pamela Smith Hill, *Laura Ingalls Wilder: A Writer's Life*.

Chapter Eight

1. Irene Gammel, *Looking for Anne of Green Gables*, "everlasting devotion," 89; "innocent," 110.

2. Carole Gerson, "*Anne of Green Gables* Goes to University: L. M. Montgomery and Academic Culture," 21.

3. Cecily Devereux, "Anatomy of a 'National Icon': *Anne of Green Gables* and the 'Bosom Friends' Affair," 36–37.

4. *Escape to Witch Mountain*, directed by John Hough. Walt Disney Productions, 1975.

5. Sonia Levitin, *Journey to America*, 34.

Chapter Nine

1. Laura Ingalls Wilder, *Little Town on the Prarie*, 11–12.

2. Ibid., 217.

3. Wilder, *Little Town on the Prairie*, 66.

4. Wilder, *By the Shores of Silver Lake*, 126.

5. Ibid., "the road . . . breaks off short" conversation, 58; Mary scolds Carrie, 58.

6. Ibid., "riding into the sun," 65; "tiger-striped," 272.

7. Wilder, *Little Town on the Prairie*, 11.

8. Wilder, *By the Shores of Silver Lake*, 60.

9. Ibid., skunk skins, 82; "one animal," 65.

10. Ibid., 73.

11. Ibid., "always be ladies," 95; "attract attention," 96; Laura forbidden, 130; "wicked" words, 96; "until the music stopped," 54.

12. Ibid., 261.

13. Wilder, *The Long Winter*, 9, 13.

14. Wilder, *By the Shores of Silver Lake*, 280.

15. Wilder, *The Long Winter*, 24.

16. Ibid., 58.

17. Wilder, *Little Town on the Prairie*, 49.

18. Wilder, *By the Shores of Silver Lake*, 144.

19. Wilder, *Little Town on the Prairie*, 89–90.

20. Wilder, *These Happy Golden Years*, 23.

21. Ann Romines, *Constructing the Little House*, 223.

22. Wilder, *Little Town on the Prairie*, 159.

23. Ibid., 173.

24. Ibid., *King Lear*, 97; "wooden swearing," 212.

25. Ibid., 203.

26. Wilder, *These Happy Golden Years*, 136.

27. John Miller, *Becoming Laura Ingalls Wilder: The Woman Behind the Legend*, 237.

28. Stanley Fish, "Plagiarism is Not a Big Moral Deal," *New York Times*, 9 August 2010, http://opinionator.blogs.nytimes.com/2010/08/09/plagiarism-is-not-a-big-moral-deal/?_r=0.

29. William V. Holtz, *The Ghost in the Little House: A Life of Rose Wilder Lane*, 15.

Chapter Ten

1. Lucy Maud Montgomery, *Anne of Green Gables*, "angelically good," 17; "clever," 109.

2. Elizabeth R. Epperly, *The Fragrance of Sweet-Grass: L. M. Montgomery's Heroines and the Pursuit of Romance*, 17.

3. Lovelace, *Betsy in Spite of Herself*, 546.

4. Abby Sandel, "Name of the Day: Maud," Appellation Mountain, http://appellationmountain.net/name-of-the-day-maud/.

5. Montgomery, *Anne of Green Gables*, 25.

6. Irene Gammel, *Looking for Anne of Green Gables: The Story of L. M. Montgomery and Her Literary Classic*, 213.

7. Juliet McMaster, "Taking Control: Hair Red, Black, Gold, and Nut-Brown," 64.

8. Gammel, 172.

9. Ibid., 171.

10. Ibid., 124.

11. Epperly, 5.

12. Gammel, 55.

13. Epperly, tries to fit in, 40; "preaching and teaching," 42; "condescending," 50; "failure," 41.

14. Ibid., "pestered," 233; "false and genuine romance," 17.

15. Ibid., 70.

16. *Anne of Green Gables* and *Anne of Green Gables: The Sequel*, directed by Kevin Sullivan. *Anne of Green Gables* was first broadcast in 1985 and *Anne of Avonlea: The Continuing Story of Anne of Green Gables* (later retitled) in 1987. A third entry, *Anne of Green Gables: A New Beginning*, was first broadcast in 2000.

17. *Anne of Green Gables*, directed by George Nichols Jr., New York: RKO Radio Pictures, 1934.

18. Montgomery, "Is This My Anne?" *The Chatelaine* (January 1935), quoted by Gammel, 255.

19. Ibid., 147.

20. Montgomery, *Anne of the Island*, 21.

21. Dawson, Kimya, "Loose Lips," from the *Juno* soundtrack, Rhino Records, 2007, CD.

22. Epperly, 180.

23. Montgomery, *Anne of Windy Poplars*, 21.

24. Montgomery, *Anne of the Island*, 18.

25. Montgomery, *Anne of Avonlea*, 212.

26. Ibid., 241.

27. Montgomery, *Anne of the Island*, 152, 223.

28. Montgomery, *Anne of Avonlea*, 237.

29. Ibid., 221.

30. Montgomery, *Anne of the Island*, 135.

31. Montgomery, *Anne of Avonlea*, 46.

32. Ibid., "sharper still," 82; "Atossa's tongue," 178.

33. Ibid., "under your curls" and education for women, 172; "metaphorical language," 205.

34. Ibid., give villains "a chance," 93; "higher things," 211; "unworthy motive," 116.

35. Ibid., "Thomas pussy," 100; "conceal our thoughts," 278.

36. Ibid., "with Diana gone," 184; "have to get acquainted with it all over again," 226.

37. Ibid., "you've tricked something out," 144; "the locust has eaten," 166; "poetical compliments," 120.

38. Ibid., 224.

39. Cecily Devereux, "Anatomy of a 'National Icon': *Anne of Green Gables* and the 'Bosom Friends' Affair," 32.

40. Epperly, 5.

41. Gammel, 235.

42. Catherine Sweet, "Secular Pilgrimages: Vacation as Pilgrimage" (PhD diss., University of Prince Edward Island, 2005), 19.

43. Mike Snow, "Pilgrimage to the Land of Anne," *American Roads Travel Magazine*, accessed 23 August 2003, http://www.americanroads.net/pei.htm.

44. Yuka Kajihara, "An Influential Anne in Japan," accessed May 2012, http://www.yukazine.com/lmm/e/Japanne.html, no longer available.

45. Mike Snow writes about the prefabricated houses, while the other examples of Japanese Anne obsession are from Yuka Kajihara.

46. Gammel, 126.

47. James De Jonge, "Through the Eyes of Memory: L. M. Montgomery's Cavendish," in *Making Avonlea: L. M. Montgomery and Popular Culture*, ed. Irene Gammel (Toronto: University of Toronto Press, 2002), 253.

48. Mary Morris, *The River Queen: A Memoir* (New York: Picador, 2008), 174.

49. Montgomery, *Anne's House of Dreams*, 60.

50. Tara Nogler, "Snapshot: My Life as Anne in Japan," in *Making Avonlea: L. M. Montgomery and Popular Culture*, ed. Irene Gammel (Toronto: University of Toronto Press, 2002), 291.

51. Jeanette Lynes, "Consumable Avonlea: The Commodification of the Green Gables Mythology," in *Making Avonlea: L. M. Montgomery and Popular Culture*, ed. Irene Gammel (Toronto: University of Toronto Press, 2002), 277.

52. Montgomery, *Anne of Green Gables*, 307.

53. Montgomery, *Anne's House of Dreams*, "glory of mingled hues," 63; "out of sympathy," 65.

54. Ibid., 56.

55. "Sister Suffragettes" by Richard M. Sherman and Robert B. Sherman, from *Mary Poppins*, Burbank, CA.: Walt Disney Studios, 1964. "How Do You Solve a Problem Like Maria?" by Richard Rodgers and Oscar Hammerstein II, from *The Sound of Music*, Los Angeles: 20th Century Fox, 1959.

56. Montgomery, *Anne's House of Dreams*, "thwarted womanhood," 78; "warped you a little," 126.

57. Epperly, 75.

58. Montgomery, *Anne's House of Dreams*, "living death," 77; "waiting on Dick Moore," 104.

59. Ibid., "rare combination," 107; "stricken eyes," 176.

60. Ibid., "stand by each other," 71; "perambulating haystack," 211.

61. Ibid., "never speak," 106; women can't write, 144; women are illogical, 175.

62. Epperly, 93.

63. Montgomery, *Anne's House of Dreams*, "queen of my heart," 81; baby talk, 192.

64. Montgomery, *Anne of Ingleside*, 114.

65. Ibid., 268.

Chapter Eleven

1. Harriet Reisen, *Louisa May Alcott: The Woman Behind Little Women* (New York: Henry Holt, 2009), 175.

2. Anne Trubek, *A Skeptic's Guide to Writers' Houses* (Philadelphia: University of Pennsylvania Press, 2011), 65.

3. Alcott, *Little Women*, "odd, blunt ways," 64; "agreeable sort," 291.

4. *Louisa May Alcott: The Woman Behind Little Women: PBS American Masters*, directed by Nancy Porter (2008: Thirteen/WNET New York), DVD.

5. Alcott, 166.

6. Reisen, 178.

7. Janice M. Alberghene and Beverly Lyon Clark, eds., *Little Women and the Feminist Imagination: Criticism, Controversy, Personal Essays* (New York: Garland Publishing, 1999), xvii.

8. Cheever, Susan, *Louisa May Alcott: A Personal Biography* (Simon and Schuster, 2010), 120.

9. Alcott, 43.

10. Judith Fetterley, "Little Women: Alcott's Civil War," in *Little Women and the Feminist Imagination: Criticism, Controversy, Personal Essays*, ed. Janice M. Alberghene and Beverly Lyon Clark (New York: Garland Publishing, 1999), 38–39.

11. *Little Women*, directed by Mervyn LeRoy. Los Angeles: Metro-Goldwyn-Mayer, 1949.

12. Ann Douglas, "Introduction to Little Women," in *Little Women and the Feminist Imagination: Criticism, Controversy, Personal Essays*, ed. Janice M. Alberghene and Beverly Lyon Clark (New York: Garland Publishing, 1999), 52.

13. Alcott, 136.

14. Reisen, 372.

15. Elaine Showalter, *Sister's Choice: Tradition and Change in American Women's Writing* (New York: Oxford University Press, 1994), 42.

16. Emanuel Levy, "Little Women (1933): Adapting to the Screen a Classic," Cinema 24/7, http://www.emanuellevy.com/comment/little-women-1933-adapting-to-the-screen-a-classic-2/. *Little Women*, directed by George Cukor. New York: RKO Radio Pictures, 1933.

17. Reisen, 1.

18. Douglas, 43.

19. Susan R. Gannon, "Getting Cozy with a Classic: Visualizing Little Women (1868–1995)," in *Little Women and the Feminist Imagination: Criticism, Controversy, Personal Essays*, ed. Janice M. Alberghene and Beverly Lyon Clark (New York: Garland Publishing, 1999), 127.

20. Ibid.

21. Fetterley, 37.

22. Alcott, "business girl," 60; "making a guy," 143; "romping ways," 180; "safe in the family," 237; "stop at home," 248; "young lady," 260.

23. Ibid., 94–95.

24. Fetterley, 39.

25. Alcott, "rich and famous," 168; "sweetest thing," 115.

26. Ibid., 876.

27. Montgomery, *Anne of Ingleside*, 268.

28. Elizabeth Lennox Keyser, "'The Most Beautiful Things in All the World': Families in Little Women," in *Little Women and the Feminist Imagination: Criticism, Controversy, Personal Essays*, ed. Janice M. Alberghene and Beverly Lyon Clark (New York: Garland Publishing, 1999), 90.

29. Showalter, 58–60.

30. Quoted in Alberghene and Clark, xxviii.

31. Ibid.

32. Douglas, 52.

33. Alberghene and Clark, xvi.

34. Lauren Baratz-Logsted, *Little Women and Me* (New York: Bloomsbury, 2011). Meg is the "prig" (20); Jo is the "rebel" (20), the one who "really rocked" (36), the "alpha girl"

(39), the one you'd never catch "wearing skinny jeans or eating salad just to impress a boy" (62). Beth, who Emily compares to Oprah (30), is the "least cool . . . but she was so sweet and kind" (20).

35. Ibid., 66.

36. Reisen, 268.

37. Nina Auerbach, "Waiting Together: Alcott on Matriarchy," in *Little Women and the Feminist Imagination: Criticism, Controversy, Personal Essays*, ed. Janice M. Alberghene and Beverly Lyon Clark (New York: Garland Publishing, 1999), 20.

38. Alcott, 116.

39. Ibid., 159.

40. *Little Women*, directed by Gillian Armstrong. Los Angeles: Columbia Pictures, 1994.

41. Reisen, 155.

42. "Orchard House" website, accessed 14 April 2013, http://www.louisamayalcott.org.

43. Trubek, 56–59.

44. Gannon, 110–11.

45. Reisen, 324.

46. Alberghene and Clark, xxvii.

47. The *Five Little Peppers* movies were *The Five Little Peppers and How They Grew* (1939), *Five Little Peppers at Home* (1940), *Out West with the Peppers* (1940), and *Five Little Peppers in Trouble* (1940), all made by Columbia Pictures.

48. Anne Hollander, "Portraying Little Women through the Ages," in *Little Women and the Feminist Imagination: Criticism, Controversy, Personal Essays*, ed. Alberghene and Clark (New York: Garland Publishing, 1999), 99.

49. Reisen, 334–35.

50. Ibid., 303.

51. Christina Rossetti, "Echo," in *Complete Poems*, edited by Betty S. Flowers (New York: Penguin, 2001), 40.

EPILOGUE

1. Rose Lichter-Marck, "Birthday Tribute: Emily Dickinson," *Rookie Magazine*, 10 December 2012, http://rookiemag.com/2012/12/dickinson-birthday-tribute/Lichter-Marck.

2. Emily Dickinson, *The Poems of Emily Dickinson*, edited by R. W. Franklin (Cambridge: Belknap, 1999). Citations refer to the page number in the text, not the poem number. "A narrow Fellow in the grass," 443; "I'm Nobody!" 116.

3. Ibid., "Bee! I'm expecting you!" 412.

4. Ibid., "I like to see it lap the Miles—And lick the Valleys up," 176.

5. Ibid., "To be alive—is Power—," 381.

6. Ibid., "A Chilly Peace infests the Grass," 553.

7. Lyndall Gordon, "A Bomb in Her Bosom: Emily Dickinson's Secret Life," *The Guardian*, 2 December 2010, accessed 21 April 2013. http://www.theguardian.com/books/2010/feb/13/emily-dickinson-lyndall-gordon.

8. Christopher Benfey, "A Fairer House than Prose," from "Emily Dickinson: The Poet at Home" (Amherst, MA: Emily Dickinson Museum).

9. Dickinson, "If I can stop one Heart from breaking," quoted in Adrienne Rich, "Vesuvius at Home: The Power of Emily Dickinson (1975)" in *On Lies, Secrets, and Silence: Selected Prose 1966–1978* (New York: W. W. Norton, 1979), 164. This version reproduced by Rich did not contain Dickinson's original punctuation.

10. Dickinson, *The Poems of Emily Dickinson: Reading Edition*, "After great pain, a formal feeling comes—," 170.

11. Ibid., "Because I Could Not Stop for Death," 219; "I heard a Fly buzz—when I died—," 265.

12. Ibid., "Wild nights—Wild nights!" 120.

13. Dickinson, *The Complete Poems* (Boston: Little, Brown and Company, 1960), 100. This poem appears in slightly different form in *The Poems of Emily Dickinson: Reading Edition*, 64.

14. Dickinson, *The Poems of Emily Dickinson: Reading Edition*, "My period had come for Prayer—" 238; "Wherefore so late—I murmured—," from "Shells from the Coast mistaking—," 320.

15. Ibid., "Tell all the truth but tell it slant—" 494.

16. Ibid., "I had been hungry, all the Years—" 203; "Amputate my freckled Bosom!" from "Rearrange a 'wife's' Affection," 119; "Inebriate of air—am I—" from "I taste a liquor never brewed—," 96; "There's a certain Slant of light," 142; "In Winter in my Room," 623; "So Keep Your Secret, Father" (which I have particularly taken out of context, from "The Skies can't keep their secret!"), 98; "Pain—has an Element of Blank—," 339–40; "He fumbles at your soul," 218.

In *Emily Dickinson and the Art of Belief*, Roger Lundin mentions the common early-twentieth-century explanation of a doomed love affair as an explanation for Dickinson's "retreat." Lundin finds evidence in her poetry for agoraphobia. Many others speculate about potential depression/anxiety disorders. According to Schizophrenia.com, "Psychologists believe famous creative luminaries, including Vincent Van Gogh, Albert Einstein, Emily Dickinson and Isaac Newton, had schizotypal personalities." ("Creativity Linked to Schizotypy," Schizophrenia.com, 6 September 2005, http://www.schizophrenia.com/sznews/archives/002372.html.)

Asperger's Association of New England asserts that "There is strong evidence that such superstars as Vincent Van Gogh, Emily Dickinson, Albert Einstein . . . among many others . . . had Asperger Syndrome" (Asperger's Association of New England, "What Is Asperger's Syndrome?" http://www.aane.org/about_asperger_syndrome/).

Heather Kirk Thomas explores the question of anorexia in "Emily Dickinson's 'Renunciation' and Anorexia Nervosa," *American Literature* 20 (May 1988), 205–25, while Camille Paglia makes a case for sadomasochism in her book *Sexual Personae: Art and Decadence from Nefertiti to Emily Dickinson* (New York: Vintage, 1990). In 2001, John F. McDermott examined the mood changes in Dickinson's poetry and how they correlated to seasons of the year to conclude that she had bipolar characteristics as well as signs of seasonal affective disorder ("Emily Dickinson Revisited: A Study of Periodicity in Her Work," *American Journal of Psychiatry* 158 [2000], 686–90). In 2006, Wendy K. Parriman argued that Dickinson displays thirty-three of thirty-seven characteristics from an internationally recognized checklist of incest survivor traits (*A Wounded Deer: The Effects of Incest on the Life and Poetry of Dickinson* [Newcastle: Cambridge Scholar Press, 2006]). Reaching back further, to 1979, Jerry Reynolds proposed that Dickinson's symptoms were consistent with systemic lupus erythematosus ("Banished from Native Eyes: The Reasons for Emily Dickinson's Seclusion Reconsidered," *Markham Review* [1979], 41–47). Most recently, Lyndall Gordon makes a compelling argument that Dickinson actually suffered from epilepsy (*Lives Like Loaded Guns: Emily Dickinson and Her Family's Feuds* [New York: Viking, 2010]).

17. Norbert Hirschhorn, "Misdiagnosing Emily Dickinson." http://www.bertzpoet .com/reviews/pdfs/livesLikeLoaded.pdf

18. Rich, 160–61.

19. Ellen Louise Hart and Martha Nell Smith, eds., *Open Me Carefully: Emily Dickinson's Intimate Letters to Susan Huntington Dickinson* (Ashfield, MA: Paris Press, 1998).

20. Lichter-Marck, "Birthday Tribute."

21. Pence, 54.

22. Dickinson, *The Poems of Emily Dickinson: Reading Edition*, "The Brain has Corridors," from "One need not be a Chamber—to be Haunted—," 188.

23. Ibid., "The Soul selects her own Society—," 189.

24. Katherine Martinez, "The Dickinsons of Amherst Collect Pictures and Their Meanings in a Victorian Home," *Common-place: The Interactive Journal of Early American Life*, Vol. 7, No. 3, April 2007 (Worchester, MA: American Antiquarian Society).

25. Frost, Robert. "The Road Not Taken," from *Collected Poems* (Henry Holt and Co., 1969), 105.

26. Mary Chapin Carpenter, "New Year's Day," from *Ashes and Roses*. Zoe Records, 2012, CD.

27. Dickinson, "I dwell in Possibility—," 215.

Bibliography

Series Books

Melendy Quartet by Elizabeth Enright
The Saturdays. New York: Farrar & Rinehart, 1941.
The Four-Story Mistake. New York: Farrar & Rinehart, 1942.
Then There Were Five. New York: Farrar & Rinehart, 1944.
Spiderweb for Two: A Melendy Maze. New York: Farrar & Rinehart, 1951.

Nancy Bruce Series by Jennie D. Lindquist
The Golden Name Day. New York: Harper & Row, 1955.
The Little Silver House. New York: Harper & Row, 1959.
The Crystal Tree. New York: Harper & Row, 1966.

Deep Valley Books by Maud Hart Lovelace
Betsy-Tacy. New York: Thomas Y. Crowell Co., 1940.
Betsy-Tacy and Tib. New York: Thomas Y. Crowell Co., 1941.
Betsy and Tacy Go Over the Big Hill. New York: Thomas Y. Crowell Co., 1942.
Betsy and Tacy Go Downtown. 1943. New York: Scholastic, 1962.
Heaven to Betsy/Betsy in Spite of Herself. 1945, 1946. Foreword by Laura Lippman. New York: Harper Perennial, 2009.
Betsy Was a Junior/Betsy and Joe. 1947, 1948. Foreword by Meg Cabot. New York: Harper Perennial, 2009.
Carney's House Party/Winona's Pony Cart. 1949, 1953. Foreword by Melissa Wiley. New York: Harper Perennial, 2010.
Emily of Deep Valley. 1950. Foreword by Mitali Perkins. New York: Harper Perennial, 2010.
Betsy and the Great World/Betsy's Wedding. 1952, 1955. Foreword by Anna Quindlen. New York: Harper Perennial, 2009.

Anne Series by Lucy Maud Montgomery
Anne of Green Gables. 1908. New York: Bantam, 1992.

Anne of Avonlea. 1909. New York: Bantam, 1992.

Anne of the Island. 1915. New York: Bantam, 1992.

Anne's House of Dreams. 1917. New York: Bantam, 1992.

Rainbow Valley. 1919. New York: Bantam, 1992.

Rilla of Ingleside. 1921. New York: Bantam, 1992.

Anne of Ingleside. 1939. New York: Bantam, 1992.

Anne of Windy Poplars. 1936. New York: Bantam, 1992.

Jennifer Books by Eunice Young Smith

The Jennifer Wish. Indianapolis: Bobbs-Merrill, 1949.

The Jennifer Gift. Indianapolis: Bobbs-Merrill, 1950.

Jennifer is Eleven. Indianapolis: Bobbs-Merrill, 1952.

Jennifer Dances. Indianapolis: Bobbs-Merrill, 1954.

High Heels for Jennifer. Indianapolis: Bobbs-Merrill, 1964.

Beany Malone Series by Lenora Mattingly Weber

Meet the Malones. New York: Thomas Y. Crowell Co., 1943.

Beany Malone. New York: Thomas Y. Crowell Co., 1948.

Leave It to Beany! New York: Thomas Y. Crowell Co., 1950.

Beany and the Beckoning Road. New York: Thomas Y. Crowell Co., 1952.

Beany Has a Secret Life. New York: Thomas Y. Crowell Co., 1955.

Make a Wish for Me. New York: Thomas Y. Crowell Co., 1956.

Happy Birthday, Dear Beany. New York: Thomas Y. Crowell Co., 1957.

The More the Merrier. New York: Thomas Y. Crowell Co., 1958.

A Bright Star Falls. New York: Thomas Y. Crowell Co., 1959.

Welcome Stranger. New York: Thomas Y. Crowell Co., 1960.

Pick a New Dream. New York: Thomas Y. Crowell Co., 1961.

Tarry Awhile. New York: Thomas Y. Crowell Co., 1962.

Something Borrowed, Something Blue. New York: Thomas Y. Crowell Co., 1963.

Come Back, Wherever You Are. New York: Thomas Y. Crowell Co., 1969.

Little House books by Laura Ingalls Wilder

Little House in the Big Woods. 1932. New York: Harper Collins, 1960.

Farmer Boy. 1933. New York: Harper Collins, 1961.

Little House on the Prairie. 1935. New York: Harper Collins, 1963.

On the Banks of Plum Creek. 1937. New York: Harper Collins, 1965.

By the Shores of Silver Lake. 1939. New York: Harper Collins, 1967.

The Long Winter. 1940. New York: Harper Collins, 1968.

Little Town on the Prairie. 1941. New York: Harper Collins, 1969.

These Happy Golden Years. 1943. New York: Harper Collins, 1971.

The First Four Years. 1971. New York: Harper Collins, 1999.

Childhood of Famous Americans

De Grummond, Lena Young. *Babe Didrikson: Girl Athlete.* Indianapolis: Bobbs-Merrill, 1963.

Gormley, Beatrice. *Amelia Earhart: Young Aviator.* New York: Aladdin/Simon & Schuster, 2000.

Howe, Jane Moore. *Amelia Earhart: Kansas Girl.* Indianapolis: Bobbs-Merrill, 1961.

Melin, Grace Hathaway. *Maria Mitchell: Girl Astronomer.* Indianapolis: Bobbs-Merrill, 1954.

Seymour, Flora Warren. *Sacagawea: Bird Girl.* Bobbs-Merrill, 1959. Reissued as *Sacagawea: Young Pathfinder.* New York: Aladdin/Simon & Schuster, 1991.

Stevenson, Augusta. *George Carver: Boy Scientist.* Indianapolis: Bobbs Merrill, 1944.

Van Riper, Guernsey. *Jim Thorpe: Indian Athlete.* Indianapolis: Bobbs-Merrill, 1956. Reissued as *Jim Thorpe: Olympic Champion.* New York: Aladdin/Simon & Schuster, 1986.

Wilkie, Katherine E. *Helen Keller: Handicapped Girl.* Indianapolis: Bobbs-Merrill, 1969. Reissued as *Helen Keller: From Tragedy to Triumph.* New York: Aladdin/Simon & Schuster, 1986.

Additional Novels, Literary Works, and Books Read in Childhood

Alcott, Louisa May. *Flower Fables.* Carlisle, MA: Applewood Books: 2005.

———. *Jo's Boys.* Boston: Roberts Brothers, 1886.

———. *Little Men.* Boston: Roberts Brothers, 1871.

———. *Little Women* and *Good Wives.* Boston: Roberts Brothers, 1868–69. Reprinted as *Little Women.* New York: Signet Classics, 2004.

Arthur, Ruth M. *A Candle in Her Room.* New York: Atheneum, 1966.

———. *Requiem for a Princess.* New York: Atheneum, 1967.

Baratz-Logsted, Lauren. *Little Women and Me.* New York: Bloomsbury, 2011.

Barber, Antonia. *The Ghosts.* New York: Pocket, 1993.

Baum, L. Frank. *The Wonderful Wizard of Oz.* Chicago: George M. Hill, 1900.

Blume, Judy. *Are You There, God? It's Me, Margaret.* Englewood Cliffs, NJ: Bradbury, 1970.

Brock, Betty. *No Flying in the House.* New York: Scholastic, 1970.

Brontë, Charlotte. *Jane Eyre.* 1847. New York: Bedford/St. Martin's, 1996.

Brontë, Emily. *Wuthering Heights.* 1847. New York: Bedford/St. Martin's, 2003.

Brooks, Geraldine. *March.* New York: Penguin, 2006.

Burnett, Frances Hodgson. *The Secret Garden.* 1911. New York: Barnes & Noble, 2002.

———. *A Little Princess.* 1905. New York: Barnes & Noble, 2005.

Burton, Virginia Lee. *Mike Mulligan and His Steam Shovel.* Boston: Houghton Mifflin, 1967.

Caudill, Rebecca. *Did You Carry the Flag Today, Charley?* New York: Henry Holt and Co., 1966.

Cleary, Beverly. *Ramona the Pest.* New York: W. Morrow, 1968.

Collins, Suzanne. *Hunger Games.* New York: Scholastic, 2010.

DiCamillo, Kate. *Because of Winn-Dixie.* Cambridge, MA: Candlewick, 2005.

Dickinson, Emily. *The Complete Poems.* Boston: Little, Brown and Company, 1960.

———. *The Poems of Emily Dickinson.* Edited by R. W. Franklin. Cambridge, MA: Harvard University Press, 1999.

Doss, Helen Grigsby. *The Family Nobody Wanted.* Boston: Little, Brown, 1954.

Duncan, Lois. *Down a Dark Hall.* Boston: Little, Brown, 1974.

———. *A Gift of Magic.* Boston: Little, Brown, 1971.

Erdrich, Louise. *The Birchbark House.* New York: Hyperion, 1999.

Evans, Polly. *Fried Eggs with Chopsticks: One Woman's Hilarious Adventure into a Country and a Culture Not Her Own.* New York: Delta, 2006.

Finley, Martha. *Elsie Dinsmore.* 1867. New York: Dodd, Mead & Company, 1867.

Fisher, Dorothy Canfield. *Understood Betsy.* New York: The Century Co., 1916.

Fitzgerald, F. Scott. "Bernice Bobs Her Hair." In *The Short Stories of F. Scott Fitzgerald,* edited by Matthew J. Bruccoli. New York: Charles Scribner's Sons, 1989.

Fitzhugh, Louise. *Harriet the Spy.* New York: Harper & Row, 1964.

Flowers, Jessie Graham. *Grace Harlowe* series. Philadelphia: Henry Altemus Co., 1910–1924.

Frank, Anne. *Diary of a Young Girl.* 1947. New York: Bantam/Doubleday, 1993.

Gilbreth, Frank B., and Ernestine Gilbreth Carey. *Belles on Their Toes.* New York: Thomas Y. Crowell Co., 1950.

———. *Cheaper by the Dozen.* New York: Thomas Y. Crowell Co., 1948.

Grahame, Kenneth. *The Wind in the Willows.* 1908. New York: Scribner, 1961.

Haywood, Carolyn. *B is for Betsy.* New York: Harcourt, Brace, 1939.

Hodges, Margaret. *What's for Lunch, Charley?* New York: Dial, 1961.

Joyce, James. *Ulysses.* New York: Modern Library/Random House, 1992.

Keene, Carolyn. *The Clue of the Broken Locket.* New York: Grosset & Dunlap, 1965.

King, Stephen. *The Shining.* New York: Anchor, 2013.

Krulik, Nancy E. *Girls Don't Have Cooties.* New York: Grosset & Dunlap, 2002.

———. *Oh Baby!* New York: Grosset & Dunlap, 2002.

Lang, Andrew, ed. *The Olive Fairy Book.* New York: Longmans, Green, and Co., 1907.

———. *The Red Fairy Book.* New York: Longmans, Green, and Co., 1890.

Lash, Joseph P. *Helen and Teacher: The Story of Helen Keller and Anne Sullivan Macy.* New York: Addison-Wesley, 1997.

Laskin, David. *The Children's Blizzard.* New York: Harper Perennial, 2005.

Lenski, Lois. *Strawberry Girl.* 1945. New York: HarperCollins, 1973.

Levin, Marcia. *Donna Parker at Cherrydale.* Racine, WI: Whitman Publishers, 1957.

Levitin, Sonia. *Journey to America.* New York: Atheneum, 1970.

Lord, Bette Bao. *In the Year of the Boar and Jackie Robinson.* New York: Harper & Row, 1984.

Lowry, Lois. *Number the Stars.* Boston: Houghton Mifflin Co., 1989.

MacDonald, Betty. *Mrs. Piggle-Wiggle* series. Philadelphia: J. B. Lippincott, 1947–1957.

Meyer, Stephanie. *Twlight.* New York: Little, Brown, 2005.

Milne, A. A. *Winnie the Pooh.* 1926. New York: Puffin Modern Classics, 2005.

Moore, Eva. *The Fairy Tale Life of Hans Christian Andersen.* New York: Scholastic, 1969.

Morris, Mary. *The River Queen: A Memoir.* New York: Picador, 2008.

Nordstrom, Ursula. *The Secret Language.* New York: Harper & Row, 1960.

Park, Barbara. *Junie B. Jones* series. New York: Random House, 1992–2007.

Parker, David. *The Best Me I Can Be: I Am Generous!, I Am Responsible!, I Can Cooperate!* New York: Scholastic, 2004.

Porter, Eleanor H. *Pollyanna.* 1913. New York: Oxford University Press, 2011.

Rodgers, Mary. *Freaky Friday.* New York: Harper Collins, 1972.

Rossetti, Christina. "Echo." In *Complete Poems,* ed. by Betty S. Flowers. New York: Penguin, 2001.

Rylant, Cynthia. *Old House in the Green Groves.* New York: HarperCollins, 2002.

Selden, George. *The Cricket in Times Square.* New York: Ariel, 1960.

Sherburne, Zoa. *The Girl Who Knew Tomorrow.* New York: Morrow, 1970.

Sidney, Margaret. *Five Little Peppers and How They Grew.* Garden City, NY: Children's Classics, 1954.

Snicket, Lemony. *The Ersatz Elevator.* New York: HarperCollins, 2001.

Sorensen, Virginia. *Plain Girl.* New York: Scholastic, 1990.

Spyri, Johanna. *Heidi.* Boston: Cupples, Upham, & Company, 1885.

Streatfeild, Noel. *Ballet Shoes.* 1936. New York: Yearling, 1994.

———. *Curtain Up.* 1944. Reprinted as *Theater Shoes.* New York, Yearling, 1994.

———. *Thursday's Child.* 1970. New York: Yearling, 1985.

———. *Wintle's Wonders.* 1957. Reprinted as *Dancing Shoes.* New York: Yearling, 1994.

Warner, Gertrude Chandler. *The Boxcar Children.* Chicago: Albert Whitman, 1977.

White, E. B. *Charlotte's Web.* New York: Harper, 1952.

———. *Trumpet of the Swan.* New York: Harper & Row, 1970.

Woolf, Virginia. *Mrs. Dalloway.* New York: Oxford University Press, 2000.

Wright, Anna Maria Rose. *Summer at Buckhorn.* New York: Viking, 1943.

Wright, Harold Bell. *Shepherd of the Hills.* Chicago: Book Supply Co., 1907.

Yolen, Jane. *The Devil's Arithmetic.* New York: Puffin, 1988.

Zafón, Carlos Ruiz. *The Shadow of the Wind.* New York: Penguin Books, 2005.

Zochert, Donald. *Laura: The Life of Laura Ingalls Wilder.* New York: Avon, 1977.

Biography, Criticism, and Commentary

Auerbach, Nina. "Waiting Together: Alcott on Matriarchy." In *Little Women and the Feminist Imagination: Criticism, Controversy, Personal Essays.* Edited by Janice M. Alberghene and Beverly Lyon Clark, 7–26. New York: Garland, 1999.

Alberghene, Janice M., and Beverly Lyon Clark, eds. *Little Women and the Feminist Imagination: Criticism, Controversy, Personal Essays.* New York: Garland, 1999.

Anderson, William. *Laura Ingalls Wilder: A Biography.* New York: HarperCollins, 2007.

Benfey, Christopher. "A Fairer House than Prose." In "Emily Dickinson: The Poet at Home." Amherst, MA: Emily Dickinson Museum.

Brown, Lyn Mikel, and Carol Gilligan. *Meeting at the Crossroads: Women's Psychology and Girls' Development.* Cambridge, MA: Harvard University Press, 1992.

Cabot, Meg. Foreword to Maud Hart Lovelace's *Betsy Was a Junior/Betsy and Joe.* Harper Perennial, 2009.

Cheever, Susan. *Louisa May Alcott: A Personal Biography.* New York: Simon & Schuster, 2010.

Corrigan, Maureen. *Leave Me Alone, I'm Reading: Finding and Losing Myself in Books.* New York: Random House, 2005.

De Jonge, James. "Through the Eyes of Memory: L. M. Montgomery's Cavendish." In *Making Avonlea: L. M. Montgomery and Popular Culture,* edited by Irene Gammel, 252–67. Toronto: University of Toronto Press, 2002.

Devereux, Cecily. "Anatomy of a 'National Icon': *Anne of Green Gables* and the 'Bosom Friends' Affair. In *Making Avonlea: L. M. Montgomery and Popular Culture,* edited by Irene Gammel. Toronto: University of Toronto Press, 2002.

Dorris, Michael. *Paper Trail: Essays.* New York: HarperCollins, 1995.

Douglas, Ann. "Introduction to *Little Women.*" In *Little Women and the Feminist Imagination: Criticism, Controversy, Personal Essays,* edited by Janice M. Alberghene and Beverly Lyon Clark, 43–62. New York: Garland, 1999.

Epperly, Elizabeth R. *The Fragrance of Sweet-Grass: L. M. Montgomery's Heroines and the Pursuit of Romance.* Toronto: University of Toronto Press, 1993.

Fellman, Anita Clair. *Little House, Long Shadow: Laura Ingalls Wilder's Impact on American Culture.* Columbia, MO: University of Missouri Press, 2008.

Fetterley, Judith. "*Little Women*: Alcott's Civil War." In *Little Women and the Feminist Imagination: Criticism, Controversy, Personal Essays,* edited by Janice M. Alberghene and Beverly Lyon Clark, 27–42. New York: Garland, 1999.

Gammel, Irene. *Looking for Anne of Green Gables: The Story of L. M. Montgomery and Her Literary Classic.* New York: St. Martin's, 2008.

Gannon, Susan R. "Getting Cozy with a Classic: Visualizing *Little Women* (1868–1995)." In *Little Women and the Feminist Imagination,* edited by Janice M. Alberghene and Beverly Lyon Clark, 103–38. New York: Garland, 1999.

Gerson, Carole. "*Anne of Green Gables* Goes to University: L. M. Montgomery and Academic Culture," in *Making Avonlea: L. M. Montgomery and Popular Culture,* edited by Irene Gammel, 17–31. Toronto: University of Toronto Press, 2002.

Gordon, Lyndall. *Lives Like Loaded Guns: Emily Dickinson and Her Family's Feuds.* New York: Viking, 2010.

Hart, Ellen Louise, and Martha Nell Smith, eds. *Open Me Carefully: Emily Dickinson's Intimate Letters to Susan Huntington Dickinson.* Ashfield, MA: Paris Press, 1998.

Heppermann, Christine. "Little House on the Bottom Line." *Horn Book Magazine* 74, no. 6 (1998): 689–92.

Hill, Pamela Smith. *Laura Ingalls Wilder: A Writer's Life.* Pierre, SD: South Dakota State Historical Society, 2007.

Hollander, Anne. "Portraying *Little Women* through the Ages." In *Little Women and the Feminist Imagination: Criticism, Controversy, Personal Essays,* edited by Janice M. Alberghene and Beverly Lyon Clark, 97–102. New York: Garland, 1999.

Holtz, William V. *The Ghost in the Little House: A Life of Rose Wilder Lane.* Columbia, MO: University of Missouri Press, 1993.

Kaye, Frances W. "Little Squatter on the Osage Diminished Reserve: Reading Laura Ingalls Wilder's Kansas Indians." *Great Plains Quarterly* 20, no. 2 (2000): 123–40.

Keyser, Elizabeth Lennox. "'The Most Beautiful Things in All the World': Families in *Little Women.*" In *Little Women and the Feminist Imagination:\Criticism, Controversy, Personal Essays,* edited by Janice M. Alberghene and Beverly Lyon Clark, 83–96. New York: Garland, 1999.

Louisa May Alcott: The Woman Behind Little Women. PBS *American Masters.* Directed by Nancy Porter. 2008. New York: Thirteen/WNET. DVD.

Lundin, Roger. *Emily Dickinson and the Art of Belief.* Grand Rapids, MI: William B. Eerdmans Pub. Co., 2004.

Lynes, Jeanette. "Consumable Avonlea: The Commodification of the Green Gables Mythology." In *Making Avonlea: L. M. Montgomery and Popular Culture,* edited by Irene Gammel, 268–79. Toronto: University of Toronto Press, 2002.

McClure, Wendy. *The Wilder Life: My Adventures in the Lost World of Little House on the Prairie.* New York: Riverhead Books, 2012.

McDermott, John F. "Emily Dickinson Revisited: A Study of Periodicity in Her Work." *American Journal of Psychiatry* no. 158 (2000): 686–90.

McMaster, Juliet. "Taking Control: Hair Red, Black, Gold, and Nut-Brown." From *Making Avonlea: L. M. Montgomery and Popular Culture,* edited by Irene Gammel, 58–71. Toronto: University of Toronto Press, 2002.

Meyer, Kimberly. "Little Log Houses for You and Me." *Brain Child,* Fall 2009, 48–57.

Miller, John E. *Becoming Laura Ingalls Wilder: The Woman Behind the Legend.* Columbia, MO: University of Missouri Press, 2006.

Miller, Lucasta. *The Brontë Myth.* New York: Anchor, 2005.

Nogler, Tara. "Snapshot: My Life as Anne in Japan." In *Making Avonlea: L. M. Montgomery and Popular Culture,* edited by Irene Gammel, 286–94. Toronto: University of Toronto Press, 2002.

Orenstein, Peggy. *Cinderella Ate My Daughter.* New York: HarperCollins, 2011.

Paglia, Camille. *Sexual Personae: Art and Decadence from Nefertiti to Emily Dickinson.* New York: Vintage, 1990.

Pearl, Nancy. *Book Crush: For Kids and Teens—Recommended Reading for Every Mood, Moment, and Interest.* Seattle: Sasquatch Books, 2007.

Pence, Amy. "Many White Dresses: Emily Dickinson and Her Biographers." *Writer's Chronicle* (December 2012): 42–55.

Perriman, Wendy K. *A Wounded Deer: The Effects of Incest on the Life and Poetry of Emily Dickinson.* Newcastle, UK: Cambridge Scholars Publishing, 2006.

Pipher, Mary. *Reviving Ophelia: Saving the Selves of Adolescent Girls.* New York: Putnam, 1994.

Quindlen, Anna. Foreword to Maud Hart Lovelace's *Betsy and the Great World/Betsy's Wedding.* Harper Perennial, 2009.

Rehak, Melanie. *Girl Sleuth: Nancy Drew and the Women Who Created Her.* New York: Harcourt, 2006.

Reisen, Harriet. *Louisa May Alcott: The Woman Behind Little Women.* New York: Henry Holt, 2009.

Reynolds, Jerry. "Banished from Native Eyes: The Reasons for Emily Dickinson's Seclusion Reconsidered." *Markham Review* (1979): 41–47.

Rich, Adrienne. "Vesuvius at Home: The Power of Emily Dickinson (1975)." In *On Lies, Secrets, and Silence: Selected Prose, 1966–1978*, 157–84. New York: W. W. Norton, 1979.

Romines, Ann. *Constructing the Little House: Gender, Culture, and Laura Ingalls Wilder*. Amherst, MA: University of Massachusetts Press, 1997.

Schrader, Julie A. *Maud Hart Lovelace's Deep Valley: A Guidebook of Mankato Places in the Betsy-Tacy Series*. Mankato, MN: Minnesota Heritage Pub., 2002.

Sewall, Richard B. *The Life of Emily Dickinson*. New York: Farrar, Straus and Giroux, 1974.

Showalter, Elaine. *Sister's Choice: Tradition and Change in American Women's Writing*. New York: Oxford University Press, 1994.

Skurnick, Lizzie. *Shelf Discovery: Teen Classics We Never Stopped Reading*. New York: Avon, 2009.

Smith-Rosenberg, Carroll. *Disorderly Conduct: Visions of Gender in Victorian America*. New York: Oxford University Press, 1986.

Spufford, Francis. *The Child That Books Built: A Life in Reading*. New York: Picador, 2003.

Sweet, Catherine. "Secular Pilgrimages: Vacation as Pilgrimage." PhD diss., University of Prince Edward Island, 2005.

Thomas, Heather Kirk. "Emily Dickinson's 'Renunciation' and Anorexia Nervosa." *American Literature* 20 (1988): 205–25.

Trubek, Anne. *A Skeptic's Guide to Writers' Houses*. Philadelphia: University of Pennsylvania Press, 2011.

Whalen, Sharla Scannell. *The Betsy-Tacy Companion: A Biography of Maud Hart Lovelace*. Whitehall, PA: Portalington, 1995.

Zochert, Donald. *Laura: The Life of Laura Ingalls Wilder*. New York: Avon, 1977.

TV Shows, Films, and Songs

Anne of Avonlea: The Continuing Story of Anne of Green Gables. Retitled *Anne of Green Gables: The Sequel*. Directed by Kevin Sullivan. Toronto: Sullivan Entertainment, 1987.

Anne of Green Gables. Directed by George Nichols Jr. New York: RKO Radio Pictures, 1934. DVD.

Anne of Green Gables. Directed by Kevin Sullivan. Toronto: Sullivan Entertainment, 1985. DVD.

Anne of Green Gables: A New Beginning. Directed by Kevin Sullivan. Toronto: Sullivan Entertainment, 2000. DVD.

Carpenter, Mary Chapin. "New Year's Day." *Ashes and Roses*. Zoe Records, 2012. CD.

Cheaper by the Dozen. Directed by Shawn Levy. Los Angeles: 20th Century Fox, 2003.

Dawson, Kimya. "Loose Lips." From *Juno Soundtrack*, Rhino Records, 2007. CD.

Escape to Witch Mountain. Directed by John Hough. Burbank, CA: Walt Disney Productions, 1975.

Hall, Kristen. "Following My Compass." *Be Careful What You Wish For*. High Street Records, 1994. CD.

"Little House on the Prairie." TV Show. NBC, Ed Friendly/NBC Productions, 1974–1983.

Little Women. Directed by George Cukor. New York: RKO Radio Pictures, 1933.

Little Women. Directed by Gillian Armstrong. Los Angeles: Columbia Pictures, 1994.

Little Women. Directed by Mervyn LeRoy. Beverly Hills, CA: Metro-Goldwyn-Mayer, 1949.

MacColl, Kirsty. "No Victims." *Kite*. Virgin Records, 1989. CD.

Raitt, Bonnie, and Don Was. "The Road's My Middle Name." *Nick of Time*. Capitol, 1989. CD.

Rodgers, Richard, and Oscar Hammerstein II. "How Do You Solve a Problem Like Maria?" In *The Sound of Music*. Los Angeles: 20th Century Fox, 1959.

Sherman, Richard M., and Robert B. Sherman. "Sister Suffragettes." In *Mary Poppins*. Burbank, CA: Walt Disney Studios, 1964.

Starr, Johnny. "I'm Moving Along." Patsy Cline. Capitol, 1959.

Williams, Dar. "Traveling Again." *The Honesty Room*. Razor & Tie, 2008. CD.

Wizard of Oz, The. Directed by Victor Fleming, King Vidor and Mervyn LeRoy. Beverly Hills, CA: Metro-Goldwyn-Mayer, 1939.

Index